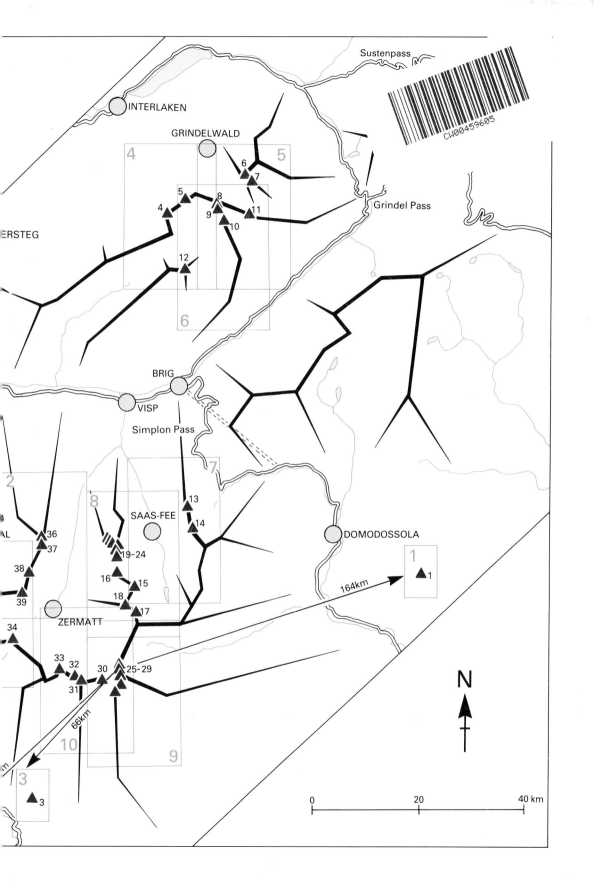

In Monte Viso's Horizon

Climbing all the Alpine
4000 metre Peaks

Gross Schreckhorn and Lauteraarhorn from the Bergli hut

IN
MONTE VISO'S
HORIZON

Climbing all the Alpine
4000m Peaks

Will McLewin

 ERNEST PRESS

Published by The Ernest Press 1991
© Will McLewin

British Library Cataloguing in Publication Data
McLewin, Will, *1940-*
   In Monte Viso's horizon: climbing all the Alpine 4000
   metre peaks.
   1. Europe. Alps. Mountaineering - Biographies
   I. Title
   796.522092

ISBN 0-948153-09-1

Front cover: Matterhorn and Dent d'Herens from the Obergabelhorn (Will McLewin)

Rear cover: Grandes Jorasses and Mont Blanc from the Tour Noire (R Everett)

Typeset by Westec
Printed by Kyodo Shing Loong

Contents

Contents

A Sort of Introduction

Beneath the surface of this book are two contradictions. One is that I have come to see mountaineering as an essentially personal activity, a private intimacy between myself and the mountain that cannot genuinely be shared. The other is that the activity of Alpine climbing is indescribable anyway. I could perhaps provide a collection of facts and impressions of events which would be instructive and possibly entertaining. They might conjure up vivid images yet they could not truly convey how it was. To know what Alpine mountaineering is like you have to do it yourself. Seeing the sunrise from a mountain in the Alps always makes me wonder how (nearly) everyone else survives without it. There are no words or pictures to compensate for that loss. Neither will change your perception of life in the way that being there inevitably would.

To find myself writing about climbing all the 4000m summits of the Alps in spite of these convictions requires explanation. The immediate one is that Peter Hodgkiss thought it was a good idea and he was persuasive, supportive and patient. Another is that my experiences, as I gradually accumulated this long list of climbs, may be of interest to others and may help them to make the same discoveries with fewer mistakes and in less time. This is not said in praise of efficient, predictable mountaineering, rather to acknowledge that life is short. Practised alpinists will find welcome echoes of days in their own lives and I hope potential alpinists will be helped and encouraged, particularly to climb in quiet places. Although it is a less forbidding activity than most people imagine, for many of them Alpine mountaineering is not an available option. That being so, perhaps the descriptions I provide will be of value.

Climbing all the Alpine 4000m peaks, many solo, may appear to be a substantial achievement. I do not regard it as such. It seems to be very rarely accomplished but it is well within the scope of many climbers. I care far more for the insights about life and the sense of being at one with the Earth that I have found while mountaineering. So although the text ostensibly deals with realising a prosaic ambition, it more importantly describes a gradual learning of how to climb in the Alps: not technically, although that too, but in the sense of discovering its meaning. The accounts of ascents are less about climbing details and more an overview of events and impressions and mountains as a whole. Climbing all the 4000m peaks has been a convenient framework for my mountaineering and it provides a simple motif for a book, but the having climbed is of no consequence. What matters is the act of climbing and the way that it neutralises questions about life by making them meaningless.

Having pointed out the sub-plot and thus revealed the true adventure that lies behind the list of climbs, there are four other explanatory admissions to make. These concern unsuccessful days, maps and guide-books, photographs and technical difficulty. Most of the text is about good days, when routes were done and something was achieved (in the conventional sense). Of course, there

GP   Gran Paradiso
G   Grivola
MV   Monte Viso
GN   Gran Nomenon
PC   Punta Chaligne
RV   Roccia Viva
AR   Aiguille Rousse
GS   Grande Sassière
PB   Punta Bianca
TGP Torre del Gran
         S. Pietro

Gran Paradiso and Monte Viso from the Grand Combin

have been many other days spent hoping the weather would improve. Alpine mountaineering seems at times to be more about waiting than about climbing. Indeed, looking back without the flattering filter I instinctively impose, my Alpine climbing is more a catalogue of missed opportunities and misjudgements than of achievements. To some extent someone else's mistakes are more enlightening, and certainly more enjoyable, than their successes, so I hope I have not been too kind to myself. On the other hand there is not much I could usefully say about days spent reading, washing clothes, or travelling from one area to another. Consequently, although these and other mundane activities make up a large part of the time spent in the Alps I have largely glossed over them.

This is not intended to be a guide-book to the 4000m peaks. Excellent guide-books are widely available. Every Alpinist makes extensive use of them and owes the authors a debt of gratitude. I have the impression however that many climbers lose sight of what should be their objective and end up following the book instead of climbing the mountain. I hope Alpinists will find my comments useful as an addition to formal guide-book descriptions. Most climbers read guide-books for general insight and pleasure in any case, and I see my accounts as complementing that information. Much the same remarks apply to maps. The diagrams and maps in the text are to give a clearer understanding of the topographical context in which the events took place. They are not a substitute for the magnificent Swiss maps which are an indispensable part of any Alpinist's equipment and objects of great beauty in their own right. Speculative enquiring study of Swiss maps of the Alps is an absorbing pleasure, almost the next best thing to climbing.

Photographs present a number of problems. A large proportion of the time spent climbing is in less than perfect weather or before dawn. Photographs taken in mist or in the dark are generally uninformative and usually uninteresting so most of the illustrations show clear air and good visibility. This selectivity creates a misleading impression that distorts the reality of mountaineering even more than filtering out all the unsuccessful days. Another problem is that high-quality, very specialised pictures of mountains are widely reproduced in calendars and magazines. These are frequently taken by photographers whose purpose is not simply to record the scene that they encountered on a route but to take interesting eye-catching pictures. Such photographs are artificial and in a sense inaccurate. Unfortunately they tend to define a pictorial style that comes to be expected. The received wisdom is that illustrations should have readily understood contents and no elementary technical flaws. They must also be well suited to the reproduction process. This means that some pictures that would require effort or charity from the reader have been omitted, despite their potential interest. I have usually carried a camera, particularly in recent years, and at suitable moments have bothered to use it. I have rarely stopped for the express purpose of taking a 'good' picture. I have never sat at a particularly fine viewpoint and waited until the light was exactly right or waited for other climbers to attain an interesting position. Nor have I flown around in a helicopter to get spectacular but unrealistic views. Most of the pictures that illustrate the book are simply what I happen to have seen as I have climbed. I rarely look at my own slides: the pictures that are important to me are in my mind.

The essential point to make about technical difficulty is that for most of the routes described it is quite low, especially by modern standards. Very few of the climbs that I have done would present substantial problems for any reasonably competent alpinist. There are plenty of people, though still a minority, who climb regularly in the Alps at a higher technical standard and many who undertake more ambitious expeditions. They know that already; I would prefer that readers knew it too. I have given the accepted guide-book grades of routes described, to provide the background for my subjective comments about routes as I found them. Equally relevant is my good fortune with respect to altitude. I never suffer from altitude sickness and my adjustment to Alpine altitudes is rapid and painless. I wish the same were true of carrying a heavy rucksack.

I have not attempted to provide a balanced view of the Alps or of Alpine mountaineering but simply to present my own impressions, so any opinions expressed arise from my personal experiences. I am conscious that quite small incidents can have a lasting influence and that if other equally likely events had occurred I might feel differently about some things. A similar comment arises from the timespan of nearly twenty years that is involved. I have not been back to several places and most routes since my first visit, in some cases many years ago. Although my impressions of them remain sharp I am conscious that they might be different now, because both they and I have changed.

The structure of the book reflects its concern with the idea of climbing all the fourthousanders both individually and overall. Each of twelve sections of the Alps is discussed as a whole in its own right before accounts of ascents of the mountains in that section. Between these twelve main parts are short essays on topics that are relevant to Alpine mountaineering in general. The treatment of individual climbs and topics varies considerably. I have allowed the events and the ideas themselves to dictate the tone and the amount of detail. Some ascents were mundane in themselves and no doubt this is reflected in their descriptions. This does not mean that I regard them with less affection. They are rather like eating good apples. Desire and enjoyment is undiminished by continued consumption, but you would not wish to read (or write) much about it. The different parts are independent of one another and can be read in any order. The sequence in which the sections appear works roughly from north-east to south-west. This structure suggests an overall plan; I never had one. To take so long over something that could be done in one year demonstrates my erratic approach. The chronological order of the climbs is listed in an appendix.

The spelling adopted for place names and the choice of words for mountain features is not something I can take very seriously. There are several places which have French and German or French and Italian alternatives and for some topographical features there is an English word as well. I have simply followed what has become my own convention in any particular instance, without great concern for a consistent overall approach. Names are spelt as they appear on the map I happen to have used most. The same applies to listed heights, which are occasionally corrected when revisions or re-surveys take place. With German language names that include an adjective I have adopted what seems to be the approach of English guide-books and used, for example, Gross Fiescherhorn instead of Grosses-Fiescherhorn. I tend to follow the local convention for nouns that are parts of names, for example Aletschgletscher instead of Aletsch glacier, and then use what is for me the most common word, glacier rather than gletscher, when referring to the object itself.

I have consciously retained my apparently inconsistent use of the definite article with mountain names. With some I instinctively insert it, 'the Breithorn' or 'the Dent Blanche' for example: with others, like 'Liskamm' or 'Mont Blanc' I do not.

Summit ridge from the Piz Alv to the Piz Bernina.   The bizarre situation of cold clammy mist on one side of a ridge and bright sunshine on the other sometimes occurs. It is a disconcerting effect, especially when it is as pronounced as this. Bad weather invariably follows, though often only briefly.

Several people helped to improve the text. Jack Baines, Peter Hodgkiss, Mike Smith, Les Swindin and Brian Wood made useful and complementary comments. Barbara McLewin rendered first drafts fit for wider circulation, bore the brunt of my stubbornness and at the proof stage relentlessly pursued the inconsistencies, errors and ambiguities that everyone else had missed. Doreen Irving and Alan Yates ruthlessly pointed out my worst excesses and rescued me from many literary crevasses.

For providing illustrations of routes views or people where I had none suitable, I am grateful to: Anne Brearley, pp 44, 236; Brian Brevitt p 242; Donald Bennet p 88; Rob Ferguson p 200; Peter Fleming p 62, 64, 108, 218; D Gaffney p 1; Richard Gibbens p 174; Ian Von Hinsburgh p 195; Peter Hodgkiss pp 33, 139, 146; Wil and Grace Hurford pp 29, 44, 158, 196, 230; Rucksack Club p 225; Les Swindin pp 26, 50, 58, 106, 120, 135, 141, 157, 162, 177, 187, 216, 221; Brian Wood p 173, 240.

The maps and final versions of the diagrams were expertly drawn by Jeremy Ashcroft.

Will McLewin,
October 1989.

Climbing the 4000 Metre Peaks of the Alps

ortunately there is no list of the 4000m peaks that is accepted as definitive. I say fortunately because it means that climbing them all is necessarily a personal affair. I assume nobody would begin their Alpine climbing with this intention because it would be a misguided approach. However, when you decide this is your aim or when you realise this is what you have embarked on then you have the problem of choosing a definitive collection of summits. The absence of an 'official' list reflects the impossibility of assembling a list that is exhaustive, consistent and aesthetically satisfying. Even if initially you accept a published list you will modify it eventually to meet criteria which strike you as the most appropriate. This is a curious situation. Climbing them all is totally inconsequential and there is no virtue in worrying about whether a particular spike of rock or a nondescript hump of snow should be included or left out, but once you adopt the basic idea then a decision has to be made. So in the discussion that follows I am conscious of a sense of the absurd, especially when I find myself wondering whether or not a nonentity like Pointe Mieulet should be included in a list of summits that excludes the magnificent Bietschhorn.

There are several lists to choose from. All are unsatisfactory in some way, reflecting the ill-defined nature of the basic concept. For German-speaking climbers the classic reference is Blödig and Dumler's book, *Die Viertausender der Alpen*. This is a comprehensive, relatively modern text by Helmut Dumler, based on much earlier material by Karl Blödig. It is a semi-guide-book, giving in outline an overall treatment of each mountain including grades and times for standard routes and some information about huts. A chance discovery of the first edition in a bookshop in Saas Fee on a rainy day started me thinking about climbing all the 4000m peaks. It is the origin, for me, of the anglicisation 'fourthousander' which is a useful word and one I use frequently.

Blödig completed his list of 57 summits in about 1900 and was the first person to complete what was then an impressive achievement. The most serious omissions from his list are the Punta Baretti and the Aiguille du Diable pinnacles. It was only when I had completed ascents of the mountains included in Blödig and Dumler and discovered it was a rare feat for British climbers that it occurred to me to look more closely at their list. At about the same time I learned about Eustace Thomas, who was the first British alpinist to climb all the fourthousanders. He worked at the task in a very business-like way from 1928 to 1932 and, after completing ascents of everything on his initial list, scurried about in pursuit of anything else that could be included.

Two years after I finished climbing the peaks in Blödig and Dumler's list, an impressive article appeared in the Spring 1983 edition of *High* magazine with a list of 75 tops. The subsequent revelation that apparently no British alpinist had completed this list was an incentive to revisit some places, mostly in pursuit of nonentities. While I was doing that Les Swindin and Peter Fleming finished climbing the 52 separate mountains in Robin Collomb's list of 79 tops.

The main difficulty when compiling a list is deciding how significant a particular local summit point has to be in comparison with nearby higher and more important ones. Useful examples to consider are the Grandes Jorasses, the Aiguille du Diable pinnacles and the grand gendarme on the Frontier Ridge of Mont Maudit. The Grandes Jorasses, number 46 in my list, has four named 4000m tops distinct from the highest point (and another unfortunate summit, Pointe Young, 3996m). Is this mountain to count as one fourthousander or five? Neither choice is satisfactory. In this case an individual number, 46, for the mountain and the highest point, and 46a, 46b, 46c, 46d for the subsidiary tops is a natural compromise. With the Grandes Jorasses and in many similar cases, there is a satisfying mountaineering resolution of the problem because a pleasing way to climb the mountain is to traverse the main ridge across all the subsidiary tops.

The Aiguille du Diable pinnacles on the south-east ridge of Mont Blanc du Tacul are more problematic. They are minor summit spikes but a striking feature of the mountain. They are rarely climbed for themselves in the sense that descending after climbing them invariably involves continuing to the summit of the Aiguille du Tacul. Their ascent requires much more demanding climbing than the normal ascent routes on the Tacul, or for that matter any other major 4000m peak. They are omitted from Blödig and Dumler's list but figure in most others. Both inclusion and omission are defensible but the frequently adopted intermediate position of including two or three of the five is a flabby compromise.

Similar to the Diable pinnacles, but usually lesser features, are gendarmes on ridges. I feel it is generally appropriate not to regard them as additional 4000m points but I have no clear criterion for deciding. The grand gendarme on the Frontier Ridge of Mont Maudit is a substantial rock tower which most parties climbing the ridge traverse round. Its ascent is out of character with the rest of the route (and the traverse is easier). This seems to me a valid reason for omitting it from the 4000m list, if only because traversing round gendarmes on rock ridges is standard practice. The grand gendarme on the north ridge of the Weisshorn is a similar example and there are many others. On the other hand, parties traversing the summit ridge of the Rimpfischhorn usually do ascend the grand gendarme that marks the north end of the ridge, so I have included it as an unnumbered point.

All lists that I have seen contain inconsistencies. One occurs when the compiler simply omits points he or she has not climbed, while including lesser points that the compiler has gone to some trouble to visit. My list does not entirely avoid this failing. Another arises when the compilation is a journalistic exercise in which decisions about debatable minor summit points are not guided by the experience of having been there. A final complication is the absence or not of a name, although I expect one could be found for almost every identifiable point if you searched long enough. The presence of a name is a quite persuasive reason for inclusion but a very inconsistent criterion. Most lists include subsidiary named points that are really of no significance while omitting nameless, but inviting, gendarmes and more substantial objects.

I make no claims for the list I present. It has been arrived at by combining all the lists I have seen, removing silly points that would be embarrassing to visit specially, and then restoring some which have historical or sentimental connections. My main criterion for the separation into major summits with separate numbers and minor summits with subsidiary numbers was whether a peak is often climbed for its own sake and descended without involving a more substantial summit. In some cases there is more than one well-defined summit point. The Matterhorn for example has an Italian summit and a Swiss summit separated by an airy ridge. Most parties stop at whichever point they reach first. For punctilious 4000m collectors, I have listed some secondary summit spot heights in brackets, but for compilations of a hundred or more minor ridge points, they must look elsewhere.

The weakest numbered entries are the Felikhorn, Pic Lory and Pointe Mieulet. Some other numbered entries are feeble and several spikes and humps on ridges will feel hard done by, particularly in the Oberland. The most controversial entry will probably be Pic Eccles, which is omitted in other lists. I like the idea of a separate 4000m summit for the lower section of each of the three great ridges on the south side of Mont Blanc, partly because each is a worthy expedition in its own right. Of well-known points that I have left out, perhaps the strongest claim for inclusion is that of the Wengen Jungfrau 4089m on the north-east ridge of the Jungfrau. Easily accessible from the main summit, it should be climbed by the east ridge of the Jungfrau.

The subdivision of the complete list into twelve sections seems to me altogether more satisfactory. Each section is a comfortable size for considering possible choices of routes and for idle, affectionate speculation. With one or two exceptions they are natural sub-sets that select themselves. Although this approach was initially a convenient way to organise the book, once I had chosen the groups they soon established themselves in my mind and I realised that I had subconsciously already accepted a tentative version. Ironically the two sections that fit my relationship with the Alps least well, the Valais South and the French Alps, are more natural for most Alpinists, who approach them from common starting points in Switzerland or France rather than from various valleys in Italy. The sections that may appear most arbitrary, the Inner and Outer Oberland, the French side of the Mont Blanc area, and the Valais West, were firmly in place in my mind before I settled on the overall scheme.

The Alpine Fourthousanders

Some Basic Preliminaries

A Typical Alpine Expedition, Snow, Weather, Grading and Condition of Routes

The phrase 'typical expedition' is doubly unsatisfactory. All expeditions develop their own distinctive character, even straightforward ones where nothing unexpected happens. 'Expedition' sounds altogether too grand for the basic activity this book is about. The alternative labels, trip, outing, climb, day and so on, are even less appropriate. Although I think of 'doing a route' rather than 'making an expedition' or 'climbing a mountain' I have found it convenient to refer to the whole business of preparation, climbing to the summit and descending as an expedition, particularly here where I can apologise for it.

While Alpine expeditions vary from pleasant strolls to fraught, exhausting epics they share the same sequence of component parts. These are outlined here for those unfamiliar with Alpine climbing.

An expedition begins with assembling the food, clothing and equipment you expect to need. You add further items to meet possible misfortunes but not in such quantity as to cause them. This preparation can be anything from a relaxing way to spend a whole morning to a mad scramble before departure in the afternoon.

Then comes the approach walk – the technically easy ascent of the lower slopes to the point where the route begins in earnest. Approach walks can feel like hard work, especially when it is hot and your rucksack is particularly heavy. In truth, the degree of enjoyment (or not) depends less on the severity of the approach walk than on your state of mind at the time. An early start when the air feels cool and crisp is invariably better for the walk itself but it demands better organisation and you lose the morning's consideration of the weather and possibly a revised forecast. Few things are more frustrating than toiling up to a hut or a bivouac and then watching your anticipated balmy afternoon and your climbing prospects for the following day disappear as the weather deteriorates. On average an approach walk needs about four hours of solid effort. Sometimes a téléphérique or a railway can relieve you of all or most of that.

The evening before your climb is mainly concerned with food, and the short night with rest if not sleep. Staying in a mountain hut or out on a bivouac offers pleasures and problems, sometimes predictable and sometimes surprising. In general, staying in a hut limits the extent of both. In either situation you hope for a clear and very cold night to freeze and solidify softened snow.

Starting time next day depends on your chosen route, its likely condition and the weather. A major ice climb may dictate beginning around midnight and climbing for several hours in moonlight or with a head-torch. Serious rock pitches early on may mean it is pointless to make a move before daylight. The aim is to strike a balance between completing the snow sections before they soften and not climbing on awkward terrain in the dark. 'Up at three and away at four' is reasonable for many routes.

An average time for the climb to the summit has little meaning. If all goes well then on a straightforward route you might expect to reach the top at mid- or late-morning. Unless there are crowds or a fierce wind you spend as much time there as you dare. It is never long enough. Always you are conscious that with every minute that passes the snow deteriorates: at best it becomes more laborious, at worst more dangerous. Snow bridges over crevasses weaken, ice cliffs are more likely to collapse, snow slopes to avalanche and couloirs to channel more falling debris. If you intend retracing your steps there is less uncertainty about the descent, but this option only applies on easier routes.

Descents are frequently as stressful as ascents and sometimes as strenuous. They are seldom as rapid as you anticipate. Reaching the last bit of the glacier is always a special moment. You stop to remove crampons and gaiters, have something to eat and look back. While you do this your rucksack mysteriously gets heavier, accentuating the pounding on the rocky path that follows. Usually you feel very tired. If you are lucky you reach your transport or your tent while there is still some afternoon sun to enjoy. You consume enormous quantities of whatever liquid is available. Whatever the company and the conversation, you think private thoughts about the enchanted world you visited that morning.

This is a convenient place to mention other topics that are relevant throughout the book. Snow is the crucial element that gives Alpine climbing its distinctive quality. Yet it is extraordinarily variable stuff. It can be feathery dry powder or wet slush. At its best, after partially melting, consolidating and freezing, it can provide the perfect surface for walking on: firm and solid but not hard like ice and not slippery. Eskimos and Lapps have many terms for different sorts of snow. With a single word they can describe subtle nuances of its condition with precision and completeness. I call it snow all the time and rely on relatively objective adjectives like crisp or subjective ones like horrid and, in this context, I rely on the reader's imagination.

Weather is a permanent preoccupation of alpinists. Reasonably good weather is a necessity, but not in conventional terms. The main requirements omit the conventional one of warm sunny days. Most important are cold nights, with temperatures well below freezing above the snow line, good visibility during the day and some degree of stability. Cold dry winds which spoil summer days in the valley are advantageous; warm, damp winds are bad news. A heavy afternoon shower may be welcome and refreshing in the town; on the mountain it may leave rock coated with a layer of ice.

I have given the grades of routes as they are listed in guide-books. This gives basic information and a context within which to interpret comments about difficulties, or their absence, on the day. The grade is an overall summary of the severity of a route assuming good conditions. Guide-book descriptions include the further refinement of technical grades for individual pitches.

In outline, the usual categories are:
F grade 1, facile = easy; undemanding snow and rock scrambles.
PD grade 2, peu difficile = moderate; snow needing care, 'easy' rock.
AD grade 3, assez difficile = fairly hard; snow may be icy and require technique, 'difficult/very difficult' rock.

D grade 4, difficile = hard; serious snow and ice, 'severe' rock.

TD and ED, grades 5 and 6, très and extrêmement difficile; very serious routes with high and sustained technical difficulties.

The harder and easier routes within each grade are denoted by + and -; sometimes sup and inf are used. Often the transitions between snow, ice and rock provide the main problems. It is not uncommon to see experienced rock-climbers very uneasy on mixed terrain; understandably so.

The terms 'good condition'and 'poor' or 'bad condition' are used to describe the state of a route or part of a route in much the same way they are used to describe the health of people or animals (or the drinkability of beer). A rock pitch will be in good condition if it is free of ice and snow, and dry. A snow-covered ice slope will be in good condition if there are several centimetres of compacted well-frozen snow, in bad condition if the snow is soft and loose. In good condition a facile snow route provides carefree walking. In bad condition it can be dangerous and very laborious.

Maps, Diagrams and Illustrations

List of maps, with the reference numbers of 4000m peaks for which each map is appropriate.

All maps are the same scale, approximately 1:90 000. The whole-page maps cover an area 13km west to east by 20km north to south. Most of the maps do not coincide precisely with one of the twelve sections of 4000m peaks.

The routes described in the text are indicated on the maps by red lines; dotted for the approach, solid for the route itself and dashed for the descent (where different). In some cases the same approach or descent was used for more than one ascent route. Any particular route is marked only on the most appropriate map. Blue areas on the maps indicate permanent ice or snow. For almost all major summits and some subsidiary ones the line of ascent and descent is shown by a dotted line on the diagram of the appropriate illustration. These diagrams give general indications; they are not intended to be sufficient for route-finding in practice. In particular, where a route follows a ridge the dotted line is drawn immediately below the ridge line in the diagram. Parts of routes that are not visible in the corresponding illustration are not indicated on diagrams.

For individual 4000m peaks the heading in the text is followed by an illustration list. The illustration with a diagram showing the route comes first, then illustrations in which the mountain appears prominently, then some of the other illustrations where the mountain is explicitly indicated in the diagram. In illustration captions the viewpoint is the summit of the mountain named unless stated as being from some other point on the mountain. The rear end-paper shows, by a blue rectangle, the area covered by each map.

Section 1
The Outliers

1	Piz Bernina	4049m	2b	Dôme de Neige des Ecrins	4015m
1a	La Spalla	4020m	3	Gran Paradiso	4061m
2	Barre des Ecrins	4101m	3a	Il Roc	4026m
2a	Pic Lory	4086m			

The Outliers provide a satisfying repetition of an underlying 'rule of three' that applies to the Alps as a whole. Climbing in the Alps involves three countries: Switzerland, France and Italy. It requires some involvement with three languages: German, French and Italian. There are three varieties of money, three kinds of eating and drinking, and three sets of national characteristics. An incidental benefit of pursuing all the fourthousanders is the perspective given by visiting many places and repeatedly experiencing this threefold diversity. You discover, by the way, that the corresponding varieties of alpinist are even less adventurous and cosmopolitan than the British are reputed to be. French or Italian climbers are rarely met in the Oberland for example. Of course, once you are established on a route, the country it happens to be in is immaterial. But much of the time you are 'down in the valley', where the differences are apparent. Given the remoteness of the Alpine areas in each of the three countries it is surprising just how different each of them feels.

If you believe in the notion of a grand design then it will surely seem right that each country has its own fourthousander separate from the main congregations. This happy coincidence has required the collaboration of modern cartography. Spare a thought for the Piz Zupo, a near neighbour of the Piz Bernina. This simple peak, whose one distinction used to be membership of this charmed class, now languishes at the curiously precise height of 3995.7m. Perhaps this exactitude, especially for a snow summit, is meant to moderate the Piz Zupo's chagrin. Associating each outlier with a different country needs a tiny sleight of hand for although strictly the Piz Bernina is in Switzerland it is effectively on the Swiss-Italian border.

The immaculate and well-signed paths of the usual approaches to the Piz Bernina and the officious, affluent, pseudo-sophistication of Pontresina typify one facet of Switzerland. The popular approaches to Les Ecrins and the Gran Paradiso also typify their nationalities. The village of Ailefroide, the brutally effective car parking at the Hotel Cézanne, the starkness of the Caron hut and the way the remains of the old hut had been left lying around (they provided a handy bivouac site) are in a way typically French. The Val Savarenche and, halfway along, the sleepy village of the same name with its quaint information-office-cum-Alpine-museum and the cheerful lack of organisation at Pont could only be in Italy.

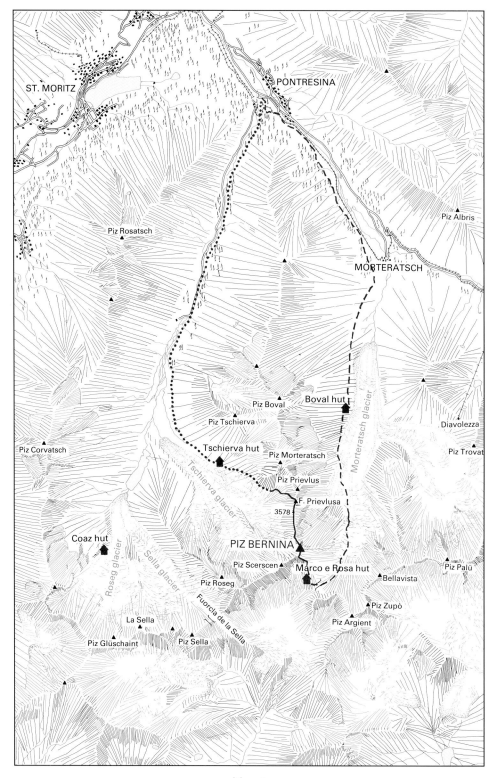

ST. MORITZ

PONTRESINA

Piz Albris

Piz Rosatsch

MORTERATSCH

Piz Boval

Boval hut

Morteratsch glacier

Diavolezza

Piz Tschierva

Piz Corvatsch

Tschierva hut

Piz Trovat

Piz Morteratsch

Tschierva glacier

Piz Prievlus

F. Prievlusa

3578

Coaz hut

Roseg glacier

Sella glacier

PIZ BERNINA

Piz Scerscen

Marco e Rosa hut

Piz Palü

Bellavista

Piz Roseg

Fuorcla de la Sella

Piz Zupò

Piz Argient

La Sella

Piz Glüschaint

Piz Sella

Map 1

Habitually approaching the Alps from the north leads me to regard these three mountains as outposts guarding each of the other directions: the Bernina in the east, the Gran Paradiso in the south and Les Ecrins in the west. In fact they lie roughly on a straight line at a compass bearing of about 240.

The most popular routes on Les Ecrins and the Gran Paradiso are very popular indeed. They both consist mostly of gentle snow slopes on simple glaciers. On a good day you will encounter a long line of pilgrims trudging along a broad path to the summit. The approach paths as far as the Caron and Vittorio Emanuele II huts will be appallingly crowded. This exemplifies an Alpine truism. The unorthodox approaches, the next valley, the other side of the ridge: these will be deserted and peaceful. On the Piz Bernina the easiest route is by the Boval hut and the Morteratsch glacier, but one of the alternatives is the famous Biancograt. This is a route of such stunning elegance that it is very frequently climbed despite being more serious.

The three mountains in this section are isolated only in terms of their 4000m height. In a true mountaineering context each just happens to be the highest peak of an interesting group with other summits that are equally challenging and worthwhile. To visit each area and only climb these three would be to underline the essential pointlessness of the 4000m enterprise.

1 Piz Bernina
1a La Spalla
    N ridge (Biancograt) (AD), descent by S ridge. With Bob McLewin
Map p 24   Illustrations pp 12, 26

Who can look at the north ridge of the Piz Bernina and not want to be there? The way the crest of snow lies neatly and alluringly along the ridge is unique in the Alps. There is something almost uncanny about its simplicity that makes it hard to believe it is the result of a chance combination of rock form, alignment and meteorological conditions. If the route does not quite live up to expectations it is because actually being on the wonderful 'heaven's ladder' of snow does not feel very different from being on any other fine snow ridge. But this is being unkind: we had an excellent outing, not exactly what we planned, and distinguished by some freak weather.

The walk from Pontresina to the Tschierva hut was pleasant enough. Our plan was to bivouac at the col where the north ridge begins, the Fuorcla Prievlusa, so after a brief stop we continued, on a less comfortable path. The hut is barely halfway so it makes a long (six hours) approach walk. The final slope of soft snow over ice was trying our patience and stamina when we were hit by a rock fall. Although it was relatively small and did no more than slide steadily down the slope it was still nasty. I was winged a bit by several smaller pieces but Bob was behind me and unsighted. The largest piece, about the size of a corgi, caught him full on and knocked him over. He slid down for a bit while he remembered instructions, as yet unpractised, about how to stop. Then he carried them out swiftly and effectively.

This was only Bob's fifth day in the mountains; the others had been on the Bellavista, the Piz Zupo, the Piz Palu and one wet one on Tryfan in North Wales. (See Matterhorn, in Section 7.) This meant that his expectations and reactions to events were simple and unprejudiced. He just accepted

Piz Bernina from the SE ridge of the Piz Morteratsch

without complaint that being knocked down an icy slope by falling rock was a normal part of mountaineering. He climbed back up to where I was standing and licking my grazed knuckles. He said he was all right while his expression said that I had not told him about that sort of thing.

At the col we found somewhere to sit comfortably but nowhere to lie down. We had our dinner, enjoying being in such a fine position. Then we became very uneasy about the weather. Early evening had been fine but gradually the dense canopy of stars, which on clear nights in the Alps seems to be almost within reach, had disappeared behind heavy cloud. This had approached ominously from all directions, signalling its progress with flashes of lightning. We were resigned to a thoroughly unpleasant night and prepared ourselves as best we could. Instead, the encroaching cloud stopped at the edge of a circle about two kilometres in diameter with the two of us roughly at the centre.

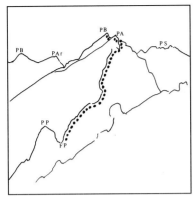

PB Piz Bernina summit
PA Piz Alv
PS Piz Scercen
PZ Piz Zupo
PAr Piz Argient
PP Piz Prievlus
FP Fuorcla Prievlusa

A small patch of clear sky was left directly above. Then for a couple of hours a tremendous storm raged around us. Lightning zipped and crackled and great waves of thunder roared across seeming to shake the ridge itself. We were astonished, excited and occasionally a bit scared. Bob said this was entertaining; his expression said that it was something else I had not told him about. When everything calmed down the world had not come to an end and our private patch of clear sky expanded as far as we could see.

Next morning the first large batch of climbers from the hut approached as we were about to leave so we waited and made another brew of tea. This let them get well in front to give us the impression of having the ridge to ourselves. It would have been better to leave a bit earlier and move quickly but that could only reasonably have followed a more restful night. The main part of the ridge is rock at first to a small saddle and then the famous snow crest to the Piz Alv, just five metres short of 4000m. All this was in perfect condition and completely straightforward. The last section, from the Piz Alv to the Piz Bernina, is a more complicated rocky crest. It has towers to be turned and a substantial gap to be negotiated. For us it was made awkward in places by some of the parties ahead of us engaging in a variety of unpredictable movements and others having great difficulty making any sort of movement at all. I realised that Bob was giving me that look again. Perhaps the other parties were disturbed by the equivocal weather which consisted of bright warm sunshine on the east side of the crest and cold dense sleeting cloud on the west side. The division was uncannily precise. It was as striking, though in a different way, as the weather had been the previous night. By the time we reached the summit there was poor visibility in every direction and steady snowfall.

We had intended to descend by reversing our ascent route but the shelter of the Marco e Rosa hut seemed a more prudent objective so we continued along the south ridge to La Spalla. From there a bit of the south-east ridge and the snow slope to the south took us easily to the hut. It would have been hard to find without footprints and other climbers doing the same thing. At the hut there was standing room only so we convinced ourselves that the weather was good enough for us to continue down. The Morteratsch glacier might have been problematic but it was merely a long ten kilometres to Morteratsch village. We had been apprehensive about the section called the Labyrinth but we simply followed the path. As soon as the weather cleared enough for us to determine our position exactly we discovered we were already below it.

2 Barre des Ecrins

2a Pic Lory

      N flank and N face (AD). With Brian Wood

2b Dôme de Neige des Ecrins

      N flank (F). With Anne Brearley

Map p 28   Illustration p 29

Les Ecrins is in the Massif de l'Oisins together with La Meije, 3983m, and Mont Pelvoux, 3946m. Driving south from the Mont Blanc region you will probably go over the Col du Galibier, 2556m. In good weather a stop here is irresistible. First, you will need to recover from the shock of realising that the massive climb you have just driven up features in the Tour de France. The numbers of brightly coloured pop-eyed cyclists underline this. Second, there is an unobscured view of the north side of Les Ecrins, about fifteen kilometres distant. As there are still eighty kilometres of driving to do, this view is useful encouragement.

    The first time I visited Les Ecrins the virtues of bivouacking were just beginning to crystallise in my mind. To be precise, the dissatisfactions of staying in huts were just beginning to be thoroughly irritating. The eleven hours we spent at the Caron hut were a case-study of frustration. They brought me to my senses more than other similar episodes. Brian and I had walked up the ordinary approach

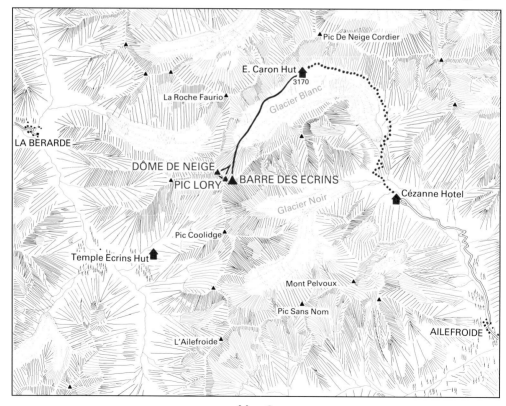

Map 2

Barre des Ecrins from the Pic du Glacier Blanc

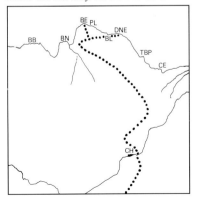

BE	Barre des Ecrins	TBP	Tour de Bonne Pierre
PL	Pic Lory	BN	Barre Noir
BL	Brèche Lory	BB	Barre Blanc
CE	Col des Ecrins	DNE	Dôme de Neige des Ecrins
CH	Caron hut		

from the Hotel Cézanne with a friend of ours, Peter Birch, who was coming just for the walk, to stay overnight and return with us the next day. The combination of two Englishmen with Austrian Alpine Club membership cards (the AAC was by far the cheapest) and another one with no card caused an immediate display of suspicion by the guardian. The ensuing session of mutual incomprehension eventually produced agreement that Brian and I would get the concessionary rates we were entitled to, but neither of us was surprised when we were assigned to a very short length of bunk nor when our food took about five times as long to arrive as everyone else's. The fact that the three of us were jammed into a sleeping space not much more than a metre wide resulted in aggravation with our immediate neighbours. They were already annoyed by the guardian's policy of cramming everyone into some dormitories and leaving others empty.

In a misguided act of kindness Brian and I had put Peter between us. He went to sleep at once and commenced a virtuoso display of snoring. We prodded him, we turned him over, we put his head in a rucksack, we put our heads in rucksacks, all without relieving our distress. When we woke him up he apologised cheerfully, said it must be the altitude and went back to sleep, and to snore, blissfully unaware how close he was to a violent death.

Brian and I were among the first up. We were keen to get on with the route and to calm ourselves with some physical effort. This was not simple to do. Apparently English members of the Austrian Alpine Club could not be supplied with hot water for breakfast until every native French speaker had been dealt with. When eventually we left to scramble down the awkward rocky buttress to the Glacier Blanc we had no need of our head-torches: we were breathing fire.

There are three kilometres of gentle uneventful ascent up the glacier in a long, anti-clockwise curve first south-west then due south. This might have been boring but we were so angry we scorched along the path overtaking one party after another. The normal route continues curving round to the south-east on easy snow slopes. Then it swings back westwards to traverse under the north face across to the little col between the Dôme and the Barre des Ecrins. About halfway across, with our ire still unextinguished, we glanced at each other and turned off the well-trodden path to go directly towards the summit. We had vaguely thought that the north face would be an instructive exercise. We had not found a description of it and were not sure what to expect. What we found was distinctly unpleasant but appropriate for our state of mind.

The face is steep enough to feel serious but that in itself did not make ascent difficult. It appeared to consist entirely of loose slabby rock dubiously held together by verglas, all of which was obscured by a few centimetres of powdery snow. The protruding bits of rock were not securely frozen in. A couple of desultory attempts to use an ice-piton as a running belay simply cracked and dislodged little sheets of ice. The north face proper has perhaps two hundred metres of ascent from the bergschrund. By the time the sense of insecurity had turned our indignation into apprehensive concentration we were quite close to the top. With an adequate covering of well-frozen consolidated snow the face would be pleasant and easy.

Once we were off the face, thankful, and seated in the sun at the comfortable summit area, several rewards became apparent simultaneously. The situation is much more spectacular than the Glacier Blanc approach leads you to expect and we were able to look at the longer and serious alternative routes now revealed. Instead of finding many other climbers there we found it almost deserted, at least until after we had had a quiet drop of Scotch and some calm contemplation. Most importantly, all our angry frustration had gone and we were back in harmony with the mountains.

We descended the little west ridge, which goes down to the col over Pic Lory. It is an easy airy arête of clean rock that is impossible to climb without squeals of pleasure. I am amazed that so many parties go just to the undistinguished Dôme de Neige, thereby denying themselves both the fine situation at the main summit and the delicious contrast between the ridge and the uneventful snow slopes. On this occasion we did not bother with the Dôme de Neige. I included it in a visit fifteen years later. The most memorable things then were several thin columns of stones that someone had constructed by the side of the broad path to the Caron hut. These were delicately and improbably balanced and obviously the result of much practice. Nowhere more than forty centimetres wide, the tallest was over two metres high. There was something very pleasing about this anonymous activity and the fragility and impermanence of the columns.

3 Gran Paradiso
3a Il Roc
      W flank (F). With Bob McLewin
Map p 32   Illustrations pp 33, 8

I am not sure why the Gran Paradiso always provokes in me such affectionate thoughts. During my visits to the area I have not enjoyed particularly good weather. I have never had a clear idea which routes I wanted to do and I have certainly not made good use of the time. The routes I have done have had their moments but for the most part have been unremarkable in themselves and uneventful at the time. On top of this there has always been an air of indecision and a feeling of 'not getting it right'. This would usually annoy me. I attribute my equanimity about the lost opportunities partly to the relaxed atmosphere that characterises the area. When you experience it, you realise it is missing in many other places, especially the Swiss valleys. Also it has not been a place of burning ambition. I have not arrived there with a particular route filling my mind, so I have been spared those most enduring of disappointments. Then there is the association with successful days elsewhere. Twice, for example, I have been entirely alone on the Grand Combin and yet had the Gran Paradiso for company, continually in view almost exactly due south. But mostly, I suspect, it is the name. The implied combination of grandeur and paradise encapsulates much of what climbing in the Alps is all about.

Bob and I tried an ascent on sight of the south-east face of the Gran Paradiso, with only a vague idea where the route went. We gave up at midday and went back to Pont when the rock climbing began to get serious and the intermittent drizzle changed to a snowstorm. The following day we just walked up and down the ordinary route. We had woken up at 06:00 to find perfect weather and set out an hour later with bivouac gear and two days' food. We left most of this near the Vittorio Emanuele II hut but still found the steady snow slopes a bit of a slog. It would have been even more tiring if all the new snow on the path had not been partly trodden down. For this we had to thank the usual daily quota of dozens of climbers from the hut who had gone up much earlier. We met most of them coming down as we went up, including two or three parties of over twenty people all roped together. Few of them looked very cheerful. Several looked positively distressed. This made us realise that climbing the Gran Paradiso is something of a national obsession. For many of these people, none of them alpinists in any real sense, this would be their great day in the mountains. I hope they were happy afterwards.

When we were close to the summit ridge we left the well-marked path and went to the point called Il Roc, at the southern end of the ridge. This is where the more interesting, but not difficult, approach from Valnontey to the north-east arrives. We were merely contriving a more sporting finish along the summit ridge so that we could feel superior to the tourists. It was rather pointless with all the new snow. The genuinely superior route is the long ridge from the Herbetet, 3778m. If we had

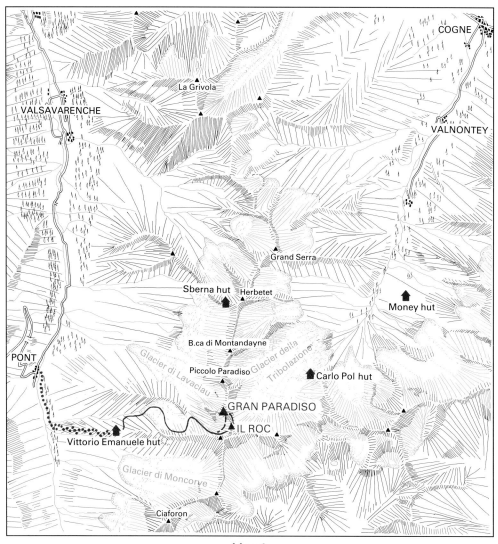

Map 3

Gran Paradiso from the Ciaforon

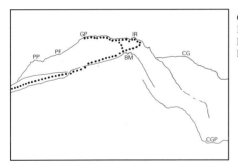

GP	Gran Paradiso	BM	Becca di Moncorve
IR	Il Roc	CG	Cresta Gastaldi
PP	Piccolo Paradiso	CGP	Colle del Gran Paradiso
PF	Punta Frassy		

gone directly to the main summit we would have had a good view of this ridge before thin cloud intervened.

The following day was a complete contrast. We did the short classic north face of the Ciarforon, 3640m. This was nicely steep, on immaculate crisp unmarked snow; a pleasing exercise, with a brief interesting bit at an icy wrinkle halfway up. This route and the normal way up the Gran Paradiso are excellent training routes. Neither needs perfect conditions. Both are of easy access and free of objective dangers.

Bivouac on the Allalinhorn summit; snow and a handy supply of flat rocks make an excellent site.

An old-style bivouac using a home-made box bag; on the Riedgletscher, below the NE face of the Hohberghorn.

Bivouacs

When I stopped using Alpine huts and began bivouacking the effects were astonishing and profoundly important. They went much further than better sleep, more congenial eating and less aggravation. Climbing became mountaineering, something done with the Earth instead of just on it, an activity shared with the mountains instead of in competition with them. Bivouacking has substantial practical advantages but the crucial changes have to be described as spiritual. So if all you care about is to say you have done a route and the manner of doing it is of no importance to you then these observations will leave you unmoved. In any case the words themselves will not be enough: personal discovery is needed.

Most climbers in the Alps walk up from the valley to a mountain hut and spend the rest of the day and at least part of the night there before leaving to do their chosen climb. This option, not available to early alpinists, has become the standard practice. Guide-book authors, by describing routes as if this were the case, ensure that it is, perhaps unintentionally. Bivouacking seems to me now almost as important as the climbing itself, yet it is generally neglected. Many climbers regard it as something to be endured in an emergency or other special circumstances and do not realise it requires preparation and practice just as climbing does.

My initial motivation for bivouacking was growing irritation with the hut regime. I rarely slept well and the inevitable snorer meant that nights were not even restful. Eating usually involved hassle unless you had plenty of money to spend. I began to feel that staying in huts was regarded as an activity in its own right and one geared to climbing only of a formalised, predetermined style. Language difficulties certainly exacerbated financial problems and magnified trivial misunderstandings. Ironically, on the now rare occasions that I stay in huts I am more relaxed about their failings and can enjoy the experience.

Bivouacs come in three basic varieties, which overlap in practice. They can be planned, when you set out with a precise site in mind. They are usually half planned, when you intend to bivouac somewhere along an itinerary, exactly where depending on how the day works out. Sometimes they are forced resulting from some degree of emergency, the seriousness of which depends on your situation, the weather, and exactly what has gone wrong. It depends also on how well prepared you are, where preparation involves food, equipment, experience and state of mind. An unplanned bivouac can be another pleasant night on the mountain if you are practised and relaxed. The same circumstances can be a traumatic ordeal if you are unprepared and tense.

Although no two are the same, an outline of a half-planned one will be relevant to bivouacs in general. The approach walk usually involves going up to a hut. On reaching it you may stop there briefly or walk disdainfully past. From the hut the first hour or so of a route often consists of boulders and loose rock. These sections are uncomfortable in the dark, worse when icy, and sometimes difficult to find. It is much easier to do them in the afternoon. When you reach the mountain proper, where the route is well defined, you look for a site. You have several factors in mind, both aesthetic and practical. You want a spot sheltered from the prevailing wind and possible bad weather and somewhere safe from falling debris. Running water is useful; at least clean snow or ice needs to be available. You want good views and it is nice to be in the sun. W.C. Fields got it right: 'If at first you don't succeed, try, try again, but there's no sense making a damn fool of yourself.'

Compacted flattish snow is best, with thin flat rocks to hand for making a seat and shelter, at least for the stove, although a bit of corrugated cardboard does that if you remember it. A rocky platform is never as flat to sleep on as one you tread out in snow, but making the best of what you find is part of the enjoyment. Even the best site needs some enhancing construction. With ingenuity very unlikely places can be made comfortable. Broken crevasses and séracs can provide good, sheltered sites but be careful you are not on a snow bridge. Once, leaving a bivouac on the north side of the Grand Combin, I idly chopped at a protruding lump of ice that had annoyed me all night. About a square metre of my bed disappeared into a vast cavern beneath.

By the time the basic construction is under way the first brew of tea is ready. As you drink it and have a snack you relax and expand out into the landscape. This is unlike arriving at a hut, which is always a contraction, a withdrawing from the mountains, however much you gaze around. Of course, this making contact with the mountain, this communion with the Earth, is a private business. It is not a question of impressing other people.

The time that remains before sunset is spent in a satisfying mixture of arranging everything, making refinements to the site, looking around to become familiar and in tune with the situation and simply enjoying being where you are. You can have a look at the next part of the route and sort out other routes on other mountains. When the sun sets it gets cold very quickly, usually with a brisk wind for about an hour even on calm days. I prefer to eat most of the evening meal while sitting in comfort in the sun. Tea, Scotch and odds and ends accompany looking at the sunset colours and settling down in bed. Equipment and the remaining food are arranged to make three things easy: finishing the evening meal and starting breakfast cocooned in bed, putting on boots and crampons and packing up at three or four in the morning when it is dark and very cold, and protecting yourself and your gear if the weather turns bad. In an exposed position you have to make yourself and everything else secure.

On top of the basics you learn many little tricks. Some paper kitchen roll weighs almost nothing and stops your tea tasting of soup. Plastic carrier bags are very useful: collections of associated objects can be assembled in them and you can store a stock of clean snow. Take a spoon: eating with pitons is only to impress the uninitiated. If you forget the plastic mug then a strip of elastoplast makes drinking tea from a metal pan less painful. (Do not forget a small reel of elastoplast.) Forgetting matches is not a total disaster: it saves messing about cooking. I take spare matches in a little bag of potentially useful items: needles and strong thread, a bandage, paracetamol, a few rivets and so on. You make your own idiosyncratic collection, gradually reducing it after years of carrying it around.

The simple-minded fussing that goes on is more important than it seems. All the time the mountains are part of your consciousness. Empathy grows. You are merely going about the ordinary business of living but it is transformed by the context, and so are you.

My sleeping and survival gear involves a Gore-Tex bivouac bag and a full-length, closed-cell carrymat. These are for basic, outer protection. As an inner layer of warm clothing I have a close-fitting pile-fabric suit, trousers, bootees and mountain shirt. Between the bivouac bag and the pile clothing is a layer of down insulation. This consists of an old sleeping bag cut down to waist length and a medium-weight duvet jacket. This arrangement evolved recently when I discovered the virtues of fibre-pile. Previously I used odd bits of spare clothing for the innermost layer and a home-made, box-shaped nylon tent-cum-bivi-bag. A tendency to bivouac higher and, I suspect, a less efficient metabolism demanded greater sophistication. For the Alps this ensemble is more than adequate except for exposed situations at the highest altitudes, so it has a valuable safety margin. I often find I am too hot at night and have to let in some cold air occasionally. The combination of down and pile is superior to either alone. Down insulates better uncompressed on top; pile fabric is better underneath. Down has better insulating properties, packs smaller and weighs slightly less; pile fabric is more robust and performs better when wet. Using garments rather than sleeping bags is slightly inefficient but provides much more flexibility. Garments can be worn during the day and are better for cooking and wriggling about when you are in the bivouac bag. The advantages of pile fabric are more pronounced when you are stuck in the bivouac bag for days on end in bad weather.

The sun disappears with a brief magic display of rosy colour. The sky darkens. You feel close to the Earth and part of its routine cycle although there is never a sense of routine about a bivouac. Strenuous efforts are appropriate to avoid having to get up during the night, which will usually be 21:00 to 03:00. You arrange inner boots into a pillow and settle down to sleep. Now the contrast with being in a hut becomes even more apparent. You sleep well or fitfully. Either way is a profound pleasure. When you are awake you look at the sky. There are so many stars. They seem not to be distant points of light but a net hung across the sky. Shooting stars flash across frequently; communications satellites, once an exciting rarity but now ever present, glide serenely across. An unbroken night's sleep is a disappointment.

Whether to bivouac or stay in huts is more a question of temperament than a weighing of practical benefits. You transform your relationship with the mountain from antagonist to communicant. 'Doing a route' becomes a more complex activity. Still, the practical advantages of bivouacking to set against having to carry extra weight are substantial. The main one is safety. You can stop anywhere and survive, and even enjoy an unexpected turn of events. If you are caught by bad weather you are not forced into a hazardous descent. Your itinerary is more flexible and you stop and start climbing where you choose. If you prefer your snow untrodden and the route to yourself this is the way to arrange it. Being first on a route is another safety factor. Other climbers are often your greatest danger.

For many participants climbing is a metaphor for life: the accepting of the challenge, the determined endeavour, the adventure. Bivouacking is superior as a metaphor for life: less of an ego trip, less false heroism, more a case of seeing what really is always there to be seen. This context for identifying and exploiting your own resources and making the most of what you can reasonably carry is less dramatic and therefore more relevant. Reaching the summit of a mountain will always be important. Equally it will always be essentially inconsequential.

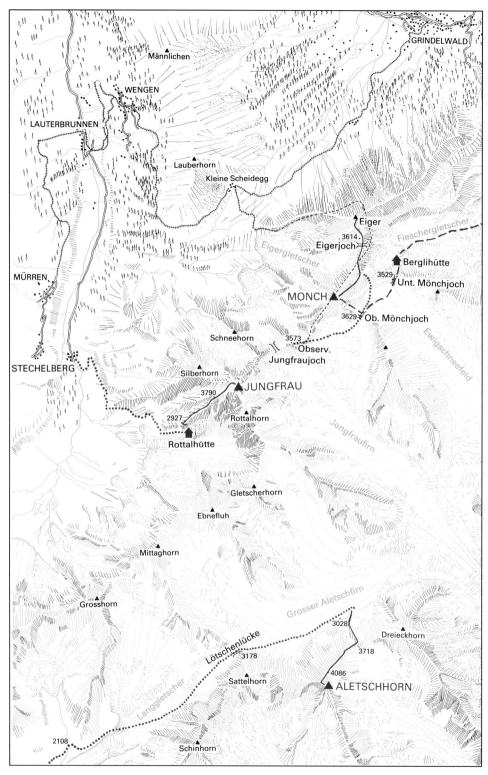

Map 4

Section 2
The Outer Oberland

| 4 | Jungfrau | 4158m | 6 | Gross Schreckhorn | 4078m |
| 5 | Mönch | 4099m | 7 | Lauteraarhorn | 4042m |

These four mountains form the north-eastern outer wall of the fourthousanders. Easy access to them from Grindelwald is emphasised by two rather grand huts which serve their popular routes. Each mountain has a distinctive character, and climbing on any one of them has its own individual feel. Some of the differences are in the mind, for this is the scene of legend, adventure stories and romantic prose: Goethe and Sherlock Holmes. Encouraged by appearances of the Jungfrau in sentimental literature many people make a laboured pilgrimage to its summit. There are few sighs of ecstacy about the Lauteraarhorn and you will find few people on it. This leads us to a distortion, small enough in itself but repeated over and over again. In truth much that is so wonderful about the Mönch and the Jungfrau is equally wonderful about many other mountains. What makes the Mönch and the Jungfrau special is that they can be viewed in comfort over lunch from chalet balconies and they can be approached in punctual and efficient Swiss trains. If poets and writers bivouacked on the Ewigschneefeld then perhaps the Gross and Hinter Fiescherhörner and the Gross Grünhorn would be the 'most famous mountain trinity in the world'. This is not quite fair, of course, because the Eiger figures in the picture. In any case I am certainly not complaining. To have so many of the people that are attracted to the mountains congregated in a few well-known places is something of a blessing because it leaves me free to enjoy long, intimate days in the sole company of, for example, the Lauteraarhorn.

Grindelwald is somewhere that I can never quite get to like. I appreciate the extensive and efficient Co-op, I know where the best bread shop is (just opposite the Co-op in fact), I know pleasant places for a beer, and I have learned the little wrinkles that come with familiarity. But there are simply too many people, in the town and almost everywhere you go. Too many notices tell you what is forbidden, and the whole place is just too pretentious. I freely acknowledge Grindelwald's virtues and its conveniences for indifferent weather. These include a number of entertaining walks. Grosse Scheidegg is a much better choice than Kleine Scheidegg, even more so when you get there. It has the option of an extension to Rosenlaui, where the narrow almost subterranean gorge is worth a visit. Also, simply for a training walk, the Gleckstein hut path is a better choice than the path to the Schreckhorn hut.

The new Schreckhorn hut has been built a bit higher up from where the old Schwarzegg hut used to be. Astonishingly, it is the obvious starting point for the north-west, south-west and south-east ridges of both the Schreckhorn and the Lauteraarhorn. Other possibilities are more remote, although the classic approach to the Lauteraarhorn from the east, starting fifteen kilometres away at

A	Agassizhorn
Hs	Hugisattel
Fj	Finsteraarjoch
S	Studerhorn
H	Helsenhorn
PC	P. Cervandone
Wh	Wasenhorn
W	Weissmies
M	Mischabel
VG	Vorder Galmihorn
Sc	Schinhorn
Ab	Albrunhorn
R	Rothorn

F	Finsteraarhorn
GW	Gross Wannenhorn
NS	Nasses Strahlegg
Fr	Finsteraarrothorn
FL	Fletschhorn and Lagginhorn

Finsteraarhorn from the Lauteraarhorn. This snowy summer landscape indicates, by implication, the poor conditions on the Lauteraarhorn when the picture was taken and partially explains the difficulties I had on the ascent.

Jungfrau, SW (Inner Rottal) ridge. The photograph is taken from the ridge itself, a few metres above the point where the path from the Rottal hut attains the ridge. The upper section of the route, on the snow slopes of the Hochfirn, is hidden behind point 3790m, and the easy-angled lower part of the ridge is greatly foreshortened.

the Grimsel pass, may appeal to some. It offers the rare possibility of starting with a boat trip, on the Grimsel lake. After that all it offers is tedium, apart from some very high-class British-style rock climbing on smooth walls beside the path to the Lauteraarhorn hut. It is hard not to feel a twinge of sympathy for the Lauteraarhorn. Everything about it is longer, more awkward and less inviting than its elegant near neighbour, the Schreckhorn. It receives hardly any visitors and the account of my solitary ascent will hardly provide encouragement to anyone else despite the grim satisfaction it continues to give me.

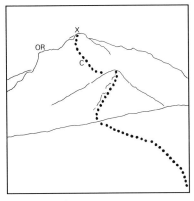

C   cliff section
X   point 3790m
OR   Outer Rottal ridge

The Jungfrau and the Mönch also are different in character. Here there is need for sympathy of another kind. Endless train loads travel up to the Jungfraujoch and do their best to trample the two of them to death. This way for community singing, hampers and Alpine fashion shows! The Jungfrau and the Mönch have much more to offer, especially the Jungfrau, which is a particularly complex mountain. The north-west sides, the long sides, both have famous classic routes. Some of these are probably a bit overrated, benefiting from their accessibility. The southerly sides, the short sides down to the Jungfraufirn, supply the popular routes, all of which are easy, elegant and interesting. In good conditions all of these routes are short enough to be climbed from the valley by catching the day's first, and cheapest, train to the Jungfrau-joch. There are several long and serious routes on the western side of the Jungfrau that are good value without being very difficult, the best of them surely being via the north face of the Silberhorn.

The enormous, fairly recent Obers Mönchsjoch hut is an impressive building but I find its presence depressing. It has had one happy consequence: the old Bergli hut, a further hour's walk from the train, is now rarely used. The Bergli hut is not all that inconvenient and offers a tranquil and more remote alternative. When it comes to choosing how to climb the Jungfrau and the Mönch the Jungfraujoch railway is a mixed blessing, because it distorts the purely mountaineering considerations. Well, everyone has to make their own choice. I did not want to climb the Jungfrau that way but I would certainly not urge anyone to use the old route via Baregg and the Kalli. Perhaps the best use of the railway is as a means of access, with several days' food, to the vast glacier complex and the surrounding peaks at the remote heart of the Oberland.

4 Jungfrau

SW (Inner Rottal) ridge (PD). Solo
Map p 38   Illustrations pp 42, 44

Despite often thinking about the routes I might do on the Jungfrau I had never got myself organised to climb any of them. Once I did set out from Stechelberg for the Silberhorn hut but found I was so totally in the wrong frame of mind that after about an hour I sat down, tried to think myself into the route, failed and simply walked back. Much later I half decided to save the Jungfrau until last. It turned out to be the last but one of my major fourthousanders.

I had just taken Anne Brearley to Zurich airport. She was somewhat the worse for wear after our encounter with the Brouillard ridge. She had caught a very early plane and I had not caught any sleep. The Sierre-Zinal race was in a few days time so I was driving towards the Rhône valley and thinking that it might be nice to do something on the Bietschhorn or the Nesthorn in the next couple of days, when I realised that I had gone through Interlaken and was heading for Stechelberg to do a route on the Jungfrau. If that was an example of 'voices in the sky' then I must have listened. They

Jungfrau E side from near the Obers Mönchsjoch; the conventional view of the Jungfrau, showing the normal route from the Jungfraujoch. This route traverses across the Jungfraufirn, then climbs to the Rottalsattel and up the broad SW ridge. Although this route can be descended very quickly there are places that are potentially interesting. These give the route character and make it more than a 'snow plod'.
In this picture I am staggering towards the Bergli hut with a heavy rucksack containing several days' food. Even at 3500m a snow-field on a windless day is very hot, so my thin shirt is protection against the sun rather than for warmth. The arab-style headgear, gloves and complete leg covering are equally important, to prevent severe burning.

had not said which route to do so I settled for a comfortable straightforward day with the south-west ridge, and that was the way it turned out.

The walk up to the Rottal hut on a very hot and bright afternoon was hard work. There was no guardian, only a party of three. Another party of three arrived a bit later and we all had a quiet and co-operative evening. I declined both offers to make up two ropes of two. After a restful night 04:30 saw us all stumbling along icy boulders towards what we hoped was going to be an easy access on to the ridge.

In fact we went right across the ridge and found ourselves with its crest behind and a bit above us. I was sure that on the crest was where I wanted to be, so I went directly to it up a dirty ice slope that was not as nasty as it pretended to be but was just steep enough to need care. One of the other parties followed. The second party watched the difficulties the first one created and perversely went further along beneath the crest to get on to it by a much longer and steeper ice slope.

I had watched enough of that. The sun was up and it was time to talk with the mountain. Past a rocky hump I could see the ridge rising pleasantly to the great broken cliff where the route climbs

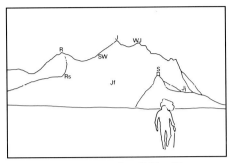

J	Jungfrau	S	Sphinx Observatory
WJ	Wengen Jungfrau	Rh	Rottalhorn
Rs	Rottalsattel	Jj	Jungfraujoch
Jf	Jungfraufirn	SW	SW ridge

steeply up and to the left. I looked all round, back towards the hut and across to the awesome Gletscherhorn-Ebnefluh north face, at the sky and down to the valley. I looked at particular bits and at everything at once. And then I grinned at the sun and just soared upwards, easily, steadily, effortlessly; physical and mental awareness fused together. There was quite a lot of fresh snow so the anticipated 'marks everywhere' were not all that obvious, but route-finding was not a problem, with the three fixed ropes acting like beacons. On the Hochfirn snow-field, conditions were immaculate, with the crisp scrunching brightness coming as a dazzling contrast to the rocks before. I began to realise that my energy was not limitless after all and it seemed natural to approach the summit in a gently ascending clockwise loop around from the north.

I did not count how many people were there, but there were definitely many. It was about 08:40 and probably the peak of the rush hour. There was a bizarre ritual in progress in which everyone had to take the same photograph but with everybody else moved round slightly. This must have been prearranged at the Jungfraujoch because as yet more groups arrived they seemed to know exactly what to do. My arrival, alone and unroped and from the opposite direction, provoked a flurry of questions in several languages. An inane smile and the single word 'English' provided a complete answer. I crept away to a peaceful spot where I could stamp out a bit of a hole in the snow. Out of the wind and in the sun I sat quietly and looked at the world. I thought fleetingly about the Wengen Jungfrau, 4089m, easily accessible along the rim of the Hochfirn. I had gone quite close to it on my way up. I decided to climb it in the proper context of the east ridge or not at all.

It was not until I was leaving, about an hour later, that I realised that there had been no sign of the other two parties. One of them appeared as I approached the end of the snow-field. Their message about what was going on further down was ambiguous, but their shock and apprehension were clear enough. I found the leader of the second party on the spacious ledge at the top of the last fixed rope. He was bringing up his two companions together, tied on to a single rope at the optimally dangerous distance apart of about four metres. They were wearing one crampon each. The second was dislodging every scrap of loose rock and snow and all three were shouting continually. The leader kindly indicated that I could descend. No way! I waited at the ledge until they had all reached it. While they were sorting themselves out I whizzed down the fixed rope and scuttled across out of harm's way. After this horror show and a minute or two to recover, I ambled on down; first to the hut and then, after a bit of lunch, to Stechelberg. I was delighted to have it all to myself until shortly before I reached the village.

Gaining access to the lower part of the Inner Rottal ridge is easy when it is in good condition. Even so an altogether better approach is to bivouac. From the hut path, where the hut first comes into view, a slaty slope leads efficiently to the end of the ridge. On a fine afternoon the ridge is a pleasant stroll as far as the steep cliff.

Mönch from the W ridge of the Eiger

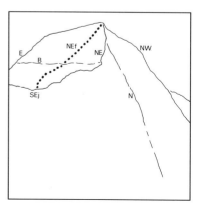

NE	NE ridge	NW	NW (Nollen) ridge
NEf	NE face	SEj	S Eigerjoch
N	N ridge	B	bergschrund

5 Mönch

NE face (D). With Brian Wood

Map p 38   Illustration p 46

This route offers a more challenging alternative to the three short ridges (NE, SE and SW). Like them it is easily accessible from the Jungfraujoch and entirely free of objective dangers. It is equally short. The north-east face is an excellent introduction to moderately steep snow/ice climbing. It is in a fine position and there is a very easy descent available, down the south-east ridge. The similar south face does not have the same elegance. Although less steep it is not quite as straightforward.

The previous day Brian Wood and I had gone up and down the south ridge of the Eiger after an excellent bivouac on the South Eigerjoch. That had left us confident for what we expected to be a test of our competence and fitness. We carried our bivouac gear round from the South Eigerjoch and left it below the face, pleased to find the bergschrund was barely a problem. We progressed smoothly up the face, climbing in pitches, although this was not strictly necessary. Slight disappointment at not finding the route technically more demanding was easily converted to satisfaction at our prowess and meant we could relax a bit more and savour the situation. Soon we were at the summit cornice, an enormous jutting overhang, which we simply smashed straight through in a burst of exuberance and energy and a great flurry of flying snow and ice. There is no alternative really. None of the parties coming up the south-east ridge was in sight, which was an unexpected bonus. We made ourselves comfortable and had finished a brew of tea by the time anyone else arrived.

We went back to Grindelwald by the pre-railway route: past the Bergli hut, across the Kalli and the Unterer Grindelwaldgletscher to join the Schreckhorn hut path at Baregg. At least that was our intention, and although we satisfied that basic itinerary I do not believe we found much of the old path. The middle section was long and tiring, in awful mushy snow. Nastily crevassed stretches gave us some uneasy moments. But do not be put off: it is probably very pleasant if you find a good line. I look back on it with grim satisfaction as one of my more trying afternoons; hard work but definitely instructive.

6 Gross Shreckhorn

SW ridge (AD), descent by SE ridge. With Anne Brearley

Map p 48   Illustrations pp 50, 52, Frontispiece

The Schreckhorn is understandably popular. The three usual ridge routes are nicely defined, give good situations and good climbing with sound rock. They are all straightforward to get at and are comfortably demanding expeditions; not long, but substantial and satisfying. The usual traversing arrangement is up the south-west ridge and down the south-east, which is what we did. A much better plan is to ascend the north-west ridge and then descend either of the other two. This is not much longer and gives more varied views. Also it avoids spending so much time in the Schreckfirn in ascent. The ridges themselves are quite short so a substantial proportion of the time and effort is spent on the steepish, less interesting approach slopes.

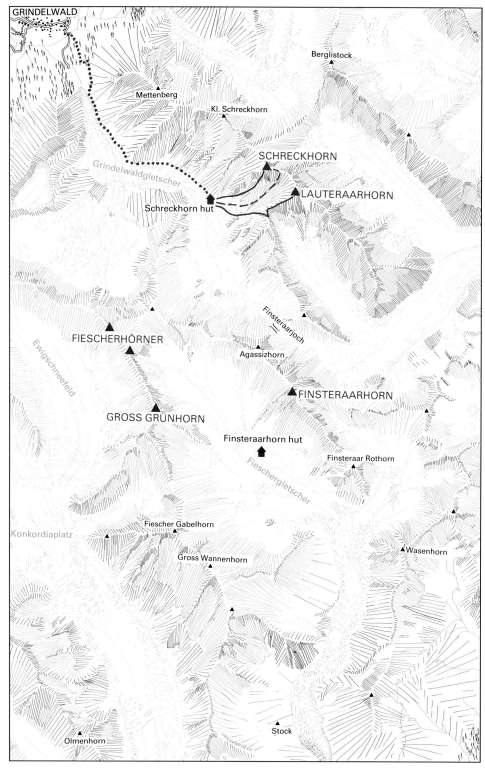

GRINDELWALD

Mettenberg

Kl. Schreckhorn

Berglistock

SCHRECKHORN

Grindelwaldgletscher

LAUTERAARHORN

Schreckhorn hut

Finsteraarjoch

FIESCHERHÖRNER

Agassizhorn

Ewigschneefeld

FINSTERAARHORN

GROSS GRÜNHORN

Finsteraarhorn hut

Finsteraar Rothorn

Fieschergletscher

Konkordiaplatz

Fiescher Gabelhorn

Gross Wannenhorn

Wasenhorn

Olmenhorn

Stock

Map 5

We were surprised to find the Schreckhorn hut completed and open so we went to have a look at it. The guardian said it was the second day it had been open to visitors. The brand new luxury and rather indifferent weather tempted us to join the few visitors already there. The next morning, about 02:30, the weather was still uncertain but good enough to be worth a try, given the moderate difficulties of the route. This provoked a not unfamiliar session of aggravation from the guardian, who did not want to provide any services and also insisted we should not use our own stove. It is sad how easily this sort of thing happens. The real problem is the mutual inability to communicate with any degree of sophistication. There is an increasing tendency for hut guardians to regard visitors who are determined to climb if at all possible as a nuisance. As approach walks are made easier and often shorter some guardians seem to have become more concerned with providing hotel facilities for tourists.

The aggravation seemed to linger on after we left. The weather for the rest of the day was windy and very cold, with occasional bright spells that faded just as we began to enjoy them. Strong winds are usually hard to live with cheerfully. They can be bracing and invigorating sometimes, when you are striding out across moorland for example, but on a mixed route, when you are roping and unroping, putting crampons on and off, continually looking about and stretching, they nag at the mind and irritate. We made only one genuine error. Instead of traversing right across to the south side of the Schreckfirn to where the bergschrund was fairly easy to cross, I thought we would save time by forcing our way across more directly. Well it was definitely a lot shorter, but it was also distinctly difficult. We gained excitement and rueful experience but not time.

The south-west ridge is ill defined in the lower section so many minor variations are possible. We did quite a bit of ascent on thin icy snow slopes on the edge of the south face, which seemed preferable to the ice-glazed rocks of the ridge itself. Higher up, another icy snow slope merged into the ridge and led us to a steeper, well-defined section of superb rock. Unfortunately this was icy. So were the one or two pitches of genuine rock climbing that followed. These involved disappearing round corners, which made communication impossible in the strong wind, so it was all a bit awkward and we took far too long. On a windless sunny day with dry rock it would be a delicious route. The final snowy crest was enjoyable, even in the wind, and we had a few minutes of calm warm weather at the summit.

The south-east ridge down to the Schrecksattel was pleasant and straightforward; occasionally quite sharp and exposed. One or two little bits were only just on the interesting side of awkward, so we were pleased to find it much less icy than the south-west ridge had been. The snow couloir down to the Schreckfirn is at exactly the angle that is efficiently and comfortably steep in ascent with crisp snow, but slightly intimidating in descent, especially when it is a bit soft. Very rapid descent is possible, perfectly safely, but it needs the right approach, which as usual is half technique and half attitude. We did not quite achieve that particular state of grace.

Once on the gentler slopes of the upper Schreckfirn we went right across to the southern corner, where the bergschrund to the lower Schreckfirn was easy. We just drifted down the centre of the glacier to the main Schwarzegg-Strahlegg path rather than traverse back north-west to the narrow snow slope that leads directly down to the hut. By now, late afternoon, the snow was soft and

Gross Schreckhorn and Lauteraarhorn from the Gross Grünhorn

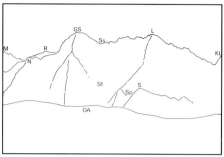

GS Gross Schreckhorn   M   Mittelhorn
L   Lauteraarhorn   KL Klein Lauteraarhorn
Ss   Schrecksattel   S   Strahlegghorn
Sf   Upper Schreckfirn Sp Strahleggpass
R   Rosenhorn   OA Ochs-Agassizhorn ridge
N   Nassihorn

Opposite: These are both summer pictures. They emphasise how much conditions can vary and how the character of routes can change. In an exceptionally dry year the ridges will be inviting and enjoyable; on the other hand the couloir from the Schrecksattel could be icy and very awkward, and give rise to unflattering comments about the hapless guide-book writer. When there is more snow than usual the couloir will be excellent, at least for the descent, but the rock ridges could be very difficult. They will essentially have become mixed routes and even the apparently clean sections may have a thin coating of ice.

frequently knee deep and there was misty drizzle. But I was reliving the same bit of descent made three years before, after climbing the Lauteraarhorn, and thinking how pleasant it was this time.

7 Lauteraarhorn

SW ridge and S face (AD). Solo

Map p 48   Illustrations pp 50, Frontispiece

I still have mixed feelings about this expedition, although they have gradually become more affectionate. At the time it felt like a total epic. In retrospect I can see that being utterly exhausted at the end was perfectly reasonable. I can also see that large sections of the route were thoroughly enjoyable and I did enjoy them. The problem was a sequence of setbacks, none of which was all that difficult. They seemed difficult because they were unexpected and because each added to the time pressure and the air of uncertainty. Something else that I have understood and learned since to recognise is that much of the anguish was self-inflicted. I had anticipated a fairly straightforward route and as it became more complicated and began to take much longer than expected I was not detached enough to adjust mentally. If it had not been my first outing of the season I would have coped better. If I had known what was going to happen I could have had a full and interesting day out. But it would still have been an epic.

Brian Wood and I had walked up from Grindelwald towards the Strahlegg hut without having finally decided which route we intended to do. The weather had not been bad enough to rule out doing a route nor had it been good; there was still a lot of new snow about. We bivouacked comfortably in the few remains of the ruined Schwarzegg hut. Though clear, the night was very warm. Next morning I was in favour of trying to get something done and Brian wanted to wait for better conditions. Eventually we decided to go up to the Strahlegg pass and we left at about 05:30. The snow on the Schreckfirn had that infuriating consistency where you break through the surface at each footstep just as you decide it is firm enough and you have almost transferred your weight. Randomly, about once in twelve steps, it is firm enough. At the Strahlegg pass, at 09:00 instead of 07:30, I looked in the guide-book for the south-west ridge. It sounded simple enough and what I

Gross Schreckhorn from the Lauteraarhorn

The ridge routes on the Gross Schreckhorn would be much less popular if they were as steep as this view suggests. The picture shows how easily photographs can mislead. The fierce-looking couloir, on the right, below the Schrecksattel is, in reality, at a comfortable angle for rapid descent. or efficient ascent, provided that the snow is in good condition.

Illustrations like this one give a false impression unless the picture's contents can be put in their proper context. In this case the steep, impressive part of the Gross Schreckhorn is the relatively short, last part of the route. A much greater distance is covered, and several times as much height gained, in the more mundane prologue to this section. A comparison with the frontispiece reveals this. Another important consideration is the prevailing conditions. The extent to which they can vary is shown in the pictures on page 50.

Considered together these four illustrations are very instructive. The observations that accompany them apply, by implication, throughout the book.

could see of it looked straightforward so I arranged to meet Brian at the Strahlegg hut at mid-afternoon.

I made good progress on the first part of the ridge even with the soft snow. I ambled up to an enormous steep step where I expected to traverse round to the right on to the south face. One look round the corner at a vast precipitous wall had me recoiling in horror. Another longer look and a walk back along the ridge for a few yards to get a better view of the prospects higher up led me reluctantly but inevitably to study more carefully the dark cliff directly ahead. Higher up, the south face was at a much shallower angle. The cliff wall was very steep and amazingly loose. But it was not so bad. I do not mind loose rock (I reminded myself). Whenever a handhold or foothold was needed one could be arranged by pulling bits off to construct it. There was not really any rock climbing to be done, just meandering from one flaky ledge to another, gradually working upwards. It was enjoyable when I concentrated on the immediate vicinity and forgot about the overall situation.

Eventually I was able again to look round the ridge on my right and to consider traversing across the south face. This was at a point where further progress up the ridge involves serious rock work. The south face was covered with a thick layer of wet soft snow. It looked beautifully clean, bright and inviting. Once on it I felt dreadfully insecure. After lurching across for a few metres, although I still felt uneasy I was not slipping much. I confirmed that the hard surface I felt occasionally under the snow was rock and not ice and carried on, eventually cheerfully, across to a little couloir leading to the south-east ridge. This took me easily to the summit, a charming rocky platform with no sign at all of previous visitors. The views were magnificent; it was 13:20; I realised I was tired; I felt terrific.

Half an hour later I started back down with wispy clouds beginning to fill the sky. There was no need for immediate concern but the situation felt faintly threatening. When I came to the point of traversing back across the south face I needed a conscious effort to push myself off the solid comfort of the ridge and into the snow. I found it hard work. My relief at regaining the south-west ridge was immediately dispelled by the intimidating prospect of threading my way down the loose ledges. Getting started on this needed another conscious effort. Once again it was not really difficult to make steady, careful progress. Even so it seemed to take ages and it was hard not to imagine the whole cliff giving way. Then I was down at the lower, easy part of the ridge and resisting the temptation to prolong a brief rest for something to eat into an extended stop .

I was only about a hundred metres from where the ridge ends at the Strahlegg pass when I fell off. I had left the crest to avoid an awkward little step and had probably missed an easy place to return to it. I was traversing awkwardly, standing on the thin crest of an icy slope where it met the vertical wall of the ridge flank. The slope had a thin covering of slushy snow and I was using rotten flakes on the rock wall for handholds. There was no real problem except that I was thinking more about reaching the Strahlegg pass than about exactly what I was doing. Suddenly I was sliding down the slope after my ice-axe, the only time I have dropped it that might have been serious. What I did not drop was one of the flaky handholds. It was big enough to dig into the snow to help arrest my descent. I went only about six metres. I watched my axe slither slowly on for at least thirty metres more before coming to rest precariously on a little rocky outcrop. It was a trivial incident and there was not really any danger but it seemed to release a flood of tiredness. I unstrapped my spare axe and climbed down to retrieve the other one, taking care not to disturb any debris. Slowly, ever so slowly, I worked my way wearily up again, veering across to an easy groove back to the ridge.

I descended the Schreckfirn like a drunken skater, reeling about in horrid soft snow, rubber legged and half asleep. I had so little control that a couple of times as I approached small crevasses I dived over them head first rather than risk a leg going in. Seeing Brian waving at me from the path suddenly brought me back to a world with other people in it. I staggered down to him and found myself unable to speak coherently. It was 18:30 and a soft drizzle was falling. We were both keen to get back to the comforts in Grindelwald, but our previous bivouac site was as far as I could manage. There we passed a wet and cheerless but not miserable night before spending most of the following morning going down.

Food

Just as equipment and clothing continually improve so there are advances in lightweight and pre-cooked food, both in variety and type. In spite of my unfriendly views about processed food I admit that food technologists have made the business of eating in extreme situations easier and more pleasant. Nevertheless, what to take to eat remains problematic.

I no longer experiment much. I content myself with small-scale variations on an established theme. Failures are so frustratingly painful. Sitting, tired and a bit frazzled, on a hard cold ledge or in a snow hole, probably in the wind as well, balancing stove and pan, carefully avoiding knocking it all over (not always, alas) while trying to organise sleeping gear and arrange all the other bits and pieces, and then finding that the menu conceived so imaginatively in the valley does not appeal is a very sad affair. I have learned to stick to a well-tried collection of items. I find that my standard dinner, which may seem boring in the valley, is always tempting on a bivouac. With the heightened sense of awareness on a mountain and the sustained intensity of my emotional state I find the same old menu satisfying. It always feels right.

It is easier when you are by yourself. There is nothing worse than feeling hungry but still not fancying the congealing mess in front of you while your companion gleefully gobbles away and almost visibly contemplates how to offer tactfully to dispose of your share too. When you are the one doing the gobbling and trying not to assess too overtly the chances of more to come, the pleasures of eating are enhanced. There are many considerations when choosing a person to do a route with! My theory about why T. Graham Brown and Frank Smythe fell out with each other so thoroughly after their admirable ascents on the Brenva face has nothing to do with arguments about whose idea it was to go where. I suspect that Brown was an aggressive eater and Smythe a fastidious one, and that while they were sitting under the Sentinelle Rouge and the Route Major with their tweed jackets and their candles, Brown was always trying to annexe Smythe's share of the pilchards.

My menu does not use the limits of food technology, and is not lightweight. I have opted to bear the weight of things that I prefer: good-quality tinned stewed steak, tinned new potatoes, and some fresh vegetables, usually onions, carrots and peppers. And large quantities. I like to eat as much as I want. I expect there are some 'complete meals in two-ounce bags; just pour on hot water and enjoy the luxury of haute cuisine' that I would like, but I persist in my old-fashioned ways. Even if such pre-packed miracles do exist I find it hard to believe that a crisp fresh onion would not improve them. I usually have some chocolate and a few raisins. Fresh figs or peaches are so unlikely on a bivouac they are worth the trouble of carrying; so is a half litre of wine, on the first day at least. Lots of tea is important, before and after the main meal. It aids digestion, combats dehydration, and helps me to get up early next morning.

On arrival at a bivouac site I usually have a cup of soup and a bit of bread at once unless it is late in the day, or construction work is needed urgently. Quickly and simply done, this eases immediate hunger. Then I can relax, immerse myself in the surroundings and make the most of the situation. Yes, instant soup; pragmatism as well as principle.

AT	Aiguille du Tour
PC	Petit Combin
A	Aletschhorn
H	Hasler rib
D	Dreieckhorn
S	Sattelhorn
B	Bietschhorn
MB	Mont Blanc
L	Lötschenlücke
G	Geisshorn
DB	Dent Blanche
GC	Grand Combin
Sc	Schinhorn

AC	Aiguille du Chardonnet
AV	Aiguille Verte/ Aiguille d'Argentière
CC	Combin de Corbassière
LB	Lötschentaler Breithorn
GA	Grosser Aletschfirn
GJ	Grandes Jorasses

Aletschhorn from the Gross Grünhorn

Breakfast is more critical. Simplicity and convenience are essential in the dark at 02:00 or 03:00 and at sub-zero temperatures. This meal took me a long time to get right and even passed through a baked beans phase. I am totally convinced by the present solution. I begin with a large mug of tea, made and drunk with conscious pleasure while still abed. A good time for a reflective look around in the moonlight or starlight, to check the weather signs and reopen communications with the mountain and the route. By then more water is hot and I emerge to begin the day proper with a large helping of muesli. This is an exotic home-made variety and I add plenty of hot water. Dried milk powder mixed in beforehand makes it very simple to prepare, usually in last night's potato tin. Muesli is easy to carry, and by taking more than I expect to need I have some excellent emergency food. It is an easily eaten, satisfying and sustaining breakfast. A large helping lasts through the business of getting boots and gaiters on, sleeping gear put away and all the other bits and pieces packed or distributed to handy pockets. Then another large mug of tea before making a move.

During the day I eat very little: perhaps a fruit-drop or a nibble of something and a 'mouthful of wet' occasionally. The most effective drink is Scotch and water in a one to five ratio. One mouthful of this is more refreshing than several mouthfuls of water.

For some climbers food seems to be simply fuel, consumed at an impressive rate and with a total absence of discrimination. This is a useful talent but one I do not possess. I take eating seriously and aim positively to enjoy it.

My favourite food incident was at the old Balmenhorn bivouac hut (since replaced). Brian Wood and I had walked up from Gressoney via the Alp Gabiet téléphérique with a vast quantity of provisions. We were determined to live in style before traversing Liskamm. The old Balmenhorn hut was a squalid snow-filled mess but we had cleared out the worst of it when two Italian climbers arrived. Possibly they were father and son, possibly both called Giorgio. Their eating philosophy was the space-travel variety: minimal-weight bits of odds and ends in silver paper. A couple of aperitifs and our first litre of wine had made us expansive and generous. Despite an almost total inability to communicate meaningfully we persuaded them that they should eat well. They joined in our six-course meal of soup, bread and salami, stewed steak and new potatoes and salad, cake, chocolate and fresh fruit followed by coffee and Scotch. Alas, our hospitality rebounded on us because they spent most of the night getting up to be sick. Entertaining for us perhaps, but not restful. When we got up and had breakfast they pretended to be asleep. We went along with this charade and left without further progress in the causes of alpine cuisine and Anglo-Italian relations.

Brian Wood.   I have climbed with Brian Wood much more than with anyone else. We have shared mistakes and frustrations along with glorious days. Whether, as we taught ourselves how to climb in the Alps, we helped each other survive or somehow managed to avoid killing each other I am not sure. He is a good man to be with on a mountain. The context of climbing days on big mountains has given our friendship qualities of affection, indebtedness and mutual respect to which nothing I could say would do justice.

In reflective mood at our private bivouac site on the Gnifetti hut balcony, Brian contemplates the extravagant collection of food and gear we have just carried up. On this occasion the approach walk turned into a relentless, exhilarating slog so the medicine he is taking is to aid recuperation.

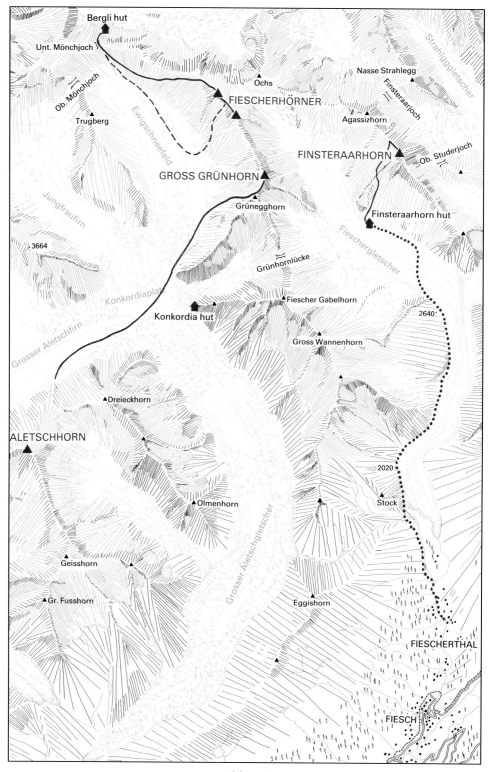

Map 6

60

Section 3
The Inner Oberland

8	Gross Fiescherhorn	4049m	11	Finsteraarhorn	4274m
9	Hinter Fiescherhorn	4025m	12	Aletschhorn	4195m
10	Gross Grünhorn	4043m			

Long days on snow, solitary and technically undemanding, are the essence of the Inner Oberland. Rugged and exciting expeditions are available, particularly major ice routes, but I did not feel a need to seek them out. Placid, straightforward routes that engendered contemplation were my instinctive choice. Perhaps, as a result, the image I have is inaccurate. I think of the Inner Oberland as a place where the landscape changes slowly as you move and where it is a background to your thoughts, only occasionally dominating them. Sometimes, of course, you lose sight of the simple pleasures and what might have been a satisfying walk degenerates into tedious plodding. When that happens what impressed you earlier as the vast grandeur of the area may become merely an endless desert of snow. Despite their simplicity the routes in this section were full of illusory impressions. On each of them the route itself or my reaction to it was different from what I had anticipated.

In this part of the Alps I was lucky with the weather. The five 4000m mountains here were climbed in three expeditions amounting to only six days, so for me much of the area remains unexplored. During those six days, spent with either Anne Brearley or Brian Wood, we encountered just three other parties. I think of it as a mysterious region that I have set on one side to await times when I want quiet uncomplicated days alone with the mountains. The sense of mystery is well founded. About twelve other mountains deserving of attention remain rarely climbed because of their relative obscurity and because they are not quite 4000m high. The most difficult peak in the Oberland, the Bietschhorn, is sixty-six metres short. It emphasises even more than the Eiger the arbitrariness of a list of mountains determined by people's obsession with round numbers.

Matching the seldom-trodden mountains are quiet undeveloped valleys, exemplified by the Bietschtal, Baldschiedertal and Gredetschtal. Parallel and adjacent to each other, north of Visp, they are simple and austerely impressive. Like most of the valleys that run northwards from the Rhone valley they are only marginally relevant to climbing the major peaks. They do however provide a refuge from busy roads and crowded towns and reinforce the area's special character. Even the attractive main access valley, the Lötschental, has remained peaceful and its villages of Wiler, Ried, Blatten and Fafleralp unspoiled. The lower section of the valley is busy because the trains carrying cars and passengers from Kandersteg emerge from the Lötschberg tunnel, at Goppenstein. All the tunnel traffic continues on southwards so the tranquillity of the long upper section of the valley is a surprising contrast. The dominant feature of the Inner Oberland is not the highest and most striking

Fiescherhörner from near the Unders Mönchsjoch

mountain, the Finsteraarhorn, but the longest glacier in the Alps. The Grosser Aletschgletscher is over twenty-two kilometres long. Its rate of flow is about 200 metres per year. It begins at the Konkordiaplatz, the plateau of snow at the heart of the Oberland. At the centre of the Konkordiaplatz the ice beneath the snow covering is 800 metres deep. The vertical distance to the summit of the nearest 4000 peak, the Gross Grünhorn, is only 1200 metres. Three other important glaciers meet here and feed the Grosser Aletschgletscher, although the word 'gletscher' is not used for any of them on Swiss maps. One is the Ewigschneefeld; the other two are the Grosser Aletschfirn and the Jungfraufirn. These two provide the shortest and most popular routes to the famous Konkordia hut: from the Hollandia hut, by the Lötschenlücke at the head of the Lötschental, and from the

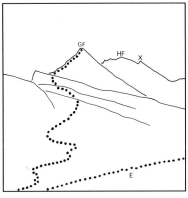

GF Gross Fiescherhorn
HF Hinter Fiescherhorn
X   point 3981m
E   Ewigschneefeld

Jungfraujoch. Curiously, and uniquely, both these hut approaches involve descending a glacier. This means that when leaving the Konkordiaplatz they are uphill. Then they do not seem short.

Other approaches to the Konkordia hut are very much longer. Those from Fiesch and from Grimsel, conventionally approaches to the Finsteraarhorn or the Oberaarhorn, are interesting expeditions in their own right. As such they have much to recommend them. The final possibility for reaching the Konkordia hut is the Grosser Aletschgletscher itself. As a geological spectacle it is magnificent: as an approach walk it is probably the most boring in the Alps.

8 Gross Fiescherhorn
NW ridge (PD), descent by W flank. With Anne Brearley
9 Hinter Fiescherhorn
NW ridge (F). Solo
Maps pp 48, 60   Illustrations pp 62, 64, 99

When we left Grindelwald on the train to the Jungfraujoch we had in mind a grand expedition lasting several days. This explains why I staggered across the Jungfraufirn to the Obers Mönchsjoch and on to the Unders Mönchsjoch with an uncomfortably heavy rucksack bulging with provisions. My discomfort was completed by dangling plastic bags full of bread, cheese and fruit. At the ancient and deserted Bergli hut the effort of haulage seemed well worth it. We sunbathed on the balcony and enjoyed a long, self-indulgent lunch that included plenty of wine and ended with fresh figs.

During the night Anne slept badly and by early morning felt unwell. She was not in pain but was heavy limbed and lethargic so it was a day later when we left for the Gross Fiescherhorn. Our progress was slow although there were no difficulties. We spent too long trying to traverse efficiently across the flank and should have gone more directly to the ridge. Steep verglassed rocks on the last part of the ridge nudged us on to a steep ice slope about fifteen metres high. This was the very edge of the great Fiescherwand, the north face of the Gross Fiescherhorn. I was halfway up before I realised that it was exposed and precarious. I pressed on to the top of the slope, which was almost the summit, relieved that it was not longer or steeper. Anne was feeling tired and unsteady, more so than I had realised. As she climbed the slope she surprised both of us by suddenly getting out of balance and falling off. I had not taken roping-up very seriously and was absent-mindedly looking to my right at the the inviting snow ridge to the Ochs. Fortunately I had a good stance and Anne was almost below me so she just swung across the slope a little.

Reaching the summit shortly afterwards was for Anne undiluted pleasure, not for the superb views all round but for the opportunity to sit down and rest. I left her there dozing in the sunshine, while I descended the easy ridge to the Fiechersattel. I continued along the north-west ridge to the

Top section of the Gross Fiescherhorn NW ridge

Hinter Fiescherhorn summit, with a loop on the north-east flank to avoid an awkward-looking tower. From the summit crest the views were enticing, like many in the Oberland. In every direction there lay vast snow-fields and gleaming ridges, smooth undulating slopes alternating with mazes of crevasses: a delight to traverse in your imagination, tedious and frustrating in practice. I retraced my steps hoping to interest Anne in the the beautiful pristine snow between the Gross Fiescherhorn and the Ochs.

I found her asleep. Ostentatiously I took out bread and cheese and began eating it. When she did not react I knew there was something wrong. She vetoed a return down the ice slope the way we had come, so we went down the ridge to the Fiechersattel and descended to the Ewigschneefeld. I had envisaged charging down to the glacier, leaping gaily over crevasses, but Anne was in no condition to charge anywhere. By the time we turned to begin trudging slowly up the Ewigschneefeld thin cloud was around us and light drizzle was falling steadily. This persisted all the way to the Unders Mönchsjoch, for four of the longest hours I can remember. Wearing head-torches in the dark we reeled and slithered down horrid wet snow and staggered at last into the sanctuary of the Bergli hut.

10 Gross Grünhorn

SW flank (PD). With Brian Wood
Maps pp 48, 60   Illustrations pp 66, 99

The previous day we had climbed the Aletschhorn and bivouacked at the foot of the Hasler rib. This meant that climbing the Gross Grünhorn was preceded by a six-kilometre walk down the Grosser Aletschfirn, across the Konkordiaplatz and up the left (east) side of the Ewigschneefeld. Crossing the Konkordiaplatz in the dark was drearily unpleasant particularly when Brian stepped in a concealed stream and found himself with both boots full of icy water. If there had been a rock close by instead of ankle-deep slush he would have stopped to change his socks for dry ones. Instead we pressed on, thinking mistakenly that his feet would get warm.

The south-west flank would be a simple snow slope without its band of deep, complicated crevasses. These create an enormous labyrinth, and crossing them is a bizarre problem. The directions in which movement is possible are dictated by the ice cliffs and channels in the immediate vicinity. Moving along the bed of a crevasse, between two séracs, you are in a strangely beautiful world of cold colours and shafts of sunlight. It is magical yet frustratingly awkward to move in because you frequently find the way blocked by fallen debris or by a deeper crevasse too wide to cross. If you climb to the top of a sérac, which is often difficult to do, you see what appears to be a rippling snow-field. Trying to walk across reveals that it is much less continuous than it seemed. Over the domed top of the sérac you are standing on you are likely to find a gaping crevasse, previously out of sight, barring your path. So you wander about trying to find snow bridges, sometimes descending from the dazzling windy surface into the eerie quiet and then clambering out on what you hope is a more helpful sérac.

We were lucky. We found a way to the unbroken upper slopes without much doubling back and before the enchantment and the sense of adventure evaporated. We came to the rocky south-west

Gross Grünhorn from the Fieschergrat, SE of the Walcherhorn

Sunrise colours from the SW flank of the Finsteraarhorn at 05:30

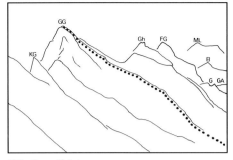

GG   Gross Grünhorn
KG   Klein Grünhorn
G   Grünegghorn
FG   Fiescher Gabelhorn
G   Grünegg
B   Bettmerhorn
ML   Monte Leone
GA   Grosser Aletschgletscher

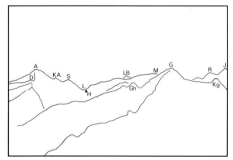

A	Aletschhorn	H	Hollandia hut
GG	Gross Grünhorn	LB	Lauterbrunnen
J	Jungfrau		Breithorn
D	Dreieckhorn	G	Grünegghorn
KA	Klein Aletschhorn	M	Mittaghorn
S	Sattelhorn	R	Rottalhorn
L	Lötschenlücke	KG	Klein Grünhorn

On the sunlight horizon is a sky-shadow of the Aletschhorn. This is an unpredictable effect. Frequently, as here, shadows of other peaks which 'ought' also to appear are absent. Presumably there is a patch of thin mist that serves as a screen on which the shadow is projected. Sometimes the shadow can clearly be seen to be in the middle distance and not at the far horizon.

ridge near the summit and scrambled up it easily. The day was bright and clear but there was a cold biting wind. This was disappointing because we were early enough, 08:00, to have stayed some time if it had been more pleasant, and if Brian's feet had warmed up. All the ridge routes to the summit looked very attractive, yet I did not regret the choice we had made. It had been fascinating in its own way, with a strange, subdued excitement. From the summit we could see an obvious modification of our line through the maze that was easier and more direct, but when we returned we soon lost our image of it and resorted to retracing our footsteps.

At the bottom of the Ewigschneefeld a warm flat rock prompted Brian to decide he had put up with cold feet for long enough. His tough, Norwegian woollen socks had shrunk tightly on to his feet and we struggled for half an hour to get them off. An ice-piton, which had been an unnecessary burden on the route, finally proved to be a decisively useful implement.

11 Finsteraarhorn

SW flank and NW ridge (F). With Brian Wood
Maps pp 48, 60   Illustrations pp 40/41, 69, 81

The Finsteraarhorn is the highest and most striking mountain in the Oberland. It is the fin-like central section of a long straight ridge running northwest to south-east. The ridge provides a classic traverse, even when only a short section of it is climbed by joining and leaving it high up. Looking back I have some regrets that we were not more ambitious. The conditions were good and we discovered we were fitter than we had thought, so we could have coped easily with a more adventurous itinerary. Instead we had two days where there was no drama and where the surprises were small and pleasant. Despite the lack of incident I remember this

expedition with particular affection. The long walk to get close to the mountain gave a superficial air of commitment which gave way to a feeling of well-being as we made rapid progress on the ascent itself.

The approach walk from the quiet village of Fieschertal to the Finsteraarhorn hut is one of the longest in the Alps. The guide-book time is seven and a half hours. The early traverses round steep rock shoulders followed by gradual progress up the right bank of the Fieschergletscher were more interesting than we had expected. At one point we stopped for a few minutes by an enormous steep wall of rock. About fifteen metres up, balancing on tiny ledges, was a large ibex with massive horns. Further progress was clearly impossible but the animal was able to make one small, precarious move higher. It edged forward, paused, and went back, waited, and stepped forward again. Apparently unconcerned by our presence or by its own predicament it repeated the movement several times as we sat watching. After a few minutes we resumed our own task in case our presence inhibited it from descending, although we could not see how it could get down or why it would have attempted to ascend such a sheer face in the first place. Brian said how impressed he was with its patience and persistence. I thought this was a bit unfair because when I behave like that on a rock pitch he usually asks what I am faffing about at.

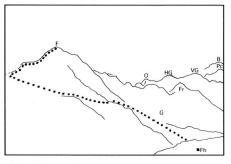

F   Finsteraarhorn
O   Oberaarrothorn
VG   Vorder Galmihorn
HG   Hinter Galmihorn
Fr   Finsteraarrothorn
Gl   Gemschlicke
Fh   Finsteraarhorn hut (out of sight)
PC   Punta dei Camosci
B   Basodino

Early morning; valley haze and bright sunlight.   The brief sunrise display of glorious colours is followed by more subdued shades which give an air of mystery to the mountains.

The upper section of the Fieschergletscher is called the Walliser Fiescherfirn; the Finsteraarhorn hut is on a buttress at the lower left bank of this glacier. As we approached the buttress we found an excellent bivouac site at its base. Despite the hut being nearby, our enjoyment of the evening meal in the comfortable situation and of the darkening clear sky was enhanced by a feeling of remoteness. We had seen no other people since we left the village. Next morning we breakfasted and left early to have the route to ourselves. Easy snow slopes, quite steep at first, lead to the incipient saddle where we crossed the long south-west rib of the Finsteraarhorn. Then more, crisp snow slopes took us to the Hugisattel on the north-west ridge, little more than five hundred metres from the summit. As we scrambled up the ridge the sun appeared. With the sun barely above the horizon the views and the colours from the summit were magnificent: blues and greys of seemingly endless, unknown misty mountains to the east; purples and rosy pinks to the west on the nearby summits as they caught the sun. I felt more than pleasure and amazement: I felt a sense of privilege. Also I was no detached observer. I was aware that in some way my life and my vision of the world had been changed.

We stayed at the summit for an hour, watching the Earth briefly blaze with colour as the sun rose. It was almost a shock to realise that this glorious spectacle happens on every fine day and usually passes unobserved.

Perhaps we should have changed our plans on the descent to take advantage of the good conditions and our being so early. We could easily have stayed on the north-west ridge past the

Finsteraarhorn from the Gross Grünhorn

Hugisattel and continued to the Agassizhorn. This fine peak, overshadowed by the Finsteraarhorn and consequently neglected, has the improbable distinction of being visible from Grindelwald and from the Grimsel pass, on opposite sides of the Oberland. We were mindful of the long walk back to Fiesch. Had we known we would find it an enjoyable stroll we might have extended our climb, but the walk back would then probably have proved to be hard work.

12 Aletschhorn

N (Hasler) rib (PD+). With Brian Wood

Maps pp 48, 60   Illustrations pp 56/57, 66, 99

It might have been all the unconsolidated fresh snow, or our heavier than usual rucksacks; perhaps we had not been in the Alps long enough to get fit; possibly the lunch-time planning session over a few beers had gone on too long. For some reason we found the walk from Fafleralp to the Lötschenlücke much more tiring than we had expected. As always the unpleasant surprise was more painful than the extra effort. Our idea had been to continue for another three kilometres down the Grosser Aletschfirn to the foot of the Hasler rib and to bivouac there. Deep unpredictable, soft snow on the glacier soon disabused us. A few hundred metres from the Hollandia hut at a point that was nowhere in particular we threw our rucksacks down and stamped out a level patch. After a soothing cup of tea we relaxed and had an enjoyable bivouac.

Next morning the snow felt much crisper and so did we. In spite of leaving most of our gear at its foot, we found climbing the rib tiring. Recent snow, although frozen overnight, was soft under the surface crust and knee deep in places. It was awkward more than difficult, particularly in the rocky sections. The north rib is a low-relief feature on the long north-west face and for much of the time, although the climbing is interesting, the situations are unexceptional. It leads to a point on the north-east ridge about two kilometres from the main summit and until the ridge is attained you do not get a view of the last section of the route. The upper part of the rib is sharply defined and feels more airy.

The north-east ridge, rounded and smooth, was at first a pleasant contrast to the last bit of the rib but then began to seem tedious. Better snow conditions in which we could have stridden briskly along the ridge would have made all the difference. We paused for a few minutes at the fore-summit, 4086m, five hundred metres from the main summit. Brian was not altitude acclimatised and decided he had gone far enough. As I ambled up the curving ridge to the top I felt slightly disappointed. The Aletschhorn had seemed beforehand more impressive than it felt at the time. It has a massive snowy bulk that typifies the Inner Oberland yet as had I climbed it an awareness of its character had eluded me.

Descending was a pleasant surprise. Any urgency climbing down the rib was removed by the anticipation of spending a sunny afternoon at our comfortable bivouac site at its foot, doing nothing but enjoying the situation. In descent the snow was accommodating and secure as we plunged down. During the afternoon I thought back to the few minutes I had spent at the summit. As on the other Inner Oberland summits I had looked down at the alternative ascent routes and seen that the mountain had much more to offer. On peaks in other areas there are specific routes that I feel I ought to do. Here I am aware of a less precise, yet more profound, longing: simply that I must spend more time with these mountains.

Equipment

Comparisons with mountaineers of the past are pointless and inconclusive. They are also inevitable, so I wonder what it was like when the routes I do were the latest achievements. If nothing else such comparisons emphasise that the mountaineer's mental equipment, fitness and attitude are more important than anything he or she wears or carries. Yet changes in material aids are profound, so much so that it seems to me impossible to imagine at all accurately what mountaineering was like when equipment that I take for granted was much more primitive or non-existent. In fact I do not take it for granted because almost every item I take on a route is significantly different from what it was when I began climbing.

Probably economic and social progress are more responsible than changes in equipment for transforming what were once great feats into commonplace events. The most important material change concerns information, especially guide-books and maps, Swiss maps at least. Adequate, freely available information enables independent mountaineering; this makes large numbers of participants possible and they sustain development and manufacture of new equipment.

My interest in 'the latest developments' is haphazard. I have tested prototypes and have usually continued using them long after improved versions have become available. The item that has not changed for me, apart from things like spoons and plastic mugs, is the two pairs of thick, blue, Norwegian wool socks I bought for my second trip to the Alps. I have worn the same two pairs, augmented by a third, on every subsequent trip.

In contrast to my socks, during the last few years leather alpine boots have nearly become museum pieces. Two-piece boots, plastic outer and soft leather inner, are almost standard. They are tough, rigid and persistently waterproof; excellent on snow, ice and difficult rock. Their rigidity makes them less comfortable than leather boots at their best and clumsy on easy broken ground. This is a small price to pay for the improvement where it really matters. They have two other major advantages that I am sure are fortuitous. They are much better for bivouacking. The outer boots do not need protection from cold at night and the inner boots make a pillow that deserves the name. This has put an end to the unsatisfactory practice of using leather boots as a pillow to stop them freezing solid. Even more important, the total rigidity of plastic boots has resulted in new style crampons. These are lighter, and clip on easily and securely. They banish the endless problems with crampon straps and with putting crampons on. I must get a pair. Perhaps this means that climbing bits of moderate rock in crampons to save the aggravation of taking them off and replacing them later will become a thing of the past, but I doubt it.

I suspect most climbers who began climbing with leather boots retain some affection for them; not for leather boots in general, but for the rare pair that was just right. I have fond memories of the boots made by Robert Lawrie. Instead of welts they were held together by wooden pegs. They were soft black leather, bendy and not nearly tough enough. On broken ground though, and there is plenty of that to be covered, they were superb: neat and comfortable and feeling as if they were part of the body. A change that has come with plastic boots, which in some cases is definitely not an

W   Weissmies
P   Portjenhorn
LS   Lagginhorn, S summit
T   Tallihorn
SWr secondary WSW ridge

Weissmies and summit crest from the Lagginhorn main summit

improvement, is colour. What character defect leads someone to buy fluorescent orange alpine boots? Someone who does is certainly not seeking a sense of harmony with the mountains.

I have no reservations at all about modern gas stoves. They are small and light and are stable and easy to shelter. They use a propane-mixture fuel and have a self-sealing detachable cylinder connected to the burner by a flexible tube. Even in very cold conditions they perform well. I look forward to seeing Camping Gaz stoves in the museum cabinet next to leather alpine boots.

Synthetic materials have transformed mountaineering clothing along with every other sort. The changes are largely cosmetic except for modern fastenings; an apparently small detail which is significant in practice. Gore-Tex is an impressive development even if it does not live up to the publicity. Expelling moisture as water vapour is not so successful when the outer surface freezes. Then the choice of inner garments is crucial. The Buffalo Double-P system, which does not aim to be completely waterproof and uses pile fabric for insulation, is a persuasive alternative. It is more comfortable to wear, moisture is expelled in the same way and it insulates well when wet. Rucksacks have improved vastly thanks to synthetic materials, although they get steadily more complicated. Are we soon to see programmable rucksacks?

Ice-axes have changed as much as crampons without such universal benefits. The angled-pick, short-shafted types are superb on steep ice. There is an extraordinary range of them. The trouble is that climbers who never climb on steep ice seem to feel obliged to buy them because they are the latest development. Or do I mean fashion? Consequently, on moderate exposed snow/ice crests where all that is needed is balance and a sense of delight, they are bent double using the axe for security, which is necessary only because they are bent double. I carry a short axe when soloing mainly in case I should lose my ordinary one. I rarely use it. The irony of ice-axes is that the pick/adze end is almost never used by most climbers. That end of the implement has largely been made redundant by crampons. Can it be just tradition that prevents more radical changes?

More significant than changes in equipment is the general availability of accurate detailed weather-forecasts. Or it will be when they are generally available. One of the redeeming features of Chamonix is mountain weather information. It means you can use your time more effectively and avoid that most awful frustration of being in the wrong place. I expect future climbers, wherever they are, will obtain the weather news on miniature portable telephones and even get pictures on tiny televisions. Probably even guide book information will be available that way. You can imagine a 2001-style conversation between a tense climber and the local smooth-toned guide computer.

'Now where do we go?' *'The next pitch traverses to your right.'*

'Are you sure about that?' *'I repeat, the next pitch traverses to your right.'*

'But it looks easier to the left.' *'The route to the left gets more difficult round the corner.'*

'But I can see pitons in place to the left.' *'They have been left by retreating parties.'*

'O.K. I'll try to the right.' *'I am sure you will enjoy it.'*

Suppose we could offer to climbers of sixty years ago, for example, all the technical and material aids that are now a routine part of mountaineering. Which single item would they be most grateful for? Probably none of the items mentioned above. Some would choose an automatic compact camera. They would all think polythene bags were wonderful.

Section 4
The Valais East

13	Lagginhorn	4010m	16	Alphubel	4206m
14	Weissmies	4023m	17	Strahlhorn	4190m
15	Allalinhorn	4027m	18	Rimpfischhorn	4199m (4108m)

These six mountains subdivide naturally into three pairs. All have undemanding, mostly short routes and easy access from the Saastal. I began my Alpine climbing here and in Arolla so I feel a special affection for this group and for the valley towns of Saas Fee, Saas Grund and Saas Almagell.

Once I would have said this was an ideal area for starting to learn about the art of Alpine mountaineering and the craft of Alpine climbing. Now I would hesitate. Saas Fee may be a great centre for tourists but for mountaineers the town has been corrupted and the mountains have been domesticated. The efforts to provide year-round entertainment for tourists have resulted in too much mechanisation. The téléphériques go high up and there are too many of them. There is even an underground railway, crassly called the Metro-Alpin, that will transfer you with clinical efficiency from the top of the Felskinn téléphérique to Mittelallin, at 3500m on the Hohlaubgletscher. Whether you regard a téléphérique or a railway as a useful amenity or an incongruous disfigurement is never clear cut. Often, ironically, the deciding factor is whether it was there on your first visit or whether it is a recent addition. But can there be anyone visiting the Saastal who is in favour of the garish advertisement hoardings for them? These developments reflect the ethos of commercialism encapsulated by the support of local councillors for a ludicrous proposal to construct a rock platform on top of the Fletschhorn to raise its height to 4000m in order to attract more visitors. Alas Saas Fee, much of your charm, once so beguiling, has gone.

The qualities of the mountains remain, of course, and they are exactly right for beginners. This means they are also exactly right for more dilapidated climbers approaching retirement as slowly as they can. These qualities are these: attractiveness, the obvious routes are varied and interesting; flexibility, there are many alternatives and it is easy to extend or curtail an itinerary en route; and safety, there are few badly crevassed approaches, there is very little objective danger and there are simple descent routes. There are a few difficult routes on the mountains of this group, mostly with fairly obscure starting points. More challenging expeditions for parties based in the Saastal can easily be arranged by combining two summits or by climbing the Mischabel peaks of Section 5. Another advantage of the Valais East is that most routes go well even in poor conditions. This makes them useful for training, if anyone still indulges in that rather old-fashioned activity, and useful in periods of indifferent weather. I have met climbers who come to Saas Fee every year and I can see their

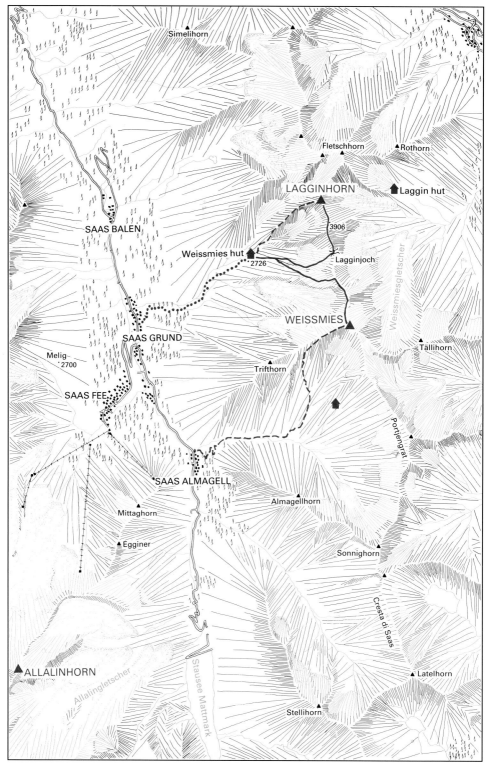

Map 7

point. There is the pleasure of familiarity, they can always find new ground to explore and they can be sure of some successful days.

The Längflue téléphérique enables the Allalinhorn and the Alphubel, or even both, to be ascended quite casually with a mid-morning start from Saas Fee. The same is true of the Weissmies using the Kreuzboden – Hoch Saas téléphérique from Saas Grund. On such excursions, as you make you way past ski-tows and piste skiers, the presence of the town and so-called civilisation remain. The voices of the mountains are but faintly heard. This is not the way to begin Alpine mountaineering.

I have only once stayed in Saas Fee itself. I prefer the humbler atmosphere of Saas Almagell. About a kilometre south of the village, by a bridge across the river, are a little wood and a flat stony meadow where ad hoc camping is tolerated provided you are discreet and do not stay too long. It is far more pleasant than the official campsites, and the rarity of such an arrangement in Switzerland adds to the satisfaction. The battle of wits with car park attendants at Saas Fee used to be an attraction until an electro-mechanical device was installed to ensure efficient removal of your money. Another attraction, the best mini-golf course in the Alps, remains. It is at the southern end of the town, near the téléphérique stations.

The routes to the Britannia hut and the Längflue Hotel, whether on foot or by téléphérique, begin near the mini-golf course. The Britannia hut is a traditional starting point for the Adler and Allalin passes and for routes on the Strahlhorn, the Rimpfischhorn and the south and east sides of the Allalinhorn, especially for those who like crowds and clamour. The Längflue is the gateway to the short Alphubel routes, to the north and west sides of the Allalinhorn and to the Alphubeljoch. The Feejoch, below the short west ridge of the Allalinhorn, does not give access to the Mellichgletscher and the Rimpfischhorn. A satisfying approach to these four mountains is to combine them in pairs. The traverse of the Feechopf provides a pleasantly interesting connection of the west ridge of the Allalinhorn and the south-east ridge of the Alphubel. All of this goes well in either direction and gives superb views all round. A bivouac at the Allalinpass or the Adlerpass would be a good way to combine the Rimpfischhorn or the Strahlhorn with the Allalinhorn and to avoid a further night at the Britannia hut and a repeat of the dreary walk along the Allalingletscher. Better still, avoid the first time at the hut as well by descending the south-west ridge of the Allalinhorn to reach the bivouac site. Combining the Rimpfischhorn and the Strahlhorn directly would involve the rarely climbed south-east flank of the Rimpfischhorn. The traverse along the north ridge of the Rimpfischhorn is more attractive and goes equally well in either direction.

The Lagginhorn is easily climbed with the Fletschhorn, usually in a clockwise traverse and descending the main west ridge of the Lagginhorn. The anti-clockwise traverse starting with the south ridge will give a better day, with glissades on the descent. You could combine the Weissmies and the Lagginhorn. The Hoch Saas téléphérique makes a high start to an anti-clockwise traverse very easy. But this begins to sound like soulless efficiency. Both mountains deserve and will repay a more relaxed approach.

13 Lagginhorn

S ridge (PD+), descent by W ridge (PD-). Solo

Map p 76   Illustrations pp 79, 81

If the four ridges on the west side of the Lagginhorn were just a bit more exciting, or if they were snow instead of straightforward rock, the mountain would not be the poor relation of the Weissmies. Perhaps just using its French name of Laquinhorn would be enough to increase its popularity. I do not share the general lack of enthusiasm. I regard the Lagginhorn with particular affection although I have only climbed on it once. I like the roof-like shape of the summit ridge. It gives the mountain a distinctive appearance, which is enhanced by the two ridges on the west side. They curve towards each other at the base, neatly defining and almost encircling the west face. More important than the appearance itself is the time of day when you often first see it. The most magical moment of any day is sunrise: the few minutes when the sun transforms the landscape and you with it. Whatever route you are on, whatever you are doing, you always pause to watch and feel grateful. For many routes on mountains of the Mischabel and the Valais West the sun appears on the horizon near the Lagginhorn's distinctive outline. On many occasions while I have paused to watch the Earth emerge from its nightly chrysalis the Lagginhorn has caught my eye and I have recalled my pleasant un-spectactular day on it.

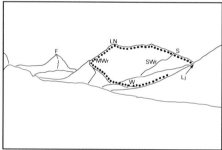

My ascent started from the Weissmies hut well after sunrise. Most parties had already left for the normal route on the Weissmies but one had gone towards the Lagginjoch. I set out to catch up with them, partly to regain some lost time and partly be-cause I did not want to be behind them on the south ridge if that was their objective. After hurrying for a while I relaxed and concentrated on the good weather and the Lagginhorn prospects. The gap narrowed just as quickly and we reached the col together. Their leader was a Saastal guide who responded to my

LN	Lagginhorn,	SWr secondary
	N (main) summit	WSW ridge
F	Fletschhorn	S S ridge
MWr	main WSW ridge	Lj Lagginjoch
W	Weissmies hut	

cheerful greeting with a fierce outburst about how foolish I was to be climbing alone. This display was for his clients' benefit. He dismissed angrily my attempts to point out how suitable the Lagginhorn was for soloing. After a minute or two I said that climbing alone was better for talking with the mountain. This made him stop shouting and waving his arms about. We gave each other a funny look and slowly he said 'Yes, you are right. But climb carefully.'

I am not sure whether I was careful or not. The south ridge was just right, absorbing but not difficult. I was conscious of the ridge itself and of the wider, distant landscape. I was conscious of moving, not exactly in the sky but as much there as on the Earth. I was quite unconscious of any effort. At one point I was on a narrow ledge that disappeared for two or three metres, necessitating

Sunrise behind the Lagginhorn and the Weissmies from the NE ridge of the Nadelhorn

Lagginhorn from near Kreuzboden

79

a very exposed hand traverse. I assume I was off route. I swung across hardly pausing at the time to give it a second thought but I have caught my breath whenever I have thought about it since. The main west ridge directly from the summit was straightforward in descent; more enjoyable, I thought, than ascending it would have been.

A lot of climbing in the Alps is like this. There is no great drama, no heroics, nobody conquers anything. Just simple, uneventful, priceless days with the mountains, which become not so much memories as part of your life.

14 Weissmies

W flank and N ridge (PD+), descent by SW ridge. Solo

Map p 76   Illustrations pp 72/73, 79

I have not climbed on the Weissmies since the second section of the téléphérique, from Kreuzboden to Hoch Saas, was installed. I have gone on the path up to the top station for a training run. The construction debris and the souvenir and fast food shacks were awful. No doubt some of the debris has been cleared and the shacks smartened up, but I expect it will still be awful. The traditional route from the Weissmies hut goes up and across the Triftgletscher and optionally on to the south-west ridge. Most of it is unexciting, though avoiding the large crevasses can provide some entertainment. I have been on it only once, in mist and with poor snow conditions, so perhaps my opinion of it is unfair. The téléphérique has changed it from unsatisfying to short and rather pointless. I suppose it will be doubly popular now. The north ridge is a minor classic but is also unsatisfactory. The short bit of difficult rock is out of character with the rest of the route. The other two ridges on the Saas side of the mountain, the south-west and the south-south-east, are straightforward. They have become more popular since the Almagell hut was built. They provide a pleasant circuit in either direction to and from the Almagellertal and they can be used in several traverses. The development of summer skiing on the Triftgletscher will enhance their charm.

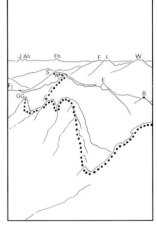

A	Allalinhorn
F	Fletschhorn
L	Lagginhorn
W	Weissmies
J	Jungfrau
Ah	Aletschhorn
Fh	Finsteraarhorn
S	Simelihorn
E	Egginer
Fj	Feejoch
GG	grand gendarme
B	Britannia hut

When I left the Weissmies hut I had not planned to climb the west flank-north ridge combination. I had not seen it described because it was not a recognised route. Since the completion of the Kreuzboden téléphérique it has begun to be used by guided parties. Perhaps it will become the standard approach from the Triftgletscher. It was a significant event for me because I had not soloed an Alpine route before. I would like to be able to relate a sudden revelation about mountaineering and a feeling of destiny unfolding. At the time it merely seemed a good way to climb the Weissmies, away from all the people on the normal route. I expected a consistently interesting but straightforward route with good situations. This was exactly what I found.

Saas mountains and summit ridge from the Rimpfischhorn

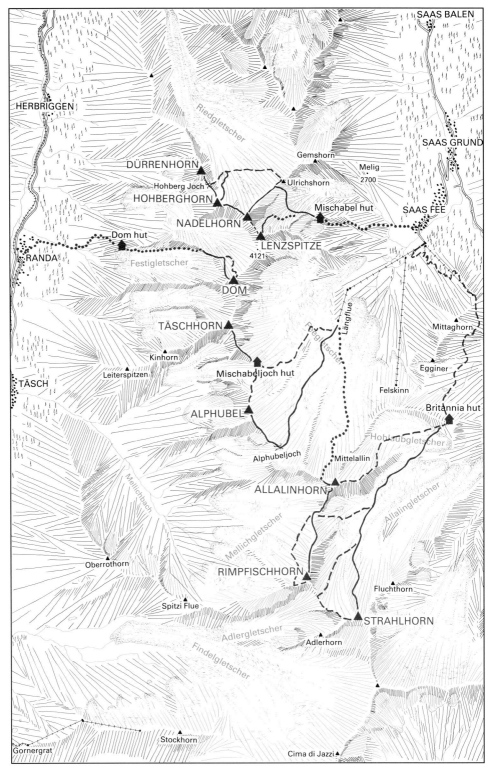

Map 8

The key is a long tongue of snow on the west side of the north ridge, narrowing as it rises from the Triftgletscher and almost reaching the crest of the ridge. It provides an easy and elegant way to gain the north ridge above the difficult rock pitch. The tongue is easily recognised because it divides into two unequal branches near the top. The shorter, left (north) arm is the most direct way to the ridge while the right arm is the most direct way to the summit. I chose the left arm because I could see more clearly that it did not finish in an icy couloir, but the right arm is equally straightforward. Reaching the end of the snow, scrambling easily up a few metres of rock and coming out on to the crest of the ridge was a delicious couple of minutes. The moments of transition on a route, when new landscapes are revealed, when you emerge from a cleft into the open or move from a flat face on to a sharp ridge, are always special. It is partly the revelations and partly the sense of progress. On this occasion there was also the relief that nothing unexpected had happened.

The ridge was nicely sharp with an entertaining succession of little problems that gradually led me to the final snow arête. Despite there being other climbers already at the summit it was comfortable and peaceful. With an easy descent in prospect there was plenty of time to look at Monte Rosa, the Mischabel and mountains further away. I enjoyed as always the ritual of identifying them all, of remembering and anticipating; half planning, half dreaming.

Descending to the Almagellertal had exciting moments after I left the ridge to enjoy some long glissades. One narrow couloir had perfect snow for fast glissades, with occasional jagged rocks to avoid. Lower down, the shady path through the trees was charming and colourful in the bright sunlight. It was a pleasing way to end the route.

15 Allalinhorn

W ridge (F), descent by ENE ridge (PD). With Anne Brearley and Bridget Hogge
Maps pp 76, 82   Illustrations pp 81, 84

The Allalinhorn was my first fourthousander. I have a special affection for it even though it was not an auspicious beginning to climbing them all. My first ascent was by the south-west ridge from the Allalinpass, with Brian and Denise Wood. The route is interesting once you get on the ridge but on this occasion there was unbroken mist almost all the time we were out. We did not know we had reached the summit until told so by another party already there. Meeting them was a pleasant surprise after our lonely and tense climb. They clearly felt the same. We had hoped that the mist would lift but this did not happen until we were nearly back at the Britannia hut. I would not repeat such an excursion now; there is no point. At the time we were inexperienced alpinists and we found it exciting and instructive.

Fourteen years later I got round to climbing it again. When I caught the Längflue téléphérique with Anne and Bridget I had a grand tour in mind: Alphubel, Allalinhorn, Rimpfischhorn and possibly Strahlhorn. This would have been a superb two-day trip in decent weather. What we had was one and a half days of frustrating indifferent weather. Never desperate, and never encouraging until it was too late. My two-day tour remains, along with so much else, an idea not a memory.

The weather signs were not good as we walked slowly up the Feegletscher towards the Feejoch, looking for a good bivouac site. This is frequently a delicate business. Almost anywhere

Allalinhorn from the Egginer.   The development of the north side of the Allalinhorn to provide year-round skiing has reduced its attractiveness. A circuit involving the Hohlaubgrat and the Feechopf takes advantage of the best climbing and avoids most of the disfigurements. When the Alphubel is included, which it is easy and natural to do, it becomes one of the most satisfying expeditions from Saas Fee. The most awkward moments are likely to be on the dry glacier just above the Längflue going to or from the Alphubel or Alphubeljoch.

will do, but you have in mind the perfect site: in the sun, sheltered from the wind, with a convenient supply of water or clean snow and some portable flat rocks to sit on. So if it is not late in the day, you walk on round the next corner, and the next, trying to convince yourself that the awkward, sloping corner you are looking at is the best there is. Often the first place you considered was the best but you do not like to return to it and lose height. The task is even more delicate when there are three of you working on it. That day we stopped at the Feejoch itself. I was tempted to breathe life

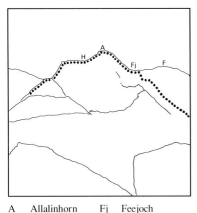

A	Allalinhorn	Fj	Feejoch
H	Hohlaubgrat,	F	Feechopf
	ENE ridge		

into what was then only an idea of bivouacking on the summit of a fourthousander, because the top of the Allalinhorn was barely half an hour away, but the Feejoch was a good bivouac site and a convenient flexible starting point. And it had started snowing.

A cloudy night with intermittent flurries of snow was followed by a similar morning. In the early afternoon the weather improved enough to lure us across the Feechopf and most of the way up the south-west ridge of the Alphubel before it began to snow again. Another poor night at the Feejoch gave us practice in the subtle art of enjoying a comfortable bivouac in miserable weather. I had not realised how much progress Anne and Bridget had made in this direction until I tried to provoke them into movement when the sky cleared at about 05:30. I thought several cups of tea and the breakfast muesli would do the trick. Instead I found myself contemplating the mysteries of the female metabolism. I did suggest that my role was to guide not to provide room service but I was outvoted.

Two parties arrived from the Längflue. They speculated on the explanation for this novel spectacle and I smiled inanely at them while Anne and Bridget began to get themselves organised. Then we joined what had become a long procession to the top of the Allalinhorn. There were too many people for sitting on top to be really enjoyable although we had plenty of time and the weather was perfect. We guessed correctly that the east-north-east ridge would be deserted so we did enjoy the descent. We abseiled over the awkward rock pitch. This is sound rock and would be pleasantly interesting in ascent.

The east-north-east ridge is the most direct route from the Britannia hut. It is much more satisfying than the normal route but few parties use it. Even fewer use the north face and the south face, although both offer routes with sustained interest and the chance to try moderately demanding ascents in very safe circumstances.

16 Alphubel

Traverse SE ridge (F+), N ridge (PD-). Solo
Map p 82   Illustrations pp 86, 94/97

This unorthodox traverse cannot be recommended as a way of climbing the Alphubel. The descent from the Mischabeljoch is potentially the most difficult part and is unpleasant in bad weather. Going in the reverse direction, anti-clockwise from and to the Längflue, would be excellent. The climbing is continuously interesting and the views are good, but I am sure it is a rarely chosen option.

My main objective was the Täschhorn. Traversing the Alphubel was a more pleasing way to get to the small Mischabeljoch bivouac hut than the direct route from the Längflue. From the summit plateau I was able to have a useful look at the south-east ridge of the Täschhorn. The direct route to

Alphubel from the Feechopf

the Mischabeljoch can be quite testing when there is not much snow. Traversing the Alphubel will usually be easier and need take less than an hour longer.

I walked up to the Längflue from Saas Fee and did not enjoy it. I had started later than intended and had tried to hurry instead of relaxing. A few metres past the téléphérique station an old damaged bivouac shelter had been dumped. It was far enough away to be peaceful and I was of a mind to stop walking. The bizarre convenience it provided restored me to good humour. The next day was delicious: perfect weather and crisp snow. Although there was no need to start moving early I made sure I was away before anyone left the Längflue. Just below the Alphubeljoch, conscious that I had plenty of time, I sat down to watch the sunrise and the usual stunning display of changing colours. Ambling up the south-east ridge I found more ice and less snow than I expected on the icy section.

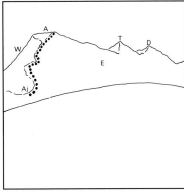

A	Alphubel	E	E flank
Aj	Alphubeljoch	T	Täschhorn
W	W ridge	D	Dom

On subsequent visits it has been equally icy. Each time the surface of the ice has been broken and crinkled, making it secure and easy to climb. In any case it lasts only for a few metres. While you pause above it, to decide exactly which line to take, you can inspect the long west ridge. This looks particularly dramatic with the sun still low in the sky. When you reach the enormous smooth summit plateau it is a surprising sight even though you are expecting it.

At the top the highest point is so ill defined that you wander about aimlessly for a minute or two instead of instinctively taking off your rucksack and sitting on it. It is an exceptionally good viewpoint. In every direction there is something of interest and the neighbouring peaks, Allalinhorn, Rimpfischhorn, Täschhorn, are very close. It is a particularly good place to sort out the Valais fourthousanders. You will come away from there with a long list of routes you must do.

After an hour or so on the summit the north ridge down to the Mischabeljoch seemed at first very sharp and exposed. When I looked back at it from the doorway of the Mischabeljoch bivouac hut, which is a few metres up the south-east ridge of the Täschhorn, the north ridge looked quite exciting whereas descending it had been nicely comfortable. Foreshortened views usually make routes seem more fierce than they really are.

17 Strahlhorn

N face (AD), descent by WNW ridge (F). With Brian Wood

Map p 82   Illustrations p 88, 90

The normal route from the Britannia hut, the west-north-west ridge, is usually easy and not very interesting. As you approach the Adlerpass up the Allalingletscher the whole route is visible. It seems to take a long time for not much to happen. The alternatives are equally natural lines and hardly more difficult. They are very rarely done although they offer better situations and involve more varied climbing. For inexperienced parties, to choose the simplest route and a beaten track is understandable. For the local guides to go repeatedly up and down the same tedious route seems feeble. When Brian and I first did the normal route we had considered the other possibilities: the north ridge, the north-east ridge from the Fluchtpass and the north face lying between them. We had no information about the north face other than what we had seen of it, but we were attracted by the prospect of untrodden snow and it fitted in with our increasing confidence about being able to cope with steeper snow/ice routes.

Access to the face was simple: we just veered off the path to the Adlerpass below the foot of the north-east ridge of the Rimpfischhorn, and walked up the glacier on the east side of the north ridge. The face slants away to the left as you approach it, so we curved round towards the left before turning to cross the bergschrund and aiming directly up the face towards the summit. There were no

Strahlhorn from the Allalinhorn

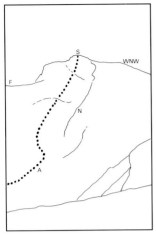

S   Strahlhorn
WNW   WNW ridge
N   N ridge
A   Allalingletscher
F   Fluchthorn

problems. The slope was less steep than we had anticipated and there were only a few small icy patches. The snow was in excellent condition and we found that we were too. We were soon on the top wishing the face had been bigger.

Descending the west-north-west ridge gave the day's only awkward moment. We had assumed the snow would be comfortably soft as it had been on our previous ascent of the Strahlhorn, so we had taken our crampons off. About halfway down we found thirty metres or so of bare ice. This is a hazard of easy routes: the snow covering gets worn away by the many visitors. Midway across we decided that crampons were necessary and had a precarious few minutes putting them on. The incident was a string of errors. We should not have taken off our crampons in the first place. Having done so we should have stopped to put them back on before trying to cross the icy section. We should have taken the trouble to chop out a bigger step in the ice so that we could put them on easily. Brian should have managed to get his crampons on without such a pro-tracted struggle and I should not have got so mad at him. It all took only a few minutes but that was long enough to learn something.

18 Rimpfischhorn

   N ridge (traverse) (PD+), descent by WSW ridge. Solo
Map p 82   Illustration p 90

My first ascent of the Rimpfischhorn differs in one respect from every other Alpine route I have done. I can remember almost nothing about it. I was with Brian Wood; we must have started from the Britannia hut and climbed the west-south-west ridge; the weather was poor and we saw few other climbers. Most of that is deduction. My only genuine memory is of one move over a bulge of rock. Where on the route this was and everything else about the day has gone. Mindful of this loss I made sure, nineteen years later, that my next ascent had some distinctive features.

I avoided the Britannia hut approach by climbing the Allalinhorn from the Längflue and bivouacking on the summit. With a mid-morning start from Saas Fee I met a few parties descending, the last of them just below the Feejoch. The perfect weather contrasted with my previous visits to the Allalinhorn. It heightened my feeling of self-indulgence as I constructed a bivouac, made a comfortable seat and simply looked at the mountains. The afternoon passed quickly, punctuated by a civilised tea. I should have spent some of the time checking the route down the west-south-west ridge. When I began to descend it in the dark next morning I was unsure of the correct line where it traverses off the ridge crest on loose rock. There was no pressing need to get down and on to the Rimpfischhorn so I had a second breakfast while watching the sunrise, and descended to the Allalinpass in daylight.

Rimpfischhorn and Strahlhorn from the Stockhorn

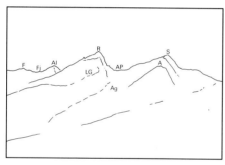

R	Rimpfischhorn	Lg	Längfluegletscher
S	Strahlhorn	Ap	Adlerpass
F	Feechopf	Ag	Adlergletscher
Fj	Feejoch	A	Adlerhorn
Al	Allalinhorn		

At the northern end of the Rimpfischhorn north ridge is a fine gendarme. It is a minor 4000m point, 4108m, never intentionally climbed for itself. The snow slope, steepening and narrowing as it leads up to the base of the gendarme, was excellent. There were useful well-frozen old footprints where the exposure became pronounced. An easy scramble led to the top of the gendarme and revealed two pitches of vertical descent. The alternative to abseiling was to return to the top of the snow and traverse past the gendarme across broken rocks on the east face. Instead of coming to a decision about whether to get out my 6mm rope and abseil I found myself spellbound by the superb views. Every direction evoked memories of past ascents and speculation about future possibilities. This reverie was ended by the arrival of another party. They were three members of Slough Climbing Club! They decided to abseil and kindly let me join in on their comfortable full-weight rope.

The north ridge, from the gendarme to the main summit six hundred metres away, was sheer enjoyment. It is sound rock, pleasantly exposed and continually interesting, and on this occasion it was clean and warm. There were three or four parties at the summit when I reached it and several more arrived in succession. None stayed very long so after half an hour I was by myself. I watched parties returning, towards Fluealp or traversing under the west face to go to the Täsch hut or the Britannia hut, and parties descending the Strahlhorn. I felt no urgency to move and no inclination to pick up my heavy rucksack. I thought about bivouacking there but I had not brought enough water. I used what there was for some tea and had a leisurely lunch. Then I went slowly across to the fore-summit and down the rock tower. I tried to remember descending it before, reluctant to admit to myself I had completely forgotten. It was quite unfamiliar.

Soloing and Safety

Soloing routes in the Alps provokes strong feelings. I have often been told how foolish it is. Usually this information is offered in a tone of voice that suggests indignation, as if soloing offends some deep-seated sense of propriety. Other climbers, particularly guides and people with 'official' positions in the climbing world, produce the most outraged reactions. They are precisely the people who should express a more sensible point of view. I assumed at first the problem was simply an inappropriate extrapolation from similar views about rock-climbing but even experienced alpinists can be equally misguided. Almost everyone thinks climbing alone is an especially dangerous activity, or rather believes it is, because clearly they have given it very little thought (and even less practice).

Climbing routes in the Alps solo is not more dangerous than climbing them as one of a party roped together, at least for easy and medium-grade routes. Soloing and climbing in a roped party are different activities, not the same activity done in different ways. Although the differences are less apparent than the similarities they are fundamental. So while it is worth explaining why soloing is not as dangerous as it might seem, and in doing so inevitably comparing it with roped mountaineering, a definitive comparison is not my purpose.

My argument refers only to the context I am familiar with, namely summer climbing and standards up to AD or perhaps D. Routes in this category have few genuinely difficult individual moves and there is not much vertical or nearly vertical terrain. Nobody would regard most of the physical moves you have to make as dangerous in themselves or dangerous if they were being done in their back garden. What danger there is comes partly from exposure, fatigue and bad visibility in poor weather and partly from the uncertain nature of the ground: crevasses, loose rock or snow, slippery ice and falling rock and ice. It is important to appreciate the distinction between this and hard rock-climbing, which is essentially about making difficult movements with small points of

Glacier hazards.   The half-blind crevasse illustrates perfectly why crossing a glacier may be very dangerous. Even in fine weather with good visibility it is difficult to distinguish between safe and unreliable terrain. Snow bridges present different problems, especially to the solo mountaineer. The path may be clear but is the structure sound; has the afternoon sun softened it too much? As the season advances bridges like this one become increasingly dubious; more of them collapse and paths become more circuitous.

contact on firm, more or less vertical rock. On moderately difficult routes in the Alps even roped parties move together most of the time.

There are two basic truths about climbing alone. First, soloing is not more dangerous; it is in fact safer, but the consequences of an accident are different. To have an accident when you are by yourself will usually be more serious. Second, whether it is safer to be tied to someone else depends on who they are. If they are more likely to fall than you are then tying yourself to them increases your danger. As soon as you think about it unemotionally, soloing is clearly safer, at least in the sense that accidents are less likely. The rope is a nuisance. It has to be managed and it distracts your attention

from the rock. It makes balanced movement in harmony with the rock more difficult. You have to adjust your speed to that of the other person and if you carry coils to ease that problem they create another one. Frequently the rope dislodges loose rocks. Speed is an important consideration. You climb much faster alone. You do not have the rope to manage and you can climb at your optimum pace all the time. This greatly increases your safety. You are less tired and on the whole you encounter better-quality snow because you get to it earlier in the day.

When soloing, I take three basic safety measures. I carry a spare ice-axe; I carry thirty-six metres of 6mm rope; and I am much more circumspect about crevassed areas of glaciers than I would be if I were roped to someone I trusted. This last point carries more weight than is apparent. It emphasises that the preceding argument is couched in terms relevant to the strictly climbing parts of routes. Crossing crevassed glaciers should perhaps be treated as a separate activity, although most of what is said still applies.

The advantages of soloing are obvious enough. What is much less obvious and what only becomes clear when you climb alone is just how different an activity it is. By yourself, you achieve a more profound rapport with the mountain. When you are with other people, their personalities interfere with that of the mountain. Your communication is more with them and less with the Earth. They hinder the changed sense of scale and time that is so striking when you are alone. On your own on a big mountain you are always conscious of being isolated and insignificant. This awareness is intimidating until you begin to experience a sense of union with the mountain, as if it were a living thing. Climbing becomes an activity shared with the mountain, whereas with other people you never entirely lose the component of combining with them to defeat it. This is still the case in the compromise approach of climbing with someone else, not roped together but carrying a rope to use at awkward places.

For many roped parties it is clear that the rope is not really increasing their safety. They just think it is. Its purpose is psychological. It is there not to increase safety but to reduce fear. Watch them at a crevasse. One by one they stand on the edge and contemplate the horror of falling down it, before jumping across. Climb with the mountain and it will look after you. You stride across the same crevasse without losing momentum. There is no danger, no need for any dramatic behaviour, and your horizontal momentum is itself a safety factor.

Climbing with other people is a wonderful activity. The relationship between you and your companions is a special one, its richness frequently remarked on and confirmed by my own experience. I began solo mountaineering by chance. Now I climb alone from choice, although I would not wish to every time. I find it enlightening and rewarding. The insights it gives, both inward and outward, the serenity, and the closeness to the mountains, are uniquely satisfying.

Section 5
Mischabel

19	Täschhorn	4491m	22	Nadelhorn	4327m
20	Dom	4545m	22a	Stecknadelhorn	4241m
21	Lenzspitze	4294m	23	Hohberghorn	4219m
			24	Dürrenhorn	4035m

Strictly, 'Mischabel' applies to the long, rather featureless east face of the Lenzspitze-Dom-Täschhorn ridge. The northern part, from the Nadelhorn to the Dürrenhorn, is the Nadelgrat. Although the mountains of the Mischabel proper are grander and much more famous than those of the Nadelgrat, they are vaguely disappointing in a way that characterises the chain as a whole. There is one magnificent face route, the Lenzspitze north-east face, and one superb high-level traverse, the Nadelgrat itself. Nothing else is indisputably a classic, although the Lenzspitze-Nadelhorn circuit on the Saas side and the Täschhorn-Dom circuit on the Täsch side come close. I cannot help feeling the Mischabel should offer more truly great routes than it does.

Although there are several excellent routes I would like to do, each has its own flaw. None has that special quality that draws me, making me feel that I must climb it. This harsh judgement stems from the situation of the mountains as much as their intrinsic character. Lying between the Mattertal and the Saastal, they occupy a prime position. Closer inspection reveals that their potential is only partly realised. Both access and opportunities from the Saas side are surprisingly limited, largely because the long Mischabel east face, from the north-east ridge of the Lenzspitze to the south-east ridge of the Täschhorn, is devoid of attractive routes. From Randa and Täsch there are more possibilities but most have long, tedious approaches and occasional difficulties that are out of character with the rest of the route. The two long west ridges at the ends of the chain, to the Dürrenhorn and to the Täschhorn, are typical. Both are fine true mountaineering routes and both require a certain bloody-minded determination. Perhaps this is in fact praise. The same applies to most other routes here, indicating that the virtues of these mountains are subtle, not on open display and not enjoyed without effort.

From most places in the valleys on either side, the ridge as a whole looks less spectacular than it feels when you are on it. The individual mountains look their best when seen from each other. These observations are the key to the Mischabel: the best routes are those which include a traverse of part of the main ridge. (The north-east face of the Lenzspitze is of course a unique, stunning exception.) Almost every part of the main ridge is exhilarating and provides superb views. The only places on it where there is genuine difficulty are between the Dom summit and the Lenzjoch. These difficulties are easily, and usually, avoided by traverses on the snow slopes of the north face. It is the lack of separation of the mountains making up the Mischabel that explains why they are collectively

Mischabel and Weisshorn from the Dent d'Hérens.   A small event of no great significance that nevertheless always gives the mountaineer great pleasure is when the 'real' world, which already seems unreal and far away, disappears completely beneath a calm sea of cloud.

disappointing: few of them have the individuality that is characteristic of the great mountains of the Alps, and in many cases routes to different mountains have long approaches in common and only a short final section specific to the mountain being climbed.

The idea of a complete traverse of the main ridge, from the Mischabeljoch to the Dürrenhorn, stands apart from my muted enthusiasm for the Mischabel as a whole. Not the least of its appeal is that it would make an ascent of the undistinguished Dürrenhorn a candidate for the best medium-grade expedition in the Alps. This ridge traverse has been an ambition of mine for many years. There are no technical problems and several escape points if needed so I wonder sometimes why I have

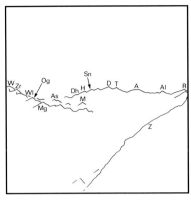

W	Weisshorn	T	Täschhorn
Zr	Zinalrothorn	A	Alphubel
Og	Ober Gabelhorn	Al	Allalinhorn
Wl	Wellenkuppe	R	Rimpfischhorn
D	Dürrenhorn	Z	Zmutt ridge
H	Hohberghorn	M	Mettelhorn
S	Stecknadelhorn	As	Äschhorn
D	Dom	Mg	Mittler Gabelhorn

never done it. Partly it is because there is no point unless you can sustain the enjoyment and the magic, and prevent it becoming an endurance test. This requires a high level of fitness and the confidence to move quickly. When I have satisfied these conditions and been in the area I have usually found poor weather. Twice I have got further than just thinking about it and each time have been driven off by a storm, once from the Mischabeljoch and once from the summit of the Täschhorn. On neither occasion had I decided which way to descend from the Dürrenhorn. That part of this persistent dream is still unclear. It will remain so until I am standing on the summit of the Dürrenhorn at the end of the traverse, when the most fitting descent route will choose itself.

19 Täschhorn

SE ridge (PD+). Solo

Map p 82 Illustrations pp 86, 96, 98, 99

Since the excellent Mischabeljoch bivouac hut was installed the south-east ridge has been the most popular ascent route. In good weather the ridge is completely straightforward so you can relax and enjoy the airy situations and superb views all round. The central part, a sharp snow crest, has lost the exotic cornices that once gave the ridge its reputation. The approaches to the Mischabeljoch are more problematic than the ridge itself, particularly on the Saas side when there is not much snow. On my first visit I traversed the Alphubel to get to the Mischabeljoch. This approach, starting from the Längflue like the orthodox route, can be recommended provided you start before the snow on the east side of the Alphubel deteriorates in the sun.

I reached the bivouac hut before 09:00 and was disappointed to find that despite its fine position the views are restricted. I tidied the hut, collected some clean snow and had an early lunch, sitting in the entrance and half dozing in the sun. An intriguing peak roughly south-east turned out to be the Stellihorn, 3436m, above the Mattmark reservoir. It has its own little glacier and would provide an excellent speculative and solitary expedition. It has joined many other meek little mountains that must wait until I am incapable of anything more demanding. In the afternoon I ambled up the south-east ridge in shirtsleeves, partly to reconnoitre the route and partly to get better views and increase my familiarity with the Valais mountains. The clean warm rock gently led me on until I was in sight of the central snow crest. By then the brilliancy of the weather had gone and it rapidly deteriorated further as I descended. Two other parties reached the hut just as flurries of light snow began.

SE ridge of the Täschhorn from the summit

Mischabel from the Alphubel

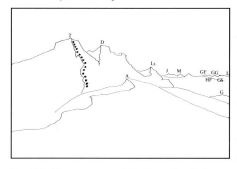

T	Täschhorn	GF	Gross Fiescherhorn
D	Dom	HF	Hinter Fiescherhorn
Ls	Lenzspitze	GG	Gross Grünhorn
G	Galenhorn	A	Alphubel, N summit
J	Jungfrau	L	Lauteraarhorn
M	Mönch	GS	Gross Schreckhorn

A half-hearted storm spluttered on for most of the night, fading away at sunrise. When it was clear that the other parties were going ahead with their plan to climb the ridge and descend the north-west face to the Dom hut, I decided that for once I would choose the easy option and let them go first. They could clear the loose snow from the rocks and tread a path across the snow crest, the crux pitch, that I could follow in comfort. I stayed in bed self-indulgently for an hour after they left. When I arrived at the snow section both parties were there each suggesting that the other should have the honour of going first. I could not see what they thought was going to be difficult. There was a problem though: it was in the sky above them. The intermittent sunshine had vanished behind thickening clouds. I trotted across the snow, sometimes on the crest and sometimes in a shallow trough a few metres down on the west side, and then pressed on as fast as I could to the summit over little shelves of loose rock.

A solid black cloud seemed near enough above to reach up and grasp, like a nightmarish counterpane. Ten minutes' contemplation of the wonders of nature was the most I could stand before tearing back down. The top part of the south-east ridge merges into a broad rounded slope. The sharp ridge crest was difficult to find on a later occasion when it was misty and snowing. This time, although

99

it was ominously dark, visibility was good. I dashed past the second party, who were ludicrously belaying themselves off the snow crest. Perhaps they were practising for their epic that was about to begin. The cloud continued to descend and I raced it down the ridge. As I dived into the hut the first hailstones hammered on the roof.

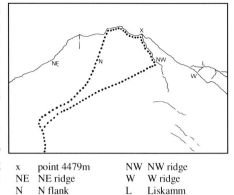

The storm, brief and vigorous, was followed by mist and occasional spats of snow. Next morning was brighter but still misty. I spent the morning reading and wondering whether I dare descend the crevassed Feegletscher to the Längflue. By mid-afternoon the

x	point 4479m	NW	NW ridge
NE	NE ridge	W	W ridge
N	N flank	L	Liskamm

mist had cleared enough to reveal most of the route down and traces of footprints. Inevitably, when I had gone about a third of the way and had just entered the heavily crevassed area, the mist descended again. The next two hours were awful. Visibility was almost zero, with mist and the snow of the glacier merged together. Great chasms would loom up suddenly in the space of a couple of paces, or what appeared to be an enormous crevasse would turn out, a step later, to be a narrow crack. Suddenly the ground underfoot that I was concentrating on became clearer and I realised that the mist had lifted. The glacier I had just crossed became visible and I could see right down to Saas Fee. I found that I was on easy terrain close to the Längflue.

20 Dom
NW ridge (PD-), descent by N flank. Solo
Map p 82   Illustrations pp 96, 99, 101, 108

The Dom is the highest mountain entirely in Switzerland but has not a single route worthy of this distinction. The two minor 4000m points, 4479m on the west ridge and 4468m on the north-east ridge, are distinguished enough to carry a name yet are unnamed. I feel guilty about the Dom. I should have made a special effort to climb one of the better routes such as the west ridge. Instead, without thinking, I just fitted in the normal route on a couple of spare days.

Despite the heat of a windless sunny day the walk up to the Dom hut from Randa was a pleasure, partly because I expected it to be harder and more tedious than it was. Continuing on to the Festijoch did eventually become hard work, rewarded by a neat bivouac site and a still evening of brilliant colours. I discovered the first of several irritating bits of carelessness, when I tried to photograph the sunset. I had only three or four frames left and no spare film. This in itself I did not mind as I often have plenty of film but cannot be bothered to take photographs. I should have used it up at once and had done with it. Instead I kept deciding not to take a picture either because I thought something better would turn up or because I had missed something that had been better. Eventually I used up the film with a picture of the path below the Dom hut! I had already found that I had brought plenty of tea but not enough sugar, that I had left some peaches on the front seat of my van and when I settled down to repair my gloves, that I had wool and fine needles but no darning needles.

Dom from the Hohberghorn

Next morning I got up too early. I wanted to have the route to myself and I thought parties from the hut would arrive at the Festijoch earlier than they did. The vision in my mind was of a leisurely ascent of the north-west ridge, a long, serene stay on the summit and then an enormous exhilarating glissade down the north face. That I achieved none of this was, like my oversights the previous day, unimportant. If my intentions had been less well defined I would not have been disappointed afterwards. There was a brisk wind which got steadily stronger as I walked easily across to the ridge. I reacted to this with an energetic pace, partly to keep warm. I reached the summit quickly, not long after sunrise. The views were tremendous, particularly with the traces of the early morning colours. The ferocious wind unfortunately made it very cold. Standing around or crouching behind an icy ridge was uncomfortable to the point of misery. I stayed about half an hour before deciding I had been quite silly enough. Then of course I found the snow on the north face was still frozen hard; very easy to descend but impossible to glissade on. I made some tea at the Festijoch, shared it with a party on their way up and was back at Randa before 11:00.

Lenzspitze NE face from the NE ridge of the Nadelhorn

21 Lenzspitze

NE face (D), descent by Lenzspitze-Nadelhorn traverse and NE ridge of the Nadelhorn.

With Brian Wood

Map p 82   Illustrations pp 99, 102

The Lenzspitze is an enigmatic mountain. It is dominated by the Dom and the Nadelhorn, both of which are close by and substantially larger, so its character is elusive. It is dominated even more by its own north-east face to the extent that it is difficult to think of the mountain as a whole or to look at it without focusing exclusively on the elegant awesome beauty of the finest ice wall in the Alps. There are many other more demanding ice routes but none has the same immaculate simplicity on such a scale. The ice-wall part of the face is almost five hundred metres high from the bergschrund and about two hundred and fifty metres wide. It is slightly concave which means that it can be seen as a whole. When you are on the face it seems flat so you are very conscious of its enormous size, and of your own minuteness.

ENE   Lenzspitze ENE ridge
LN   Lenzspitze-Nadelhorn ridge
B   bergschrund

This photograph of the NE face, from the lower part of the Nadelhorn NE ridge above the Windjoch, was taken while descending the Nadelhorn, two weeks after we had climbed the face. On that occasion we descended the same way and could see the line of belay steps we had cut, leading directly to the summit. The overhanging bergschrund clearly presents a problem.

There are several peripheral features of the north-east face that enhance its quality. The approach from the Mischabel hut is easy and the descent via the Nadelhorn is interesting yet uncomplicated. It is framed neatly by the east ridge of the Lenzspitze and the north-east ridge of the Nadelhorn, which both provide superb views of the face. This gives the route two advantages that few others possess: you can easily get close to the face before you climb it, so that your deliberations are based on your own first-hand impressions; descent by either the Nadelhorn or the Lenzspitze ridge enables you to see exactly where you have just been and to relive the climb as you descend. Seeing the route from one of the ridges immediately puts climbers into one of two categories. Either they recoil in horror or they feel drawn to it. In the second case it may be only a dim secret hope, and at the time they may be unaware that seeing this superb face is changing their climbing horizons.

The face gives a route of great simplicity; the only question for the prospective climber is not about the route but about his or her mind. In good conditions there are no technical problems, just repetitive crampon climbing on front points that needs fit calf muscles, balance and steady nerves. All the usual complications about where the route goes and what difficulties you might find are absent. The important question is whether you can concentrate instinctively and let your mind and awareness open out to embrace the vast, smooth steepness or whether you are forced to shut this out and fill your consciousness with immediate preoccupations: the next step, the rope, the condition of the snow, the time.

I have heard the Lenzspitze north-east face described as boring and I met someone who said that he had spent every minute on the route terrified by the situation and had effectively climbed it with his eyes shut. The day Brian and I climbed the north-east face seemed to me to have a quality that made it significant even in the context of days with mountains, all of which are special. It was an ascent that left me a different person. It is more than unforgettable: it is present always.

We had first looked at the route while climbing the Nadelhorn. Now, four years later, we were having a good season and beginning to complement our enthusiasm with a more instinctive assurance. We were confident about the Lenzspitze, yet still apprehensive, and were lucky that we both felt ready for it at the same time. We had begun bivouacking instead of staying in huts, so our visit to the Mischabel hut was a brief one to inform the guardian of our intentions and to get his views on the weather and the condition of the face. There were several parties in the hut. Our plan to bivouac below the bergschrund caused some hilarity and the usual knowing smiles about mad English climbers. These must have been repeated next morning because we were both still sleeping when two parties from the hut approached the face. We had intended making an early start, to be well established on the route before anyone else. Our embarrassment produced a frenzy of activity and a gasping, eye-popping sprint to the bergschrund.

The difficulties there were substantial. The horizontal gap was only a metre or so but the upper lip overhung and was out of reach above us. Our frenetic state allowed no time for contemplation. Trying not to inflict too much damage with my crampon spikes, I stood first on Brian's back and rucksack then on his shoulders. I reached up as far as I could, rammed his ice-axe into firm snow at the edge of the overhang and hung a tape sling on the axe head. By leaning against the overhanging snow and standing on Brian's helmet I got one foot into the sling. I sprang upwards and plunged my own ice-axe into the snow above the overhang. I scrambled up on to the moderate slope above, showering Brian with snow to ease the pain of his wounds. Then I went up a few metres more before helping him up using the rope. His flurry of snow as he squirmed over the bulge landed on the first party from the hut.

Conditions were excellent. There was a clear sky and almost no wind. The snow on the face was solid, well-frozen and perhaps fifteen centimetres deep. We climbed up rapidly, moving together with about thirty-five metres of rope between us. We soon relaxed into a steady rhythm, making efficient progress at a comfortable pace and using ice-pitons as running belays. Every rope's length, when Brian reached the last piton I had put in, we both stopped. I cut a step, scraped away the snow at shoulder level, hammered in another ice-piton and clipped the rope to it through a karabiner. Brian chopped out the previous one and we moved on another pitch. It may sound monotonous. It was just the opposite: enchanting and exciting.

The simplicity of the situation and the repetitive nature of the physical effort produced a sense of unreality and allowed subtle emotions and insights to emerge clearly. Although Brian and I were tied together and consciously alert to our responsibilities to each other, we were climbing with an instinctive harmony that left each of us in his own world and in closer contact with the mountain than with each other. The regular pauses were relaxing breaks in the obsessive tension of front-pointing. They punctuated our ascent, allowing us to measure our progress against the nearby ridges. We were calm yet excited about our situation, and pleased with our competence. The other parties must have decided our circus tactics at the bergschrund were beneath their dignity. We were about two hundred metres up the face before they appeared over the bergschrund.

About halfway up the face I chopped out a large step and brought Brian up. We clipped in to an ice-piton and paused for a conference. At this point the face shimmers off tangentially to infinity in all directions. It is intimidating and uniquely beautiful. The snow covering had gradually got thinner so it was time to climb in pitches, properly belayed and with more frequent protection. The rope was irritatingly twisted so we decided to untie and shake it down the face so that when we retied it would run freely and be easier to handle. I had been careful to attach our piton hammer to a loop clipped to the rope round my waist. I overlooked this when I untied the rope. The hammer dropped over the edge of the step and bounced down the face. We stood in silence watching it descend in what seemed to be slow motion.

There was no danger to the other parties because they had already veered off to their right and were climbing the gentler and shorter slope to the Nadeljoch. In any case the hammer's path curved slightly the other way, to the south-east. When it cleared the bergschrund and came to rest in the softer snow below we turned and looked at each other. It was not an authentic piton hammer; our finances did not run to such luxuries and we did not take ourselves that seriously. We had been making do with a cheap roof-tiler's hammer. Even so we were disappointed to lose it. Brian was still silent although his expression was eloquent. Then, calmly pragmatic as ever, he asked whether he should throw the ice-pitons after the hammer as now we had nothing to bang them in with.

We pressed on, less euphoric than before, using two ice-screws for belays. The gradient gradually increases, though nowhere is it much more than 55 degrees. The snow covering became thinner and had softened in the morning sun. The condition of the face was less predictable: essentially ice in places, sometimes with a slushy covering of snow, sometimes with a surface crust of thin brittle ice. We had intended to follow the usual line near the top of the face. This moves to the left, where the gradient eases, to reach the top of the east ridge below the summit. Instead I aimed directly for the highest point of the face. The snow covering improved slightly on the last two pitches; the cornice was negligible. We stepped off the face on to the summit and exchanged grins.

The descent, north-westwards along the summit ridge, involves more ascent when you reach the Nadeljoch. This was straightforward and we were pleased to revisit the Nadelhorn. After descending from the Windjoch we walked back in tedious soft snow up the Hohbalmgletscher to retrieve our bivouac gear. We found the piton hammer fairly easily although it was never used again. As we passed the Mischabel hut the guardian insisted we come inside for some tea. I hoped to subject the other parties to at least a quizzical look but either they had already gone down or they were hiding in the dormitory. The guardian said he had watched us on the upper part of the face through his binoculars. He must have been impressed because a couple of days later in the square in Saas Fee he called us over and with evident satisfaction introduced us to two guides.

Nadelhorn from the Lenzspitze

22	**Nadelhorn**	23	**Hoberghorn**
22a	Stecknadelhorn	24	**Dürrenhorn**

Nadelhorn: NE ridge (PD), Nadelgrat: Nadelhorn-Stecknadelhorn-Hohberghorn

Dürrenhorn traverse (PD+), descent via Hohbergjoch.   Solo

Hohberghorn: NE face (AD+), descent via Hohbergjoch and Windjoch.   Solo

Map p 82   Illustrations pp 96, 106, 108, 110

This curious two-day expedition devoted to the peaks of the Nadelgrat was the result of conflicting desires. The ridge traverse is the best route the four mountains offer, yet I felt they deserved something more. I had, and still have, what strikes me as a perverse liking for the long west ridge of the Dürrenhorn. This route needs an approach from the Mattertal and I prefer the Saastal. My familiarity with the approach from the Saas side, which gave me a better chance of success in the unsettled weather, led to my unadventurous choice. The traditional plan for the Nadelgrat is north to south from the Dom hut, using the Stecknadeljoch and the Lenzjoch for access to and exit from the ridge. I walked up to the Mischabel hut on a drizzly afternoon with a heavy rucksack and only a vague idea what I might do. If I had been sure of the weather I would have bivouacked on the east ridge of the Lenzspitze just beyond the grand gendarme. At the hut I waited hopefully for the weather to improve. It did, but only when it was too late to take advantage of it.

Next morning the weather prospects were indifferent. I walked, without much enthusiasm, across to the Windjoch and then on up the north-east ridge of the Nadelhorn. The problem in situations like that is not that you mind being out in dreary weather. The possibility that nags at your mind is that if you persist then your return to the valley for more food may coincide with excellent weather. The ridge to the Nadelhorn tends to be underrated because it is the trade route from the Mischabel hut. Although the climbing is uncomplicated it is never totally simple and the situations and views, dominated by the north-east face of the Lenzspitze, are good. By the time I had reached the summit the weather had brightened. There was plenty of clear sky above though not enough bright sunshine to drive away the mist around the ridge.

The first part of the ridge to the Stecknadelhorn is rock. It was cold and slippery, with patches of icy snow. With a heavy rucksack I found it awkward while being aware that it would be pleasant on a warm day or if I could relax and let myself enjoy it. As soon as I was past the rocks and on the crest of snow the day changed. The snow was crisp and the situation superb. I strode towards the Stecknadelhorn and either the mists thinned or I imagined they did.

The top part of the Stecknadelhorn is rock again. I wandered across the summit looking more at the fine ridge to the Hohberghorn than where I was going. Suddenly I found myself in a very precarious position in a steep groove of rock. There were plenty of small holds, all full of verglas, but nothing substantial. I was facing outwards with

N	Nadelhorn
S	Stecknadelhorn
H	Hohberghorn
LN	Lenzspitze-Nadelhorn ridge

Hohberghorn and Nadelhorn from the Dürrenhorn.　　*This view of the NE face of the Hohberghorn gives a fair impression of its slope, although the increased steepness directly towards the summit is not obvious. The awkward access at the foot of the face is not apparent.*

one cramponed boot on each side wall. I had descended only three or four metres and there was an easy horizontal exit two metres below. My initial reaction of amused surprise disappeared when I realised that if I came off and got a bad bounce I could go a very long way. I knew I had descended from the top of the groove on large holds and I was trying to recall where they were behind me. As I adjusted one foot to look back the other one slipped off. I slithered and bumped down about three metres, out of the groove, then stopped. I was in exactly the same position, just lower. I looked at both hands and both feet in turn. All four were secure on large holds. There seems to be a tradition of pausing at such moments for profound revelations about the mysteries of life. I simply walked across the face and resumed my cheerful progress along the ridge. The whole incident took only a few seconds.

Traversing the Hohberghorn was simply an enjoyable walk on a fine snow ridge. I left my rucksack at the Hohbergjoch to saunter easily up the clean rock of the Dürrenhorn south-east ridge. For a few minutes it was warm and sunny, emphasising the contrast with the crisp snow on the Hohberghorn. I do not think my profound feeling of well-being was a delayed reaction to falling off and escaping unharmed. Nor could it have been any sense of achievement, because there was none to speak of. Perhaps both falling off so neatly and my feeling of harmony with the mountains as I walked along the ridge were equal minor miracles. They seem like it now. At the time, sitting on the top of the Dürrenhorn, I had no such thoughts. I just felt pleased.

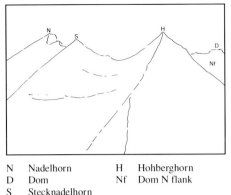

N   Nadelhorn   H   Hohberghorn
D   Dom   Nf   Dom N flank
S   Stecknadelhorn

By the time I was back at the Hohbergjoch misty cloud had drifted in and the day had turned grey. The couloir down to the Riedgletscher looked steep and horrid. I could not tell whether the snow covering was firm and deep enough. There was no cornice but the first two or three metres were almost vertical. Logically there was no problem but I felt intimidated. Eventually I dropped a large rock down the couloir. It bounced once and was then held by the snow so I slithered down after it. My first few steps were tentative; then I descended rapidly, spurred on by some gentle thin snowfall.

Below the north-east face of the Hohberghorn are two complicated sérac zones which hinder access to the face. The lower one is much the larger but it peters out below the couloir leading up to the Hohbergjoch, so there is a smooth crevasse-free slope from the couloir to the main part of the Riedgletscher. At the edge of this slope a huge fallen sérac provided a convenient sheltered bivouac site. The sky cleared during the night and the bright early morning matched my mood.

I would probably have done better to loop round the upper sérac barrier to get to the north-east face instead of forcing a direct route below the rock wall at the north-west end of the face. There appeared to be a way through to the main face that would avoid any possible problems with the bergschrund. It was frustrating and increasingly difficult. Each few metres led to a corner round which I expected to find the smooth crisp snow of the face. Instead I found another steeper and more icy slope, even more precarious and exposed than the one I was on. At last I plunged thankfully into deep snow and paused to regain some composure. I looked down and saw a longer, much easier approach route to the face where I could have come instead, if I had known about it.

After the unexpected tension the north-east face was lovely: steep enough to be exhilarating, not so steep as to be uncomfortable. Apart from some small patches of ice the good-quality snow covering persisted until near the top of the face. There it began to get consistently icy and I veered to the left for an easier line on to the ridge. At the summit two Swiss climbers were enjoying the sunshine. They invited me to join in their second breakfast. My contribution of malt whisky surprised them and then helped them over the shock. They asked where I had come from. When I told them they stood up, walked over to look down the face, then sat down again without a word. We left the summit in opposite directions. They were climbing the Nadelgrat; I trotted down the north ridge towards the Hohbergjoch thinking that I should have stayed longer at the summit. The descent couloir from the col was totally simple the second time round.

From the summit of the Hohberghorn the west face of the Ulrichshorn had seemed a good idea. I thought it would give the day a satisfying symmetry. By the time I had retrieved my bivouac gear the snow on the Riedgletscher had begun to soften and I found even the gentle gradient approaching the west face hard work. I soon changed my mind about the Ulrichshorn and contoured round eastwards to its north face. I rapidly felt very tired and was glad the slope was at a comfortable

Hohberghorn and Dürrenhorn from the Riedgletscher, below the Ulrichshorn. The ridge from the *Hohberghorn to the Dürrenhorn is as benign as it appears. The Hohberghorn NE face and the descent couloir from the Hohbergjoch are less so. Although the face steepens slightly towards the summit, ascent is comfortable once the face is attained. From the Windjoch (out of sight to the left of this view) an easy direct route to the lower part of the face can be seen. This avoids the complication of negotiating the séracs directly below the face.*

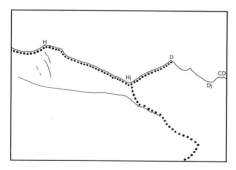

H   Hohberghorn
Hj   Hohbergjoch
D   Dürrenhorn
Dj   Dürrenjoch
CD   Chli Dürrenhorn

angle as I ascended with slow steps and frequent pauses. The Ulrichshorn summit is only seventy-five metres above the Windjoch. It is a rewarding viewpoint for the Nadelgrat, well worth the short detour. From there it is clear that the north-east face of the Hohberghorn is unjustly neglected. At the very least it offers an ideal proving route for climbers who are not quite sure whether they are ready for the corresponding route on the Lenzspitze.

Snow Technique

The basic snow technique of many alpinists is poor. This is true even of some accomplished climbers who are capable of very difficult routes. For them it hardly matters as it is compensated by their greater strength and fitness. For the average climber doing ordinary, unexceptional routes it means that moving on snow is often more tiring and more stressful than need be. So it takes longer. More of it than is necessary takes place later in the day in worse snow conditions and so it becomes yet more tiring and stressful. More subtle consequences are loss of rhythm and loss of harmony with the route. Descent even more than ascent can become a struggle. The sense of serenity and elation that can overlay the most strenuous physical activity is lost.

Effective progress in tune with the alluring environment of snow slopes is a precious part of Alpine climbing. There your immediate field of vision changes slowly and smoothly and the repetitive movements require less of your attention than the more detailed scrutiny demanded by rock work. Consequently more of your mind can be devoted to the wider scene and to more profound contemplation. Losing this because of a misguided approach is deplorable.

Level, or nearly level, and solid well-frozen snow that takes crampon points firmly presents no difficulties to anyone (which is not meant to imply that everyone uses crampons correctly). At the other extreme, steep hard snow climbed on front points with positive use of the ice-axe pick is essentially easy ice climbing. In between is a range of conditions characterised by significant but not precipitous gradients and snow at least soft enough to give way underfoot: in other words, conditions that are not desperately difficult but where technical competence will make a difference. These situations make up sizeable portions of many routes.

I suppose part of the reason that poor technique on snow is so widespread is that many accomplished climbers who get it right themselves have not isolated the essential point. When giving instruction, either in practice or on paper, they concentrate too much and too soon on more sophisticated details. Usually they also expound a view of safety which further confuses the issue. Even Rébuffat fails to make the crucial point. The root of the problem is depressingly simple. Most people who climb begin on rock. When they climb on snow, they see themselves engaged in the same activity, namely climbing. They recognise that this new medium, snow, has different characteristics from rock, that frequently it is less solid. Instead of developing a different approach they behave as if they were climbing or scrambling on a particularly unreliable sort of rock.

Rock-climbing is a sequence of discrete movements between existing firm points of contact. Snow climbing is a smoother, more rhythmic activity where the movement itself is creating the points of contact. I am not saying that rock-climbing cannot be rhythmic, but this is not its essence. Rhythm there applies to the larger activity surrounding the smaller individual movements. The main aim when climbing rock is not to slip, for no handhold or foothold to give way. Most people adopt the same aim on snow, whereas what they should do is move more normally, as in ordinary walking, be relatively unconcerned about stability of individual points of contact, but concerned to stop a slide of the whole body quickly should one start.

On a snow slope or snow crest you should aim to move swiftly, easily, smoothly, not bothering whether the feet slip a bit, but ready to get into the correct braking position immediately should you happen to slide. The essence of snow climbing is moving comfortably, in balance and upright. The ideal use of the ice-axe to aim for, especially in descent, is to hold it in both hands: one hand on the head, with the thumb round and under the adze side, the other on the shaft near the spike. This encourages you to walk in balance and you are holding the axe correctly for the braking position. Aim to use the spike gently, not as a walking-stick to lean on, nor with the shaft buried and with the head as a handhold to pull on. The crucial judgement always is knowing whether and how quickly you can stop if you do come off. The crucial ability is that of stopping yourself instantly and instinctively. In essence, moving on rock is about not falling, whereas moving on snow is about stopping if you do. Most alpinists have not spent enough hours on safe snow slopes, in all sorts of snow conditions, deliberately falling off backwards, sideways and head first, time after time, to practise stopping and to become proficient at it and confident about it.

Some examples of inept behaviour may clarify the principle. Ascending a fairly steep slope of softish snow is hard work however you do it, but not nearly as hard as many climbers make it. Somewhere in their past they have heard the phrase 'kicking steps'. It has so captured their imagination that kicking steps is what they are going to do. That it is unnecessary never occurs to them. In any case kicking steps is not the bizarre activity they practise. They stand on one leg and stamp and kick vigorously with the other to create a firm platform. Then they stand on this with the by now tired leg and repeat the procedure with the other leg. All this energetic leg waving demands a firm handhold so it is preceded by vigorous arm movements to ram in the ice-axe. This manoeuvre can only be performed a small step up from the stationary foot. Instead, all that is needed is to take a much higher step up into the slope and to let the increased downward pressure compress the snow and create a firm enough platform to enable upward movement. The foot finds its own stationary point and as soon as it does the body moves upwards and the other leg begins its own high step. It can be relaxed and smooth, but it does need some agility.

For descending, the contrast between the two approaches is even greater. The obsession with kicking steps is again misguided. When facing inwards, just swing the higher foot out backwards and allow it and the whole body to drop down. As the now higher leg bends more – and really acute leg bending is important – the lower foot sinks into the snow and the movement itself creates the solid point of contact. As soon as this begins to happen the weight comes off the higher foot and the next step starts. The essence here is taking big steps in a continuous movement, not small stuttering ones. The same principles apply when facing outwards, which if feasible is to be preferred. Having to leave a nice solid ridge at a col and descend a steep couloir of soft snow is quite common and is frequently regarded as an unpleasant business. Given a reasonable depth of snow it can be done very rapidly and comfortably by aiming to control slips instead of going to a lot of trouble to prevent them.

One of the supreme delights of mountaineering is a sharp crisp exposed snow crest: more walking in the sky than climbing. There is no need to pound away alternately with each foot while bending double to achieve a solid handhold with the ice-axe. That is fighting a mountain not climbing it. Instead, decide which would be the better side to come off should you slip, and then walk normally: upright, physically in balance and mentally poised. Always aim to be in balance on snow (and ice). Let each footstep find its own point of stable contact and feel the mountain rather than tread on it. The state of soaring exhilaration this can produce is not always achieved of course, but it should always be sought. Good technique helps.

Another component of technique that is commonly very poor is lack of flexibility. Snow is highly variable stuff and so good technique needs to be correspondingly adaptable. A forty-five degree slope of soft slushy snow over smooth ice is a serious proposition if the snow is ten centimetres deep, merely strenuous if it is a metre deep. Both situations change if you are one metre up the slope from a yawning crevasse instead of twenty. Everybody knows this, but not everybody adjusts the way they climb. One last point concerns crossing crevasses. I have never been able to see any sense in the common practice of standing on the edge of a crevasse and stamping out a firm stance before jumping across from a stationary position. The edge of a crevasse is the least sensible place to spend any time stamping about and the more horizontal momentum you can take off with the better.

Section 6
Monte Rosa

25	Nordend	4609m	28	Parrotspitze	4432m
26	Dufourspitze	4634m	28a	Ludwigshöhe	4341m
26a	Grenzgipfel	4618m	28b	Schwarzhorn	4321m
27	Signalkuppe	4556m	29	Piramide Vincent	4215m
27a	Zumsteinspitze	4563m	29a	Punta Giordani	4046m

Whenever I see it I am aware that I have a soft spot for Monte Rosa. It looks particularly good seen from the Mont Blanc area or the Grand Combin, well to the west. As the sun comes up and with a bit of hazy mist lower down, everything in the Alps looks fantastic but Monte Rosa is special. It looks comforting rather than awe inspiring and has a satisfyingly heavy appearance. However, the main reason for my affection is the massif's unique quality: it provides the best high-level strolling in the Alps.

Thanks to the long west ridge of the Dufourspitze the whole place is like a vast ampitheatre, with a crest of comfortable 4000m summits round the rim. It is about two kilometres across, roughly round, and open at the west side. The central arena is complicated by the intruding south-west ridge of the Zumsteinspitze. Diagonally opposite, outside the circle to the north-east and south-west, are the spurs of the Nordend and the Piramide Vincent. Nowhere else in the Alps offers the possibility of spending such relaxed and enchanting days simply promenading around.

There are plenty of comfortable long ridges in other places of course but only on Monte Rosa can you wander about with the same exhilarating ease and sustained combination of views. Almost every important mountain in the Alps is visible. There is also the apparently infinite outlook to the south, down and across Italy, emphasising the feeling of being high up and on the edge of the Alps. Monte Rosa is large enough to accommodate quite a few other people, while still feeling quiet and remote. It is the sort of place where the paths are helpful without being beaten tracks, which is not to deny that at certain times, when you are tired and the weather is poor, a beaten track can be a great comfort.

The Monte Rosa summits themselves are nicely varied; mildly craggy on the Schwarzhorn, a long broad crest on the Parrotspitze and suitably imposing rocks on the Dufourspitze. Everywhere you go there are the surface snow patterns, glittering and shimmering and delicately coloured as you look across them to the other planet of hot dry valleys far below. And always, on the distant skyline, far away in the Po valley is Monte Viso, mysterious and intriguing. Given enough good days on the southern peaks of the Alps, Monte Viso will become a special object that you always look for. Eventually you will succumb and go there to look in the opposite direction. (You do not need a guide book. From Crissolo the south face of Monte Viso via the Quintino Sella hut is a straightforward

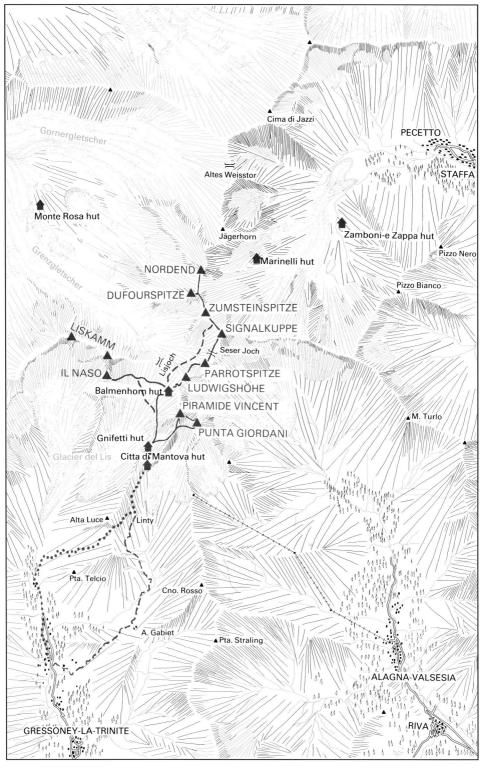

Map 9

Monte Rosa and Liskamm from the summit crest of the Breithorn

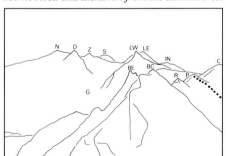

N	Nordend	LE	Liskamm, E summit
D	Dufourspitze	LW	Liskamm, W summit
Z	Zumsteinspitze	R	Roccia Nera
S	Signalkuppe	BC	Breithorn, central summit
IN	Il Naso	BE	Breithorn, E summit
C	Castor	G	Grenzgletscher
P	Pollux		

and well-marked scramble, PD-). Incidentally, the compass bearing for Monte Viso from Monte Rosa is 200, and for the Gran Paradiso 225.

Access to Monte Rosa from the Swiss side via the Monte Rosa hut is long and mostly tedious. I prefer to approach from Italy. From Alagna it is very easy to reach the Gnifetti hut and even the important bivouac hut on the Balmenhorn, if you use both stages of the téléphérique. Gressoney is a less busy valley, which retains some of its charm despite developments for piste skiing. Below the Gnifetti hut, on the path from Gressoney, is the newer and quieter Citta di Mantova hut. From the vicinity of either hut the Piramide Vincent and Punta Giordani offer the rare possibility of pleasant equipment-free afternoon scrambles.

None of this talk of casual high-level swanning about is to deny the importance of the long and serious routes to the various Monte Rosa summits, particularly on the great east face. Routes such as the Marinelli couloir and the Cresta Signal are indisputable classics, as in their different

Monte Rosa from the Schwarzhorn (Corno Nero)

ways, are the Cresta di Santa Caterina and the Cresta Rey, and they deserve the same praise and reputation as routes on the south side of Mont Blanc for example. But they are more remote for British climbers and less written about (just as here). I regret continuing this dismal tradition. I have not spent days in Macugnaga looking at the east face and waiting for good weather so these routes have not taken hold in my mind.

29 Piramide Vincent
  SW ridge (PD-). With Brian Wood
29a Punta Giordani
  WNW ridge (PD-). Solo
Map p 116 Illustrations p 124, 127

  Brian Wood and I walked up from the northern end of the Gressoney valley by the old route. This approaches the derelict Linty hut from the west, where it meets the usual route to the Gnifetti hut going northwards from Alp Gabiet. On our first visit to the area, fired with the enthusiasm of our first outing of the season and the need to get fit, it seemed appropriate to spurn mechanical assistance. The derelict téléphérique to Alp Gabiet was working then. As it happened we found thick fog and few signs of any path so it was quite hard work. At the Gnifetti hut we discovered a curious secluded patio affair which made an ideal bivouac site.

  Overnight the weather improved so next morning, not very early, we ambled over towards the south-west ridge of the Piramide Vincent. This is just right as a first-of-the-season route. It is

118

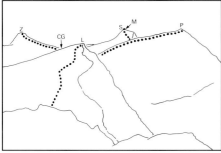

Z	Zumsteinspitze	S	Signalkuppe
CG	Colle Gnifetti		(Punta Gnifetti)
L	Ludwigshöhe	M	Margherita hut
P	Parrotspitze		

In good conditions of well-compacted snow and clear visibility the easy slopes present no technical problems to overcome. They offer instead a robust serenity, provided that you are altitude acclimatised.

short, uncomplicated but not trivial, comfortably interesting and a nice mixture of rock and snow. That uniquely special pleasure of being back in the Alps again was enhanced by having the mountain to ourselves. Brian was not altitude acclimatised and was suffering a little, so he opted to make a circuit back to the hut via Colle Vincent to the north while I went along the ridge to Punta Giordani. The west-north-west ridge (or the east-south-east ridge of the Piramide Vincent if you prefer) was delightful; the essence of airy charm. I remember it as more interesting than I had expected; perhaps I deliberately found bits to linger on. The traverse to Punta Giordani is mostly downhill so I could look past the summit and down to the hills of North Italy. Walking along the ridge was like stepping off into space. Descending from the summit was simplicity itself. An almost level snow path led back westwards to join the south-west ridge of the Piramide Vincent.

After a leisurely brew of tea and an early lunch we set off for Gressoney the orthodox way via Alp Gabiet. Inexplicably, I suppose I mean carelessly, we wandered off the path and got ourselves mildly lost. As is quite often the case the result was a dazzling display of alpine flowers, this time in a little ravine complete with tiny stream and still enough dew to sparkle in the sunlight.

28 Parrotspitze	**27 Signalkuppe**
traverse W to E (F+)	SW flank (F+)
28a Ludwigshöhe	27a Zumsteinspitze
NW flank (F+)	SE flank (PD-). With Brian Wood
28b Schwarzhorn	
NE ridge (PD-)	

Map pp 116, 128   Illustrations pp 117, 118, 122

This time we did indulge ourselves by using the Alp Gabiet téléphérique. To compensate for this and for a late start after an even more indulgent lunch-time session we walked up to the Gnifetti hut in one long burst of sustained hard work. When you are in the mood, of course, that sort of thing is not work at all, even with a heavy rucksack. We might have gone on directly to the Balmenhorn bivouac hut but decided instead to spend a comfortable evening and night at the lower altitude of our private site at the Gnifetti. Next morning, again not very early, we plodded up to the Balmenhorn, left most of our gear and food there, and set out for a stroll round Monte Rosa, expecting to enjoy ourselves without knowing then just how satisfying it was going to be. The Schwarzhorn (sometimes called the Corno Nero) is really an insignificant appendage of the Ludwigshöhe, itself a not very

N	Nordend	S	Strahlhorn
R	Rimpfischhorn	L	Lagginhorn
A	Allalinhorn	F	Finsteraarhorn
Ad	Adlerhorn	Al	Aletschhorn
Sh	Simelihorn		

Nordend from the Dufourspitze

Dufourspitze and Zumsteinspitze from near the Lisjoch

significant extension of the Parrotspitze. But they are pleasing summits: the first nicely craggy, the second an immaculate snow dome. Both are worth visiting.

The Parrotspitze was superb: a clean snow ridge, mostly quite broad, curving round from east to north and down to the Seserjoch. From there the climb up the broad snow slope narrowing to a crest to the Signalkuppe was not as far as it looked. The Margherita hut has been sited with depressing insensitivity directly on an otherwise elegant summit. It spoils a fine situation. Still, as it was there we thought we might as well make use of it to have lunch. So we sat on the end of the balcony and enjoyed the knowledge that there was more carefree strolling to come and that we were free of the usual concern, however slight, about descending.

The view to the south-east is stunning. The south-east face falls away steeply from the summit accentuating the airiness of your position. Alagna, far below, seems remarkably close. The east ridge of the Signalkuppe, the Cresta Signal, was particularly impressive and I regret that I have not been back to climb it. As we left, someone sprang out from inside the hut and demanded 1000 lire from each of us. Totally taken aback we assumed he was talking to the wrong people. But no, this was for the privilege of having sat on the balcony and, no doubt, for not having gone inside and bought some food. It was too late now to pretend we spoke only Hungarian so we said we had no money. Several more hut-dwellers emerged. It began to have all the signs of an international incident. I wondered whether a chit for two free nights at our bivouac site at the Gnifetti hut might do the trick. Brian thought not. Face was saved all round when they took an old karabiner that was dangling from a sling I was carrying.

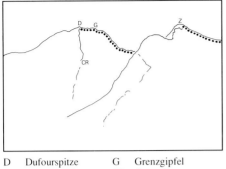

Then we resumed the day's delights: down to Colle Gnifetti and up the Zumsteinspitze. At the flat col the surface snow patterns, in bright sunlight and with wisps of spindrift, were enchanting. I took some photographs but did not capture the magic that my awareness added to the visual picture. Everything was in perfect condition except Brian's head, for which the cure was lower altitude. So we ambled back to the Balmenhorn hut where the only medicine we had was likely to make matters worse. I took some just in case. Brian went down for an afternoon sleep on our patio, returning later for dinner and the rest of the medicine.

26 Dufourspitze
26a Grenzgipfel
      SE ridge (PD-)
25 Nordend
      S ridge (PD). Solo
Maps pp 116, 128   Illustrations pp 117, 120/121, 122

The weather was only reasonable the following morning and Brian was still not altitude acclimatised. We abandoned our plan to climb the Cresta Rey up to the Dufourspitze. I retraced our route of the previous afternoon back to Colle Gnifetti. On the way I was overtaken by a solo dog, presumably on its way to the Margherita hut to make sure the next visitors paid. The north ridge of the Zumsteinspitze was excellent: crisp and narrow, with tremendous views down and across the great east face. About two-thirds of the way up the broken rocky ridge to the Grenzgipfel the rocks began to get icy so I stopped for crampons, a breather and a bit of a think. As I looked back a chamois appeared over the Grenzsattel where I had just been. It trotted round on the lower part of the ridge below me and bounded without the slightest pause directly up towards the Grenzgipfel and over the skyline. I wondered if it was breathing as hard as I was. It did not look like it.

The collection of little towers from the Grenzgipfel across to the Dufourspitze and back were icy. They felt more awkward than they probably were. Having decided that the worsening weather was going to hold long enough I should have stopped thinking about it and concentrated more on choosing a better line for the steep descent to the Silbersattel. The nearly vertical rocks were undemanding enough although their covering of verglas made me feel insecure. From the saddle, the ridge across to the Nordend was a treat. Enormous flaring cornices made the easy ridge seem exotic.

As I came back, wispy bits of cloud began drifting in. By the time I had regained the Dufourspitze, mist completely obscured the east side of the Nordend ridge. When powdery snow began to fall it was clear why the only other people I had seen all morning were two parties on the Nordend. I was glad, in the mist, that all I had to do was to retrace my steps. When I arrived at where

Piramide Vincent, Monte Viso and Schwarzhorn from the Ludwigshöhe

Piramide Vincent from near the Gnifetti hut

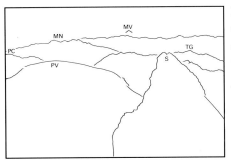

MV	Monte Viso	PC	Punta di Ciampona
PV	Piramide Vincent	MN	Mont Nery
S	Schwarzhorn	TG	Testa Grigia

In this picture Monte Viso appears as a relatively insignificant blur on the horizon. In practice, once identified it becomes a prominent landmark that draws your attention.

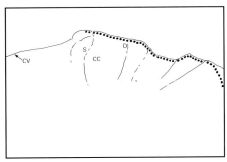

SW	SW ridge	CC	central couloir
CV	Colle Vincent	D	direct route
S	via della Spalla		

The SW face of Piramide Vincent is convenient for afternoon training at altitude (or diversion). There are several possibilities in addition to the three named lines indicated, and easy snow slope descents via Colle Vincent to the Gnifetti or Balmenhorn huts.

I expected the Balmenhorn hut to be there was no sign of it except too many bits of path to choose from. I carried on along one of them and just as I began to feel uneasy about finding the hut there it was, with Brian just beginning to feel uneasy about where I had got to. After a quick cup of tea we charged off down, past the Gnifetti hut, on to Alp Gabiet, and then down to a nice sunny afternoon in the Gressoney valley.

All the tops in this section could be visited in one superb two-day outing by an energetic party. This would be a good introduction to the whole area and an excellent preparation for the more serious routes. Done the right way it would still be a relaxed stroll around and not a frantic race against the clock. From either side, make an early start from the valley and approach the Monte Rosa or the Gnifetti hut, but then carry on further to bivouac at the foot of the Cresta Rey. Take this elegant and efficient line directly to the Dufourspitze. Then go to the Grenzgipfel, out to the Nordend and back, and just continue on round in a lovely undulating semicircle. Going from the Italian side gives a less tedious descent to finish. It also gives the two useful options of stopping overnight at the Balmenhorn hut and leaving some gear there, and of doing the Piramide Vincent and Punta Giordani on the first day.

Bad Rock

Bad rock has strange powers. It can provoke startlingly irrational behaviour in otherwise competent climbers. I have seen strong, resourceful cragsmen turn into neurotic ditherers when faced with a pitch of loose, crumbling rock. An innocent phrase in a guide book like 'continue up the friable buttress', instantly rules out that route from their consideration.

Climbers habitually use the terms 'good rock' and 'bad rock'. As my purpose here is, if not praise, at least mitigation on behalf of bad rock, a complaint about such language is in order. Are not the terms good and bad unnecessarily prejudicial? 'A ridge of bad rock' suggests something sinful on the mountain's part; a feature of a route that the impressionable climber is almost encouraged to endure instead of enjoy. The prevalence of such loose talk exacerbates the problem without explaining why some climbers react so strongly. From now on I will refer to firm rock and loose rock. Even as simple a device as this could alleviate the trauma felt in some quarters. It still exaggerates the issue. To be strictly accurate I would have to say something like 'not entirely firm' instead of loose.

So what is the problem with loose rock? In truth there is none. The problem is in the mind of the climber. He (or she) has a fixation with an ideal vision of firm, totally reliable rock. His passion is for this material and his technique is designed for it. Presented with something else, instead of cheerfully and pragmatically adjusting his approach, he concentrates on bemoaning his situation. I suggest such a person is essentially a rock-climber who has yet to become a mountaineer.

I am no stranger to the delights of firm rock. I agree that there are few activities so profoundly satisfying as steady progress on it. The mixture of delicacy and power, the continual assessing and solving of the problems the rock presents, these are some of life's great joys. Similar, albeit muted, views can be sustained regarding loose rock. You need to approach it with enthusiasm and adjust your technique. Regard it as a different situation rather than a debased version of the other. In particular, concentrate on the splendour of the mountain as a whole rather than on how much you would prefer to be somewhere else.

A definite change of technique is needed: less tactile and more visual assessment, a more continuous spread of supporting points of contact, less total reliance on single holds, smoother transfer of weight, fewer abrupt pulls and less swinging about. However the greatest change required is not in physical technique but in mental attitude. There is no need for a hold to be absolutely solid, merely firm enough for what you require. It does not matter if you can lift a spike out or if it moves when you pull it sideways, when all that is necessary is a downwards pull of a few kilograms. You never need total security, merely enough security.

So if you instinctively shy away in horror from loose rock, I propose this therapy: seek out a spectacular situation on a fine mountain where there is notoriously loose rock and set out to enjoy it. Loose rock is very common. There is a vast amount of it in the Alps that can give you a wonderful time if only you will let it. Plenty of classic routes are spoiled for many climbers by their stretches of loose rock. They do not have to be spoiled: you can choose to enjoy the loose parts along with

Punta Giordani – Piramide Vincent ridge from the Balmenhorn

the rest. Most of the climbing that is involved is relatively easy so your instinctive craving for sound rock is simply greediness.

Take the Grand Combin as an example. A terrific mountain. The south side of the west ridge is almost entirely loose rock. One section is worse than loose: it consists of thin crumbly sheets like mica. I have climbed it twice and found it engrossing and thoroughly enjoyable each time. The quality of the rock did not diminish the splendour of the situations on the route. These were not great days in spite of the loose rock: they were great days without qualification.

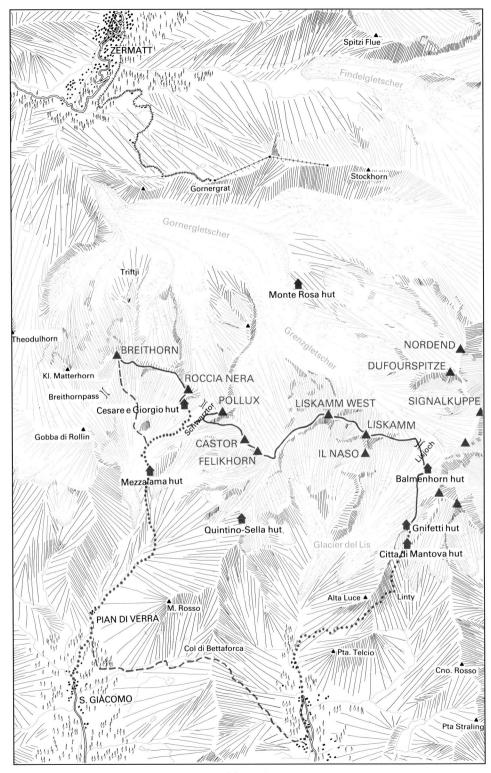

Map 10

Section 7
The Valais South

30	Liskamm	4527m	33	Breithorn	4165m
30a	Liskamm West	4480m	33a	Roccia Nera	4075m
30b	Il Naso	4272m	33b	Breithorn East	4141m
31	Castor	4226m	33c	Breithorn Central	4160m
31a	Felikhorn	4174m	34	Matterhorn	4477m (4476m)
32	Pollux	4091m	35	Dent d'Hérens	4171m

The mountains in this section are not naturally associated with each other despite their geographical proximity. The relative insignificance of Castor and Pollux is one obvious disparity. Even setting aside these two, each of the others, Liskamm, the Breithorn, the Matterhorn and the Dent d'Hérens, has a sharply differentiated character. The Matterhorn of course is so special that it almost insists on individual consideration. A superficial link between them all is provided by Zermatt, which is often a common starting point. In my case however the opposite pattern evolved. I climbed them from the Italian side in four expeditions, each approach beginning in a different valley.

Collectively these mountains are like a summary of the Alps. Every type of route is available. Some will usually be crowded; on many you can expect total privacy and a sense of remoteness. Emphasising the stature of the four major peaks here are magnificent classic routes that provide lasting pleasure or equally durable regret. Those you climb provide some of your great days; those you do not give rise to a wistful longing. Each of my climbs in this section had a special quality and a sense of completeness that I look back on with great satisfaction, yet each mountain has a route that I should have done; a route that will continue to haunt me until I climb it.

Castor and Pollux are overshadowed by their illustrious neighbours. They would be charming and useful mountains in a different context. They are usually climbed by their easy routes as a simple exercise or as a make-weight to something else. From the Swiss side in particular, where the approaches are awkward, their more demanding routes seem perverse when there are such attractive alternatives nearby. Their strange names give them a sentimental attraction even though it is misleading to think of them as twins. Castor is a much larger, more snowy hump.

Liskamm and the Breithorn lie on either side of Castor and Pollux. They have the same basic topography of a long ridge running roughly east-west. This makes both of them distinctly two-sided mountains. The two enormous flanks facing north and south offer many climbing possibilities, with those on the southern sides being much less demanding and more easily accessible. In spite of these similarities Liskamm and the Breithorn are quite different in character. The former is massive, with a brooding intensity. The clean lines give well-defined and starkly uncompromising routes. Yet its

Liskamm and Il Naso from the Lisjoch

fierce appearance is deceptive, for Liskamm is stern rather than intimidating. Even the committing routes on the north side excite desire more than awe, especially the direct line to the east summit, up a thin, shallow rib. The Breithorn, while still a large mountain, is altogether more delicate. Its routes are more intricate and suggest an immediate intimacy. The north side is complicated by secondary ridges and shoulders. These make it a less impressive spectacle than Liskamm's north side but provide attractive routes, none more so than the famous Younggrat.

The elegant spire of the Matterhorn makes it probably the most widely recognised mountain in the world. The well-known views are from the east and tend to exaggerate its relatively isolated position, its steepness and its exceptionally well-defined four-sided shape. Seen from the north-west or the south, the prominent shoulder called Pic Tyndall on the Italian ridge gives it a different appearance. Among the mountains of the Alps I find the Matterhorn an enigma. For such a dominant peak it offers me relatively few attractive routes. These are of such high quality that I should not complain, yet the one I most want to climb, the Zmutt ridge, is uneven, disjointed and in some ways the least satisfactory. A problem with the Matterhorn is that the endless publicity and its flamboyant history come between you and the mountain. I am sure that no other Alpine summit has been visited by such a variety of animals, although I do not suppose it was ever their idea. Dogs, cats, monkeys and a bear have been recorded, but not, as far as I know, an ant-eater.

Another, more tangible, problem with the Matterhorn is its obsessive and self-perpetuating popularity. The enormous numbers of people attempting the easy route on a good day make it unpleasant, dangerous and pointless. Scrambling up the easy rocks of the Hörnli ridge with two hundred others, harassed by faster parties, frustrated by slower ones, bombarded by rocks from

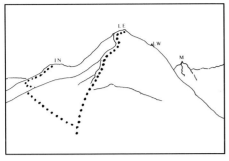

parties above and then queuing up on the last slope for a brief sojourn on the small, overcrowded summit is not what I have in mind when I go to the Alps. The Matterhorn's picturesque uniqueness is both its essential attraction and its weakness. No other summit in the Alps is besieged by so many climbers whose purpose is not so much climbing it as saying they have climbed it. In retrospect, our problematic ascent in uncertain weather and bad conditions when almost nobody else was on the mountain was amazing good fortune.

In total contrast to the Matterhorn, its near neighbour the Dent d'Hérens is mysterious, relatively rarely climbed and truly a mountaineer's mountain. Access to any part of it is awkward and requires effort. The snowy north face is steep, and complicated by ice cliffs. The traditional route from Zermatt traverses across the face on a long terrace. The south side is easier yet still interesting. The long east ridge is an exotic expedition on rock, sustained and serious without being particularly difficult at any point. This ridge continues across the summit crest and then splits into the west and north-west ridges. Between them is the delectable west-north-west face. This is narrow, wedge-shaped and airy; a complicated hanging glacier topped by a simple snow slope. When I was climbing the Tête de Valpelline, 3802m, the next peak to the west of the Dent d'Hérens, I did not think about what I would see from the summit so the view to the east was an amazing surprise. My feelings, as I gazed at the west-north-west face, were a mixture of astonishment and desire.

30 Liskamm
30a Liskamm West
     traverse, E ridge/SW ridge (PD+)
31a Felikhorn traverse, N to E (F)
31 Castor
     traverse, SE ridge/NW flank (PD)
32 Pollux
     NW face (PD). With Brian Wood
Map p 128   Illustrations pp 130, 132

Most people associate Alpine mountaineering with excitement and precipitous situations. This expedition was yet another demonstration that simple undramatic days can be equally memorable. Only a few metres of it felt technically more demanding than a walk in the Peak District but I look back on it with great satisfaction. It began as efficient climbing in a superb context and achieved distinction by gradually changing to a grittily cheerful endurance test.

It began at the old Balmenhorn hut, between the Piramide Vincent and the Ludwigshöhe. This primitive shack has since been replaced in a more prominent position directly on the Balmenhorn

Castor and Pollux from the Stockhorn

by a cosy modern hut. Outside is a large statue of a bearded gentleman making an ambiguous gesture with one hand. Brian Wood and I had walked up briskly the previous day from Gressoney via the Gnifetti hut. We had carried extravagant provisions and after clearing up the squalor inside the Balmenhorn hut we had eaten and drunk very well. We left the hut just before sunrise. The snow was wonderfully crisp and the air still. We climbed the east ridge from the Lisjoch as the sun rose. Our lingering feeling of apprehension about Liskamm disappeared as we realised the ridge was not difficult.

The panorama was magnificent, and astonishingly varied. The Matterhorn was impressive as always though the snowy humps of the Monte Rosa massif, when we looked back, were a match for it. Smooth and shining, delicately coloured by the early sun, they looked like the enchanted

132

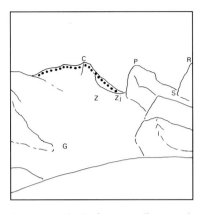

C	Castor	Z	Zwillingsgletscher
P	Pollux	Zj	Zwillingsjoch
R	Roccia Nera	G	Grenzgletscher
S	Schwarztor		

mountains of a fairy tale. From the Lisjoch to the east summit, across the crest to the west summit and down to the Felikjoch is five kilometres. There is plenty of time to enjoy the views, and plenty of opportunity because the terrain is easy.

By the time we had crossed the insignificant knoll of the Felikhorn the early clarity had changed to a faint haze. On the south-east ridge of Castor the snow had lost its crispness. Though still pleasant it was soft enough to make us glad of the two parties in front treading a path. The north-west flank was steeper and the snow slightly harder. It was perfect to plunge down with enormous bounding strides. As we veered to the left to pass under the south face of Pollux we saw the Cesare e Giorgio bivouac hut. This brought a wry smile. We had not been sure of the location of this hut and as our plan had been to climb the Breithorn the following day we had carried bivouac gear from Gressoney and over Liskamm and Castor. At least we were able to leave everything behind to climb the north-west face of Pollux. This was little more than an exercise on the short uncomplicated slope, because as we reached the summit the haze thickened to a thin mist, and instead of the splendid views of Castor and Liskamm that we had anticipated all we could see were vague outlines.

By the time we had descended and were sitting on our rucksacks the mist had turned to drizzle and then to snow. The cloud cover was thick and barely above us. We decided to return to the valley as the weather prospects for the following day seemed hopeless. This was an emotional decision rather than a rational one, influenced by the disappointing change from a glorious bright morning to such a dreary afternoon.

Getting back to Gressoney the same day was another factor in our decision to descend. Once we had concluded that it was possible it became a challenge. The shortest route would have involved reversing our traverse of Castor, in wet steady snowfall and with very soft snow underfoot. The alternative via the Mezzalama hut, visible and almost sunny, was irresistible. Two kilometres past the hut, at Pian di Verra, the opportunity for a comfortable sit and a few beers was equally irresistible. Ahead of us was a fourteen-kilometre hike, with six hundred metres of ascent over the Bettaforca pass. I barely managed to hang on as Brian produced an inspired stint of determined walking to get us back by dusk.

30b Il Naso

SE flank (PD). Solo

Map p 116   Illustration p 130

Unkind words are spoken about the claim of this shoulder on the south side of Liskamm for inclusion in the list of fourthousanders. They can come only from people who have never actually climbed it because other mountains far less worthy are accepted without comment. Clearly it is insignificant in comparison with Liskamm, yet it is quite distinct from the main mountain, well defined, and has an excellent knife-edged summit ridge. It is ascended for its own sake by parties from the Gnifetti hut. I have no regrets about spending an enjoyable morning climbing it in solitude, except that I should have been more ambitious.

For parties based in Gressoney, the traverse of the summit ridge is a common way to climb Liskamm. The route goes equally well in either direction linking the Gnifetti and Quintino Sella huts. A much more adventurous but still straightforward version of the same circuit would be to use the south and south-west ridges of the east summit. The south ridge has Il Naso as a fore-summit. Whichever ridge is used for ascent, rucksacks can be left at the east summit of Liskamm to make the most of the pleasantly delicate main ridge to and from the west summit.

33 Breithorn

33a Roccia Nera
33b Breithorn East summit
33c Breithorn Central summit
     traverse E to W (PD+). Solo
Map p 128   Illustration p 135

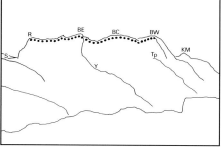

BW	Breithorn, main	R Roccia Nera
	(W) summit	S Schwarztor
BC	Breithorn, central	Y Younggrat
	summit	Tp Triftjiplateau
BE	Breithorn, E summit	KM Klein Matterhorn

The approach walk from St Giacomo in the Valle d'Ayas to the Cesare e Giorgio bivouac hut turned out to be more arduous than I had expected. The last two kilometres in knee-deep soft snow were particularly tiring and also disappointing because I had thought I was fit. I made myself some tea, which was ready just in time to cheer up two Austrian climbers who arrived. They had come from the Margherita hut on the Signalkuppe and had endured the soft snow for longer than I had.

They were a guide and client on a four-day expedition from Zermatt taking in Monte Rosa, Liskamm, Castor and the Breithorn, if the weather permitted. We had an interesting evening comparing our different approaches: my solitary method, carrying plenty of food and bivouac gear for safety; their more confident lightweight style, staying in huts and relying on the guide's previous experience. When I produced a tin of new potatoes as part of my dinner the guide shook his head in disbelief. On the other hand when they shared my litre of wine he admitted that my system had its advantages.

This was a regular tour for the guide. The following week would see them on the Matterhorn and a similar trip north and west of Zermatt. Having hired the guide for two weeks the client was more at the mercy of the elements than I was. On good days he would have a marvellous carefree time with no worries about route-finding and unforeseen problems. In bad weather he would either be towed around in mist and unpleasant conditions, seeing nothing, or else endure the frustration of sitting idly in huts. I was amazed when the guide said he had never climbed in the French Alps.

Breithorn from the Stockhorn

Summit crest of the Breithorn from the Roccia Nera.   The unlikely spire of the Matterhorn is entirely in keeping with the air of enchantment produced by the sunrise colours and the serpentine ridge.

H   Hörnli hut
MV   Monte Viso
A   Abihorn
M   Matterhorn

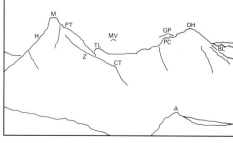

BL	Becca di Luseney	Z	Zmutt ridge
GP	Gran Paradiso	TL	Testa del Leone
PT	Pic Tyndall	PC	Punta Carrel
DH	Dent d'Hérens	CT	Colle Tournanche

Matterhorn and Dent d' Hérens from the Ober Gabelhorn

When I asked was he not tempted by the Grand Combin, which he saw so often, he said he was but it was too far away.

Next morning conditions were perfect. The complete traverse of the Breithorn summit ridge starting at the Roccia Nera is about two and a half kilometres. It is a superb route, airy and delicate, with many transitions between rock and snow and several intricate sections. Along the ridge are a variety of minor 4000m points. The guide planned to take a diagonal line to reach the ridge near the easternmost of these subsidiary summits. I wanted to take advantage of his knowledge of the route along the ridge so I left hurriedly as they were getting ready and worked hard on the steep snow slope that leads directly from the hut to the Roccia Nera. I reached the summit, eyes watering and gasping for breath, just as the sun appeared. Briefly the fourthousanders were highlighted in rosy colours above the cool dim valleys; the fresh snow on the ridge was an iridescent pink, contrasting with the rich-chestnut-coloured rocks.

I caught up the other two and we continued along the ridge together, exchanging the lead amiably. Even when you miss the easiest line the difficulties are modest and short lived. After the central summit the rocky outcrops give way to a gentle snow ridge. We ambled across to reach the west summit, the highest point, shortly before 09:00. I was surprised and pleased to find nobody else there. On fine days two hundred people visit it by the south-west flank, taking advantage of téléphériques and easy snow slopes. The guide hesitated over my offer of Scotch, then declined. His client had no such inhibitions and while we celebrated the guide went over to my rucksack. He lifted it for a few seconds, then said 'You go very fast, with a heavy rucksack'.

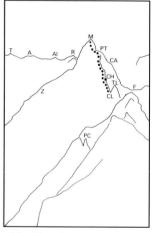

34 Matterhorn

SW (Italian) ridge (AD). With Bob McLewin

Map p 144   Illustrations pp 139, 136/137, 152/153

M	Matterhorn
PT	Pic Tyndall
CA	Cresta di Amicis
CH	Carrel hut
CL	Colle del Leone
TL	Testa del Leone
F	Furggjoch
T	Täschhorn
A	Alphubel
Al	Allalinhorn
R	Rimpfischhorn
Z	Zmutt ridge
PC	Punta Carrel

Bob is my younger brother. It was his idea to climb the Matterhorn when we did. I usually call in at our parents' home in East London on my way to or from the Alps. One year when he was still living there he asked what the Alps were like and what climbing was all about. I suggested that he should come with me next time to find out, so one weekend the following spring he visited Manchester for some training. On Saturday we had a wet afternoon on gritstone and on Sunday drove to Wales and went up and down Tryfan in the rain.

In the Alps he was amazing: tireless and nerveless, a natural alpinist. After we had done three routes in the Bernina, with heavy storms on our first two bivouacs, we went to the Gran Paradiso and did two climbs there. Then Bob said that when he was back at home people would ask what he had done, so could we climb something they would have heard of? That gave us only three

Matterhorn from the Dent d' Hérens

Left: Bob and Will McLewin on the Italian summit of the Matterhorn, with a nostalgic collection of clothing and equipment.

Right: Bob McLewin descending the fixed rope below the Carrel hut.

possibilities: Mont Blanc, the Eiger and the Matterhorn. The Matterhorn was nearest and as we were in Italy we went to Breuil.

Our difficulties began early, in the gully where the approach route to the Carrel hut begins in earnest. The gully provides the way past a steep rock wall and is a natural channel for debris. This had accumulated in intermittent loose heaps that were obscured by wet recent snow. We felt very insecure in several places where the walls of the gully were smooth and the ground awkward and uncertain. Above this first obstacle is a long section of scree and shattered rock where the ascent line is vague. With the liberal covering of snow hiding all traces of the path and concealing the quality of the surface the climbing was irritating and our progress tentative.

Eventually, after several minor detours, we reached the Colle del Leone, 3580m. This col separates the Matterhorn from the insignificant Testa del Leone and is the beginning of the Italian ridge proper. Our problems had eased in so far as the correct route was now easy to find and adorned with fixed ropes and iron spikes. On the other hand the conditions made the slabby sections delicate, the weather had gradually become overcast and threatening, it was already late afternoon and we were still two hundred and fifty metres below the hut. The absence of footprints in the snow indicated that the hut would be unoccupied. We had enough food for several days and the prospect of a comfortable, peaceful stay high on the Matterhorn, even in poor weather, encouraged us to press on. Despite several brief flurries of sleet, steady progress helped to quell my unease about whether it would have been more prudent to retreat.

We reached the hut and were in the middle of our dinner when two Austrian climbers arrived. Like all the Austrian climbers I have met in the Alps they were charming and friendly. They had been told at the Abruzzi hut that the Italian ridge was in bad condition. Seeing us enter the initial gully they had left the Abruzzi and followed our path. They asked whether we would take them to the summit the next day, a request that Bob found very amusing. At the time the weather looked so unpromising that it seemed an academic question. I said they would be welcome to follow us and we would help them if necessary. That was exactly what happened and all that we did was to wait once or twice for them to catch up.

Several centimetres more snow fell during the night, but before dawn the sky cleared. For once there was no need for an early start so we had a leisurely breakfast and left the hut shortly after sunrise. Ours must have been one of the more bizarre ascents of the Italian ridge. On what is one of the classic rock ridges we stepped on clean rock for about fifty metres in total. All the rest was snow, sometimes shallow and slushy, mostly deep and pleasantly firm. The guide-book description was irrelevant and barely recognisable apart from major features. Two of the fixed ropes were useful and we located one or two more. All the others were completely buried in snow. The famous Enjambée, the narrow cleft that separates the final shoulder of Pic Tyndall from the main summit ridge, was full of snow. Instead of a daring leap we merely stepped across the snow.

The strange conditions did not make the ridge particularly difficult, although it took me some time to overcome the vague uneasiness caused by the discrepancy between the reality and my preconceived idea of the route. Constantly exploring to find the best line and taking care on variable snow maintained a feeling of tension and took time. It was early afternoon when all four of us reached the Italian summit. I walked across to the Swiss summit and back. There were no other climbers and no marks on the snow. No other parties had climbed the mountain that day. Our Austrian companions hurried off to descend the Hörnli ridge, probably only as far as the Solvay hut that day. Bob and I sat eating lunch in solitary splendour by the iron cross at the Italian summit of the Matterhorn. Quite by chance Bob had achieved one of the rarest prizes in the Alps, one that many alpinists with vast experience would envy.

Although the clouds that almost surrounded us were bright and seemingly benign we did not dare stay longer than forty minutes. Descending was like the ascent, not difficult but slow and tense. With wispy cloud swirling around us, route-finding would have been difficult without our footprints to follow. Bright sunshine above the cloud produced strange and slightly eerie penumbral and rainbow effects. We were relieved when the cloud cleared and we saw, and then reached, the Carrel hut. The round trip had taken us over thirteen hours.

Next morning we waited for yet more snowfall to stop before leaving. Descending was frustrating and unpleasant. I slipped and sat down in soggy snow with just the frequency needed to maintain a cold clammy feeling where it was least appreciated. The final gully was particularly grim and we emerged frazzled and wet on to the snow slope below. We sat to coil the rope and calm down. As we began to relax there was a dull rumbling sound. Before Bob had finished asking I suddenly realised what it was. I yelled at him to run. We grabbed our gear in armfuls and tore down the slope like madmen, pursued by the torrent of crashing, bounding rocks and lumps of ice that issued from the gully. They gradually subsided behind us and we stopped, gasping for breath and laughing hysterically with fear and relief. A cheer reached us faintly from the Abruzzi hut.

35 Dent d'Hérens
SW flank and W ridge (PD-). With Anne Brearley
Map p 144   Illustrations pp 136/137

When I first visited the Aosta hut, the problematic approach route, mostly on the east side of the river, had been a nasty surprise. On this occasion, with my previous experience reinforced by a damning guide-book description, we stayed on the west side. Instead of the unpleasant day we expected we found the walk straightforward and enjoyable. Because we arrived in good spirits the dilapidated state of the hut was welcome. In its remote location it felt like a refuge should, instead of incongruously smart like some modern huts.

Soon after we had made ourselves at home our peaceful solitude was disturbed by a large party of Yugoslavian climbers with a guide. Their behaviour seemed strange until we realised that they had just climbed the Dent d'Hérens and were simply pausing at the hut before continuing their descent to the Valpelline. This seemed unequivocally good news because they must have left a clear and safe path through the badly crevassed section of the Grandes Murailles glacier. With hindsight the presence of this path on the south-west flank and its seductive promise of a simple and relaxed ascent led my thoughts away from the west ridge. I am not sure why I regret this particular missed opportunity as much as I do. Perhaps I feel that the reticent character of the Dent d'Hérens demands a special effort. Perhaps it is just that even my logic was wrong: the presence of a path to follow in descent should positively have encouraged a more adventurous ascent.

Whether the decision was feeble or not, as an ascent route next day the south-west flank was lovely. Following the track in the snow we serpentined through the crevasses to the snow slopes above. These were firm and just the right angle for efficient comfortable progress. We climbed energetically to the narrow final section of the west ridge, which gave interesting scrambling to the top.

The immediate benefit of our uncomplicated route was a long stay at the summit. To the east, with the sun still barely risen, the Matterhorn looked magnificent. Even though there had recently been a long spell of poor weather its Italian ridge looked more rocky than when I had climbed it with my brother. This made me think of the Welzenbach route on the Dent d'Hérens' north face, which I expected to appear snowy and relatively attractive. Instead, as I started directly down the steep face, the last few rocky pitches with their thin icy cover looked dreadfully insecure. The other side was a total contrast. The amiable snow slope of the south-west flank was inviting and far below on the glacier the curves of our path looked simple and elegant.

The feeling of serene splendour stayed with us when we eventually descended and ambled back to the Aosta hut and then down to Prarayer and the Place Moulin. Even the dreary last section, by the depressingly ugly reservoir, passed pleasantly. The hot and dusty road seemed less real than my recollection of the cool summit.

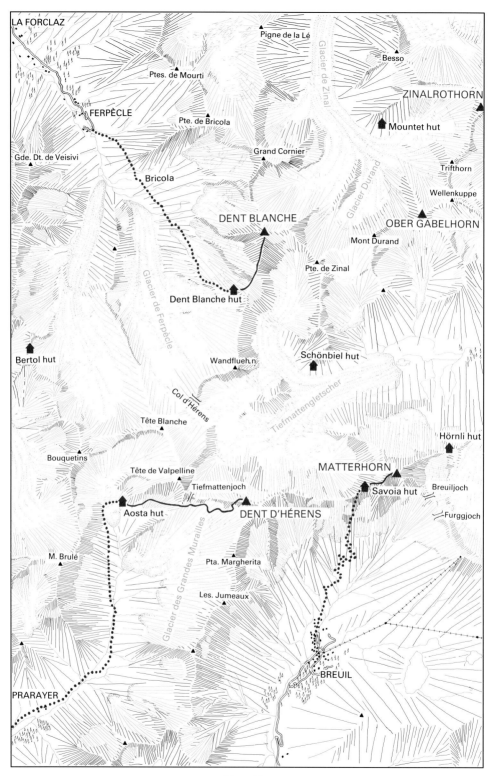

Map 11

144

Approach Walks and Alpine Plants

I took far too long to understand about approach walks. Getting yourself and a heavy rucksack up to a hut or a bivouac is hard work and I used to see it as nothing more than that. I have excuses for having been so misguided. Some hut walks are described in guidebooks with phrases like 'a noted slog'. Such prejudicial descriptions make a big impression on innocent minds. What is worse is that they are not always used correctly. The steep path up to the Mischabel hut frequently receives unfavourable comment, although it seems to me less dispiriting than the tedious trudge across the Mer de Glace on the way to the Couvercle, which is usually described as pleasant.

There are practical considerations too which tempt you to 'slog it out'. The faster you move the less time you bear the burden of the rucksack. When you are on any particular approach walk for the first time, feeling an element of anxiety to reach your destination is understandable. Often you are not sure how much more there is to do until you are so close to the hut that you may as well press on and get there. Descending after a climb, you are genuinely tired and usually sore in one or two places and the only worthwhile source of relief is getting it done with. And to be fair there is a deep satisfaction to be had from accomplishing this act of transportation in a solid relentless effort. It helps to get you fit as well.

I realise now that the slog is just the superficial, almost incidental part. The approach walk presents and emphasises the change of environment from what we ironically call civilisation to the austere enchantment of the mountains. Your slow progress upwards is measured by the changing display of diverse plant life and the plodding walk is an ideal context in which to observe it. You begin in the lush jungle of sub-alpine meadows, pass through dark or dappled woods and end with improbable delicate-looking plants growing in harsh places. When you reach the hut or the beginning of the climb you are usually at the point where plant life ends.

When you learn to look at alpine plants instead of just seeing them, every approach walk brings new delights. The less used the path the better. You find the best displays when you lose the path altogether. Then you discover that edelweiss for example, which seems scarce, is quite common. On the other hand I am still hoping to come across a good plant of the fabled Eritrichium nanum to see whether the 'King of the Alps' lives up to its name. A plant that is popular with everyone is the small deep-blue gentian, Gentiana verna. It is not rare, but scarce enough to give a jolt of pleasure whenever you see it. Everyone develops their own favourites. I am surprised to find I have become particularly fond of two very common plants. These are the two gentians that most people do not realise are gentians: Gentiana lutea with spikes of yellow flowers, and the dull-maroon Gentiana purpurea. Neither is conventionally attractive; in fact both are coarse and inelegant. Perhaps I like their persistent teasing. When they look as if they are about to produce a spectacular display they are in fact just past their prime.

Alpine plants are a source of embarrassment. My botanist friends expect me to know much more about them than I do. My excuse is that good weather is needed for serious study and then I am too busy giving all my attention to climbing. There are signs, especially from my knees, that nature is taking a hand to change that.

I still tend to confront approach walks with solid effort, but now I am more relaxed and I enjoy them. Instead of a penalty to be paid before doing a route the approach walk is an integral part of it. The preliminary ritual of assembling everything and deciding what to include and what to do without always takes ages. This too is part of the climb and I no longer fret over it. The almost inevitable realisation that something has been forgotten no longer seems a disaster. What might have been the most ludicrous omission did not actually happen. Brian Wood and I were on our way to the Schmadri hut to do the Lauterbrunnen Breithorn. We were still a bit inebriated even after two hours' hard work when we stopped for a rest. Whether to walk up comfortably in trainers and carry stiff climbing boots or to opt for less weight and walk up in boots is still a decision I remake every time.

On this occasion we had gone one stage further and were trying trainers and shorts. Our stop was traumatic instead of restful. We were engulfed by a herd of goats who went crazy licking our legs and trying to eat their way to the food inside our rucksacks. As we started walking again to escape I suddenly thought 'I have forgotten my trousers!' I had intended to strap them to the lid of my rucksack. Brian insisted I unpack everything and there they were, wrapped round some fresh peaches.

Gentiana verna in the Valpelline on the way to the Aosta hut

146

Section 8
The Valais West

36	Bishorn	4153m (4134m)	39	Ober Gabelhorn	4063m
37	Weisshorn	4505m (4331m)	40	Dent Blanche	4357m
38	Zinalrothorn	4221m			

The long ridge separating the Mattertal and the Val de Zinal is part of the dividing line between French-speaking and German-speaking Switzerland. The summits linked along the ridge provide a wealth of splendid routes and at its southern end the ridge curves south-west towards the magnificent Dent Blanche. The whole ridge is like a larger, grander version of the Mischabel ridge on the opposite side of the Mattertal.

The topographical similarity with the Mischabel diminishes with closer inspection. Here the mountains stand apart from one another and have distinct identities, which is possibly why the ridge as a whole does not have a name. The individuality of the 4000m peaks of the chain, apart from the Bishorn, is emphasised by the presence of at least one important mountain between each of them. These intermediate mountains, particularly the Schalihorn, the Trifthorn and the Pointe de Zinal, should not be dismissed, even though their status is inevitably diminished by their higher neighbours. Their contribution adds substantially to the area's mountaineering riches, particularly of shorter routes that are useful in poor weather and for acclimatisation.

The impression of endless possibilities, all of high quality, for climbing at a moderate level of difficulty characterises this group of mountains. Each of the five 4000m peaks has a pleasing appearance and a simple structure with well-defined ridges and faces. Every ridge suggests a natural line and in practice provides a satisfying route in almost every case. The fine ridges mean that you always have a clear sense of position. This gives an underlying feeling of comfort and security and enhances the pleasure of movement.

In common with every accessible mountain no face has been left unclimbed, but the face routes here are not the major attraction. Mostly they lack the compelling elegance of the ridge routes and are rarely climbed. The main exceptions, apart from extremely difficult possibilities like the north-east face of the Dent Blanche, are on the Bishorn and the Ober Gabelhorn. The two Bishorn face routes, the simple north-west flank and the complicated impressive north-east face, together with the beautiful north face of the Ober Gabelhorn are the pure snow and ice routes in this group. The Ober Gabelhorn south face provides a pure rock route. Another face route is on the long west flank of the Weisshorn, which uses a vague rib descending from the grand gendarme to fashion, on the Zinal side, relatively easy access to and from the upper part of the Weisshorn's north ridge. There are iron spikes in places, installed by the Zinal guides.

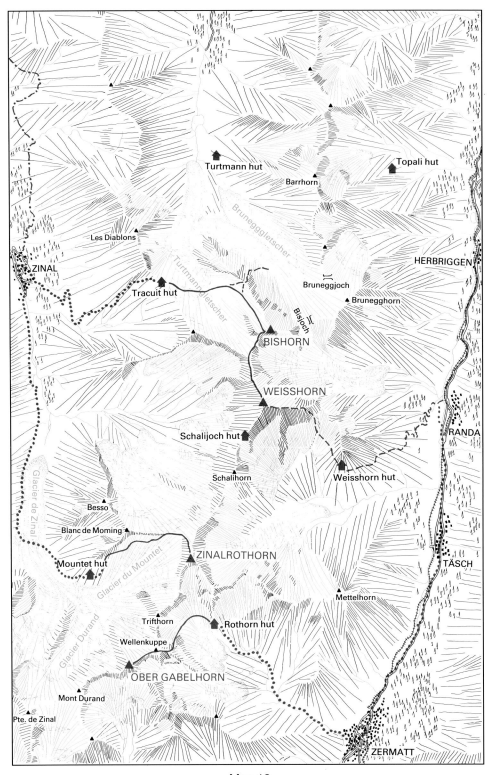

Map 12

148

The Bishorn is the poor relation in this group because it runs on without a significant drop in height from the north ridge of the Weisshorn. The whole of the connecting ridge and shallow col that separates the two mountains is over 4000m. As a result the Bishorn can seem merely a shoulder in the Weisshorn's distinctive and dominating outline. Frequently the Bishorn is overlooked altogether, as it is by the Sierre-Zinal race. This is sub-titled 'The race of the five 4000s', because competitors can see during the race the Weisshorn, the Zinalrothorn, the Ober Gabelhorn, the Matterhorn and the Dent Blanche. The Bishorn is deemed unworthy of inclusion in such illustrious company. I never overlook it. The closest I have ever been to disappearance and death was on the Bishorn.

Access to the mountains in this group is straightforward. There are well-used paths and a generous supply of popular huts. The Matterhorn is the dominant feature, of course, luring endless throngs of visitors to the area. Most of them do little more than sample and sustain the crowded opulence of Zermatt. Zinal, in contrast, retains a simple charm and is relatively quiet.

Zermatt is the starting point for a larger number of famous mountains than anywhere else in the Alps. The very name encapsulates mountaineering for many alpinists and is enough to evoke their own and more celebrated histories. I do not share this reaction. I find Zermatt crowded and smug – an amalgam of Singapore and Tunbridge Wells. Its immediate environs undeniably provide pleasant walking and running. The paths are liberally supplied with bench seats painted bright red: ironic as well as intrusive. Higher up, above the tree line, construction of ski-runs has left many places looking like abandoned building sites. Although in the town anti-litter notices are frequent and strident, large-scale commercial litter is apparently acceptable.

Despite its prominence I have scant affection for Zermatt. I use a vehicle as a base and my aim is always to find secluded spots for a day or two at a time. As the last section of the Mattertal road, from Täsch to Zermatt, is for residents only and ordinary visitors have to walk or use the train, Zermatt does not even have the appeal of convenience. Consequently I hardly know the town despite many visits to the Valais West. It remains an unimportant part of my experience.

The five 4000m mountains in this section provide a refreshing contrast to my lack of enthusiasm for Zermatt. Each one was a very significant experience and all of them have routes and traverse combinations that still attract me. The Ober Gabelhorn and the Zinalrothorn have the most possibilities although, unlike some other mountains, no particular route beguiles me. This is partly because neither mountain is conspicuous when seen from other areas. The Weisshorn and the Dent Blanche on the other hand stand out as two of the great mountains. It is not just their size that impresses. Each is unmistakable and has a distinctive outline that draws the eye. No mountaineer can look at them without wondering how he or she might climb them.

36 Bishorn

NW flank (F). Solo

Map p 148   Illustrations pp, 150, 155

The gentle snow slope of the Turtmanngletscher leads directly and easily to the col between the two summits of the Bishorn. The twin peaks are nicely shaped snow humps, five hundred metres

Bishorn W summit from the E summit.   To the uninitiated, alpine mountaineering is about braving the elements, or effort and struggle in exposed situations. Some participants never learn to see it any other way. For most alpinists the activity is more about special, almost secret, delights. One of these is the enticing prospect of smooth, untrodden snow. This is an uncertain pleasure because the snow is often uncompacted and laborious to traverse. Another, that is unfailingly pleasing, is looking back at an expanse of clean snow and seeing it marked only by your own footprints. The ephemeral nature of this historical evidence does not diminish the satisfaction it gives.

apart. They are connected by a crest that is corniced just enough to provide visual interest. This unusual summit arrangement gives an ascent of the Bishorn by the uneventful north-west flank the distinction that the route lacks. The proximity of the great east face and north ridge of the Weisshorn adds to the interest. The pleasant stroll that constitutes this route is quite short and free of objective danger so it can be enjoyed even in the afternoon. Yet this route, the easiest of all 4000m ascents without mechanical assistance, gave me a few of my worst minutes in the Alps. I learnt from it that one of the most serious dangers of Alpine mountaineering is to miss public transport connections.

I was camping with friends in Saas Fee. Several routes on the Mischabel had given me repeated views of the Weisshorn and left me fit and confident enough to attempt the north ridge via the Bishorn. This meant a bus to Visp, a train eastwards along the Rhône valley to Sierre, then another bus back south to Zinal. At Sierre I took too long over some odds and ends of shopping, missed my intended bus to Zinal and found I had a two-hour wait for the next one. I rapidly dispelled my disappointment by purchasing an English newspaper and settling down at the station café for a few beers and a civilised lunch.

When I left Zinal to walk up to the Tracuit hut it was mid-afternoon. For most of the way I had a niggling feeling of unease and several times stopped to convince myself I was on the correct

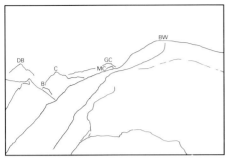

BW	Bishorn, W summit	C	Grand Cornier
DB	Dent Blanche	GC	Grand Combin
B	Besso	MC	Mont Blanc de Cheilon

path. Eventually I realised the discomfort had nothing to do with my over-indulgence at lunch-time. I had seen no-one else on the path, even though it served a popular hut. The reason, which should have been obvious enough, became apparent when the brilliant, sunny weather was replaced with low clouds. Occasional spots of rain turned to steady drizzle before I reached the hut. The guardian was surprised to see me and clearly undecided whether to believe me when I managed to explain what my intentions were. Eventually he got me to understand that the north ridge of the Weisshorn was 'not ready' and that only one party had attempted it so far that season.

The rain stopped during the night. By mid-morning next day the mist had lifted and there were breaks in the cloud. If the weather continued to improve and then stayed fine overnight the Weisshorn was a possibility. Then a consequence of my session at the station café struck me. Were I to stay a second night at the hut, I would not have enough money if bad weather forced me to return to Saas Fee the way I had come. Ideally I would descend the east ridge of the Weisshorn. This would take me to Randa, giving me a shorter return journey, down the Mattertal to Stalden and back up the Saastal to Saas Fee. Even if poor weather ruled out the Weisshorn, a descent to St Niklaus in the Mattertal would be possible by a tortuous route over the Brunneggjoch and down by the Topali hut. Unfortunately the only map I had with me ended south of the Topali hut.

In any case I did not like the idea of crossing the Turtmanngletscher to the Brunneggjoch in mist without looking at it beforehand. Copying the large map on the wall of the hut, I sketched in the top margin of my map the continuation north as far as the Topali. Then I left to walk up the Bishorn. The guardian had observed me with perplexed amusement and a familiar air of knowing superiority. I regarded my behaviour as a logical consequence of the price of Swiss beer. We had so little vocabulary in common that I did not even attempt to explain.

The Bishorn was a simple delight. I ambled up the Turtmanngletscher feeling liberated from the hut and the morning's clammy mist. The weather was steadily improving. The thin layer of fresh snow glittered in waves as more and more breaks appeared in the cloud cover. I went to both summits and chose the slightly lower east peak for a bit of lunch and a careful look at the Weisshorn. There was no-one else to be seen of course. The only signs that the Earth was inhabited were my own footprints. The north ridge looked magnificent: awesome and serious yet powerfully alluring. Although it was clearly not in condition I found it irresistible and felt very confident about climbing it.

As I walked back I was optimistic about the following day's weather. Nevertheless I thought I should look at the route to the Topali hut, at least as far as the Brunneggjoch. The north-west flank of the Bishorn is an elevated tongue on the east branch of the Turtmanngletscher. It is joined to the east branch by a moderately steep rocky slope. Near the bottom of the tongue I turned away from my footprints which curved leftwards towards the Tracuit hut. A shallow saddle gives access to the

M	Matterhorn
W	Weisshorn
B	Bishorn
H	Hotälli
Br	Brunegghorn
Bj	Bisjoch
Ws	Wildstrubel
SH	Schalihorn
Og	Ober Gabelhorn
W↓	Wellenkuppe
T	Trifthorn
ME	Mettelhorn
LM	Le Mammouth
R	Riffelhorn
Bq	Bouquetins
MD	Mont Durand
GC	Grand Cornier
DB	Dent Blanche
PZ	Pointe de Zinal
Wf	Wandfluelücke
Sb	Schönbielhorn
Wa	Wandflue

PM	Pointe Sud de Moming
N	Pointe Nord de Moming
Mt	Pointe du Mountet
Ug	Unter Gabelhorn
G	Gornergletscher

Valais mountains; Matterhorn to Brunegghorn, from the Lisjoch.   An added attraction of approaching Liskamm and the Monte Rosa massif from the S is the fine view of the Valais from the Lisjoch. Everything is in your favour: you will usually be there early in the day, the morning sun is behind you as you look towards the NW and the appearance and relative positions of the Valais moutains when first seen from the SE are often a revealing surprise. In addition the Lisjoch is high, 4151m, so you will be doubly pleased to pause for a few moments.

rocky slope and I went easily down a vague rib to the glacier. A third of the way to the Brunneggjoch my carefree progress vanished as I realised I had entered a crevassed area. There were a few small open crevasses visible but I felt sure there were plenty more blind ones under the surface.

I edged forward carefully, unsure whether to go on or back. Suddenly my right leg plunged down into emptiness and I pitched forward. Instinctively spreading my arms and left leg to cover as much area as possible I lay on the snow and gently swung my right leg to find the nearest crevasse wall. My foot made no contact at all. I squirmed forward, trying to extricate my right leg and stay spread out in contact with the surface. Just as I began a sigh of relief there was a soft plop and I was on my way to the centre of the Earth.

Before I was aware of falling I was stationary again. The smooth walls of the crevasse curved away in both directions and went down for ever, so I was pleased to find that I had landed about a metre from the end of a bridge of snow debris about five metres long. It must have fallen from the surface some previous summer, wedged and frozen between the walls and lain there ever since, waiting for this moment to snatch me out of the air.

W	Weisshorn	BG	Bisgletscher
SW	SW ridge	L	Leiterspitzen
	(Schaligrat)	R	Alphubel W ridge
E	E ridge		(Rotgrat)
N	N ridge	A	Alphubeljoch
B	Bishorn	WS	Weisse Schijen

With two tape slings and an ice-screw I secured myself to one wall and jumped up and down to confirm the snow bridge was solid. Then I could look around. Cold greenish-blue half-light and profound silence: not a cheerful place. The hole I had made was about six metres above but it seemed tiny and far away. Towards the other end of my platform the polished walls of the crevasse were just close enough together to back-and-foot upwards. It was easier than I expected but felt very precarious. Near the surface the walls were further apart so I had to wriggle sideways to a narrower place. Butting through the layer of snow covering the crevasse I was able to straighten out backwards, ram my ice-axe into firm snow, roll over face downwards and squirm on to the surface.

I grinned a greeting to the sun and walked fairly easily to safe ground, using the exact line of the crevasse as a guide. I had been calmly deliberate the whole time and almost carried on to the Brunneggjoch. Then sitting at the Tracuit hut as a lovely summer afternoon ended seemed a much better idea.

As I walked back, and later that evening, my thoughts were of the Weisshorn rather than the crevasse. Lying on the snow, suspended above an unseen crevasse of unknown size; dropping into it; landing comfortably on a snow bridge that just happened to be there; wedging up the glassy walls to the world of warmth and life: somehow, at the time, I simply assimilated the whole episode as though it were a commonplace event. Since then, if I choose not to regard it as a miracle or a message from the Earth, I can argue that the point where the snow covering had previously fallen into the crevasse to form the bridge is exactly where the new cover would be weaker and least able to bear my weight. Usually, when I remember that crevasse, I simply shudder.

Weisshorn from the Feechopf

37 Weisshorn

N ridge (AD), descent by E ridge. Solo

Map p 148   Illustrations pp 155, 152/153, 157, 158

The Weisshorn! A long day of magnificent mountaineering: exhausting, though I never felt weary, and tiring, emotionally as much as physically. The significance of events usually becomes clear only when the immediate preoccupation with physical activity has ceased and there is time to reflect on them. That is true of this ascent yet a special quality was apparent at the time. Throughout the day I seemed to have a heightened consciousness. Everything was more vivid than usual, as if my perception had been retuned. At the same time I had a sense of detachment. I could see myself, tiny and insignificant on the Weisshorn's inert brooding vastness, but moving and undaunted by it. Enjoyable and exhilarating, the day was both of these, yet somehow it was more about revelation than climbing.

It began strangely. There were few people at the Tracuit hut and none of them got up early when I did, even though the sky had been clear during the night. There was no sign of the guardian either. This meant helping myself to water from the kitchen and heating it with my own stove on one of the hut tables. I was happy to be left to my own devices but being alone and using a head-torch in the darkness of the hut was eerie. As I had breakfast I reviewed my finances. On the table, with a note, I left what I thought was the correct amount of money, and for once I did not find myself paying for unexpected items. There was not much remaining to take with me.

Outside it was cold and clear and quiet, so quiet that my crampons scrunching in the crisp snow seemed obtrusive. I began walking up the Bishorn almost stealthily. I had intended to be brisk and relentless on the initial easy snow slopes. The western sky, as it lightened, made that impossible. If I cannot stop to look at such splendour then mountaineering is pointless. There were two broad horizontal bands of even and intense colour: deep indigo-blue below rosy purple. Above them, the rest of the sky was a cool pale blue. In this pale blue, to the right of the Grand Combin and left of Mont Blanc, was the new moon, no longer shining (just before sunrise) but softly luminous. A bit later I sat on the west summit of the Bishorn to watch the sun rise and the colours flare and then fade.

I wondered about the rest of humanity. What do they see that compensates for not seeing this? Nobody could experience this view of the world and not be moved and enriched by it. The vision as the sun rises in the Alps is a fleeting one yet its effect on your life is permanent. But I think you have to be there; you have to be involved; you have to be a part of it. Being alone makes a big difference. Although I wish more people saw such splendours I was pleased none of them was there that morning.

An easy crest of exquisitely clean unmarked snow led me down from the Bishorn and on to the Weisshorn in a long curve. The first difficulty is two fifteen-metre, flat-topped, almost vertical steps to descend. I almost began climbing down the first one before I told myself there was too much snow and ice on the rock. In a deliberate act of caution to counter the feeling of being in a dream I took out my thirty-six-metre length of 6mm rope and abseiled down. At the second step the wind threw the rope about so that halfway down the little cliff I had to pause awkwardly to untangle it. This interruption, and the uncoiling and coiling of the rope, was irritating. Returning to serene progress along the ridge and down an easy third step I told myself that even if I had not needed to use the rope, it had been sensible.

The three steps in the ridge are a prelude to the grand gendarme, 4331m, which presented me with a genuine difficulty. You ascend the ridge for a few metres towards the base of the gendarme and then traverse on slabs across the east face to the foot of a thirty-metre chimney. The sudden change from the comfort of the ridge crest to the enormous steep face accentuated the exposure, yet even on the icy slabs I felt at ease. The chimney was intimidating and repellant, covered in ice and awkward to enter. I went back across the slabs and got the rope out again.

Weisshorn N ridge and E face, from the E summit of the Bishorn

Mischabel from the Weisshorn

D	Dom	B	Balfrin
L	Lenzspitze	Gj	Galenjoch
N	Nadelhorn	Fg	Festigletscher
S	Stecknadelhorn	Kg	Kingletscher (N)
H	Hohberghorn	Dh	Dom hut
Dn	Dürrenhorn	Ls	Lagginhorn

When I descended it the E ridge of the Weisshorn did not seem quite as exposed as it appears here. There was more snow than when this picture was taken, which made rapid descent straightforward. In any case, my attention was held by the panorama of the Mischabel on the other side of the Mattertal. The long rock ridges on the W side of the Dürrenhorn seem ideal for a fast, lightweight, scrambling circuit on a pleasant sunny day. The climber is Grace Hurford.

I tied the middle of the rope to a karabiner on a sling doubled round my waist, the two ends to another karabiner and sling round a rock bollard, left the rucksack clipped to the second sling and returned to the chimney. Without the rucksack it was straightforward although very precarious. Two places for reasonable running belays using metal chockstone wedges reduced the insecurity. Just as the rope began to tighten the holds became bigger and more plentiful and there was a convenient spike for another sling. I untied the rope from my waist, fastened it to the sling, and clipped the karabiner on my waist sling round the rope. All I had to do now was climb down and back across the slabs, retrieve my rucksack, remove the sling belay from the bollard, tie myself on to the ends of the rope and climb up again.

The whole of this pantomime seemed unreal. I went back and forth with a detached calmness, unperturbed by the enormous drop beneath me. I must have been tense yet I felt relaxed and unhurried. I seemed to be looking down on myself, separate from the person who was moving about. Totally absorbed with the immediate problem, I was at the same time conscious of the larger landscape: the east ridge, the west face of the Bishorn and, across the Mattertal, the familiar peaks of the Mischabel. I hardly climbed the top part of the chimney; it just slid past as I approached it, to leave me back on the ridge crest with an easy scramble to the top of the grand gendarme.

Seen from other mountains the top section of the ridge appears to be a gentle smooth two-dimensional arc. The foreshortened view of the route from the grande gendarme, nearly a kilometre from the summit, was a surprise. The ridge twisted about in swooping curves, icy rock at first, then mostly snow, sharp and exposed and in places extravagantly corniced. The snow was in quite good condition and unmarked; the weather was perfect; the situations along the airy crest magnificent. To call it climbing gives the wrong impression. It was another example of walking in the sky, effortless and tranquil. Every few metres presented a minor problem, interesting rather than difficult, needing care rather than effort. Although I was tired I had no feeling of fatigue and although I made steady progress there was no sense of movement. The overriding impression was of stillness. Reaching the summit, coming to the end of the ridge, was almost a disappointment.

I was glad to find nobody there. I had assumed other parties, coming from the Weisshorn hut, would have been and gone and I was surprised to find untrodden snow. For the first time since leaving the Tracuit hut at 04:30 I looked at my watch. It said 11:40. Seven hours. It had not felt that long; time had seemed not to be involved. It felt only a few minutes later when I looked again at 12:30. I gazed back down the north ridge, shaking my head in wonder. It was now marked with my own footprints. A tangible, yet ephemeral, record of my presence. At last, and quite slowly, I began to understand about mountaineering.

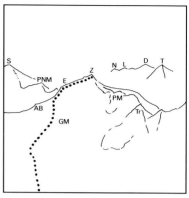

Z	Zinalrothorn	L	Lenzspitze
E	L'Epaule	D	Dom
PM	Pointe du	T	Täschhorn
	Mountet	Tr	Trifthorn
S	Schalihorn	AB	Arête du Blanc
N	Nadelhorn	GM	Glacier du
PNM	Pointe Nord		Mountet
	de Moming		

When I turned my attention to the east ridge and descending I was amazed to see, far down the ridge, a party of three climbing up. This immediately removed any apprehension I had about the descent. I left before they reached the summit. Not far down the ridge I found that the new uncompacted snow was soft and in places deep. Thanks to the other party's tracks, descending to the Weisshorn hut was straightforward; even so it took three hours of hard work.

Near the hut I stopped, had something to eat and brewed a large quantity of tea. The path down to Randa was pleasant enough and I was still elated, but the afternoon was hot, my rucksack felt heavy and there was not much spring in my step. My sleepy grin as I walked into the station signified pleased relief. The next train was due in about forty-five minutes; time to cool down and relax in a shady spot. I went to buy my ticket and found I did not have enough money.

I stood in the ticket hall with my eyes closed, half asleep, trying to think. I could use some of the money I had set aside for the bus fare from Stalden back up to Saas Fee and perhaps hitch a lift. I looked at a map on the wall. The next station was at Herbriggen, a further five kilometres. I had nearly enough money. I heaved my rucksack on, staggered out into the blinding sunlight and half walked, half trotted down the road. I reached Herbriggen station, put my little pile of sweaty coins on the counter and heard the train in the distance. Delicately, with the tip of one finger, the ticket clerk spread them out. I was still thirty centimes short. I stood in front of her, absolutely spaced out, mouth open but unable to speak. As the train rumbled into the station she solemnly took two coins from her purse, added them to my collection, smiled, and gave me a ticket.

38 Zinalrothorn
N ridge (PD+). With Brian Wood and Andy Hartley
Maps pp 148, 144   Illustrations pp 161, 162, 168/169

Climbing the Zinalrothorn was memorable and very instructive. Sadly, the mountain was just a backdrop for other, more significant events, and the ascent itself was an anti-climax.

Zinalrothorn from the Dent Blanche

A comfortable bivouac above the Mountet hut and a steady start at first light seemed to indicate the beginning of a relaxed uneventful expedition. That was what we had in mind when we decided simply to go up and down the north ridge. More ambitious ideas had faded during several days of frustrating indifferent weather. We had now an excellent morning and fairly crisp snow as we walked across the Glacier du Mountet towards the sharp snow ridge that leads to L'Epaule on the north ridge proper. The route looked totally straightforward. In the right frame of mind such days bring a special cosy pleasure, which I was already anticipating.

Shouts and screams from the centre of the glacier signalled an accident. A party from the hut had been traversing diagonally across the glacier eastwards to reach the south-west ridge. Their leader had fallen about nine metres into a blind crevasse, hit its icy bed and broken his right femur.

Top section of the Zinalrothorn N ridge; the tower called the Bosse

Later we learned that he was from Chamonix and was with his wife, sister, brother-in-law and two friends. He had graduated as a fully fledged guide a few days before and this was their expedition to celebrate. Even so he was lucky! Had the crevasse been two metres deeper the whole of his party would have followed down on top of him, crampons and all. When we reached the scene the second was sitting on the edge of the crevasse with the rope tight between her and her husband below.

They had been crossing a crevassed glacier carrying coils of rope as most parties still do, and exactly the way I had been taught to by Austrian guides. If the person in front falls cleanly into a crevasse the coils are snatched from the hand of the next person, who is then swept off his or her feet by the momentum. The sensible method is a tight rope between climbers so that any fall immediately meets resistance from the next person. The disadvantage of this approach is that it requires concentration and involvement from the whole party. The first way gives a veneer of safe climbing technique in situations where it is unnecessary. The illusion of safety is the greatest danger. The members of the graduation party, stunned by their calamity, were still roped together but not yet belayed. They resisted our attempts to organise them because they had an Alpine guide in charge: a ludicrous impasse which Brian resolved by pointing at me and proclaiming 'Guide Anglais!' Two of them went back to the Mountet hut to arrange for the famous Swiss Mountain Rescue Service and I abseiled down to do what I could for the poor guide. Not much. A couple of ice-screws and a tape sling made a back rest. His rucksack and mine made some cushioning. Various items of clothing and sleeping gear helped keep him warm. The presence of another person gave him the most benefit. We agreed, by sign language, to do nothing else until the helicopter and a stretcher arrived. Still in shock in the numbing cold, his embarrassment was giving him more anguish than his injury, but not for long.

The roar of the helicopter was followed by angry argument on the surface. I began to wonder whether the rescue team's strategy was to fill the crevasse with snow. They all had to walk to the edge of the crevasse to see for themselves what the situation was, kicking loose snow down in the process. I crouched over the guide while a stream of fine snow mixed with icy lumps poured down on us. It felt endless. Every time I looked up, more hit my face and went down my neck. Whenever I sheltered my face somebody shouted something that made me look up. Eventually Brian explained to me, and the guide's wife explained to the guide why no stretcher was being lowered. The rescue team had not brought one.

Then a net landed on top of us. I was to wrap the guide in the net and then the rescue team would haul him up. Both of us found this very hard to believe. It was also difficult to accomplish. The narrow, sloping crevasse floor was a jumble of icy blocks covered by now in loose snow. To get past the guide I had to climb over him. Our conversation, of necessity quite complicated, was pure Laurel and Hardy. To ask him something I bawled up at Brian in English. A bit later some French would come screeching down. The guide would bawl up a reply in French and after another pause his translated answer would reach me. Once or twice, receiving these garbled messages, we gawped at each other in amazement.

At last, our protestations exhausted, I wrapped both his legs in my carrymat, tied them together with a tape sling and wriggled him into the net. He was hauled to near the top of the crevasse, where the overhanging lip made further progress impossible. The guide's groans died to a whimper and a lot more snow poured into the crevasse before he was pulled out using the helicopter. I heard it depart and felt very cold. I was disturbed and dispirited by what I had seen. My carrymat had been blown away and had disappeared when the helicopter took off. For the rest of that season I made do with a short spare piece. There followed an awkward unreal Anglo-French breakfast by the hut. Then the three of us went back to Zinal. We had taken up only one day's food.

Two days later we did the route in the uneventful way the beginning of our first attempt had presaged. Brian and Andy wanted to make more fuss over the trickier bits than I felt was warranted, particularly little verglassed traverses off the ridge crest. I thought the situations on the ridge were ideal for relaxed scrambling and found their caution irritating. They were mindful of an incident a few days before. An English party descending in the afternoon, had had a fairly serious accident at L'Epaule, which is the transition point at the bend in the ridge. The narrow rock crest changes to a sharp icy snow ridge descending westwards. Forewarned and taking care, there is no danger at all, though it was easy to see how an unsuspecting party could get into difficulties. The snowy ridge was harder and smoother than it looked, and while the inclination on the very crest was quite shallow it rapidly steepened at the sides.

The Rothorn was a rare occasion when I finished a route feeling disappointed even though the weather was fine and the route in good condition. Perhaps the events two days earlier had been more disturbing than I realised. The route is enjoyable and I did enjoy it, but I was unable to get completely in tune with it.

39 Ober Gabelhorn

ENE Ridge (PD+). Solo
Map pp144, 148   Illustrations pp165, 168/169, 152/153

My ascent of the Ober Gabelhorn was a bonus at the end of a successful season. While enjoying a relaxed evening in Sierre, after climbing the Dent Blanche earlier in the day, I realised there was time for another route before my planned departure. The Dent d'Hérens was too far away and the Ober Gabelhorn was the only other 4000m summit in the Valais I had not climbed. The surest and most straightforward way, Zermatt, the Rothorn hut and the east-north-east ridge over the Wellenkuppe, chose itself. I had often tried to settle on which way to climb the Ober Gabelhorn; now circumstances resolved the problem for me.

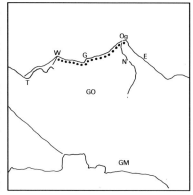

Og   Ober Gabelhorn
W   Wellenkuppe
E   ENE ridge (Arbengrat)
N   NNW ridge
G   grand gendarme
GO   Ober Gabelhorn glacier
T   Triftjoch
GM   Glacier du Mountet

This view exaggerates the steepness of the N face, although the impression that it is a serious route in anything less than perfect snow conditions is the appropriate one. Another, more general, message clearly conveyed is that getting to Alpine routes may be more problematic than climbing them. Here, the Mountet and Ober Gabelhorn glaciers can be seen to be complicated and badly crevassed. They present a substantial barrier to be overcome before the elegant pleasures of the ridges can be enjoyed.

When I arrived at Randa in the early afternoon next day there was a roadblock and police were ordering visitors to return down the valley. A short distance beyond Randa a landslide of rock and mud had swept across the road and the railway. The two policemen who refused to let me park there were so insistent that it was impossible to get to Zermatt, even on foot, that I almost believed them. I drove back a short distance, found a place to leave the van unobtrusively and walked across the railway. There were more police turning back sightseers on the footpath, so a little detour through a wood and across a boggy meadow was needed before I could pick my way over the tip of the tongue of rubble and scramble back to the road.

The twelve kilometres to Zermatt was a preliminary exercise that I could have done without. The novelty of the eerily deserted road had worn off well before I arrived. The path up to the Rothorn

Ober Gabelhorn from the NW edge of the Mountet glacier

hut was also deserted, which surprised me until I realised that guide-book time would get me there at 21:15, well after sunset. I worked hard at the ascent, intending to go past the hut before looking for somewhere to bivouac. I reached the hut at 20:05 but before then I felt tired from the previous day's effort on the Dent Blanche. The most convenient flat spot was the helicopter landing pad, where I enjoyed my dinner and spent a satisfying night, looking at the sky and sleeping well.

I intended using the first parties from the hut to guide me up the early part of the route. By 04:30 no-one had appeared. I had finished a leisurely, extended breakfast; there was plenty of light; it was a wonderful morning. I left, wondering whether everyone else knew something I did not.

On some days you do not climb mountains, you ride up with the sun. The rock and snow flow smoothly past under your feet. The Earth unrolls and displays itself and you stop being an observer and become part of it.

At the snow dome of the Wellenkuppe I sat for a few minutes' enchantment. I could see no moving dots of people. More crisp snow led me down to the col and up the Ober Gabelhorn ridge as far as the grand gendarme. The rock was mostly clean and almost warm. The fixed rope, by now fully in the morning sun, was comfortable to grasp and seemed to haul me upwards. Past the grand gendarme the ridge is superb: interesting without being difficult, undulating at first, then quite steep. The contrast on the narrow ridge between empty space on the left and the shimmering snow-sheet of the north face on the right gives a pleasant tension which enhances the actual climbing. At one point the north face was irresistible so I traversed out to the right for a few metres. It was steeper and more icy than I had expected. I felt insecure and soon veered back to the ridge. Verglassed rocks and a snow groove near the top led to awkward jumbled blocks immediately below the small snow summit. The chilly breeze had been absent on the ridge. I made a comfortable sheltered seat in the sun and sat down, to look, and see, and be aware. Time stopped, and an hour sped by.

It was only 08:40 yet somehow I knew it was time to leave. There was no need to stay longer: I could always return in my mind. The ridge was just as good in descent, the snow still beautifully crisp. As I left the fixed rope two parties were approaching. I could hardly believe it. I had forgotten all about other people. We passed each other with mutual curiosity. At the top of the Wellenkuppe, in distinctly soft snow, a third party was resting. They asked me where I had been. I asked them where had they been. They shook their heads and said I was crazy. Then they left to fight their way up rapidly deteriorating snow and probably to spend most of the afternoon struggling back.

I stopped by the Rothorn hut for a brew of tea and some lunch, reluctant to begin pounding down to Zermatt. The railway was running again but it was not a day for train rides. By 15:00 I was back at the van, drinking tea and beer alternately and soothing my sore feet in a stream.

40 Dent Blanche

S ridge (PD+). Solo

Map p 148   Illustrations pp 167, 170, 168/169, 152/153

My first attempt at this route was with Brian Wood and Andy Hartley. Our intention was to bivouac past the Dent Blanche hut. We took minimal gear as we were optimistic about the weather. It was sunset when we reached the hut, even though we had taken less than the guide-book time of six hours from Ferpècle. Instead of the clear calm evening we had anticipated, there was a cold breeze and thickening cloud. The only flat snow we could find was at the side of the hut. By the time we had finished our evening meal a thin drizzle of sleet was falling. Short of money, we hoped to avoid using the hut. Our combined waterproof covering was adequate only while we remained immobile.

As we tried to sleep hut-dwellers on their way to the privy paused to make witty conversation. Most of it we found unintelligible even though they repeated it when we failed to respond. Thin wet snow fell intermittently throughout the night and cold trickles fed growing patches of damp. Every so often one of us would fall asleep and emphasise the misery of the other two. At one point a strong wind drove all three of us into the sentry-box privy. The absurd impossibility of sharing equally the available comforts broke our spiral of deepening rancour. 'Convenience' was the wrong word for

Dent Blanche S ridge. Several short traverses on the W flank avoid towers on the ridge. The rocks on the flank are frequently verglassed and can be almost as awkward as the problems they avoid.

that privy. We returned to our earlier arrangement and laughed hysterically at the thought of the contraption toppling from its exposed perch with the three of us inside.

At first light a procession of hut-dwellers began visiting our discarded bedroom. For most of them, it was an excuse to look at the bizarre spectacle outside. After several demands to explain ourselves Brian revealed his genius for language. He sat up like a glove puppet and proclaimed 'Pas de money!' Andy and I sat up beside him and chanted 'Oui, pas de money!' and we all flopped back in unison. This little sketch was repeated with increasing finesse for successive visitors until the guardian's nerves gave way and he insisted we come inside the hut to have our breakfast.

A few days later, in beautiful morning weather, Andy and I were back at Ferpècle. Better equipped to bivouac we went up to the hut again. The weather deteriorated in the evening exactly as it had before. This time the guardian said we should sleep on the floor inside the hut. His kindness rebounded on us because it was hot and stuffy and we slept badly. Next morning, in a very strong wind, we climbed the lower part of the route to work off our frustration. Heavy snowfall during the afternoon followed by clear sky left the route totally out of condition, making an ascent the next day out of the question. In beautiful evening weather we went back to Ferpècle.

Four years later there was the longest spell of perfect Alpine weather I have known. I had been climbing with Brian Wood in the Inner Oberland: long, quiet days of steady tramping. Before Brian and his family returned home we stayed overnight at Sierre, enjoying the unfailing relaxed hospitality of the station café and the Auberge des Collines. I had to leave in two days. There was just time for the south ridge of the Dent Blanche. At Ferpècle that evening there was no sign of the weather

167

DB	Dent Blanche
W	Weisshorn
Z	Zinalrothorn
PZ	Pointe de Zinal
Wl	Wandfluelücke
Bh	Balmhorn
Bl	Blüemlisalp
D	Doldenhorn
WS	Wildstrubel
BH	Bishorn
B	Besso
J	Jungfrau
LD	Les Diablons
Bn	Bietschhorn

LB	Lauterbrunnen Breithorn
T	Tschingelhorn
Og	Ober Gabelhorn
Ds	Dammastock
G	Gspaltenhorn
BM	Blanc de Moming

168

Dent Blanche and Weisshorn from the Dent d'Hérens

Bivouac site at the NW edge of the Mountet glacier.   The situation is perfect: sheltered flat snow, a convenient supply of rock for various bits of construction, and a fine view of the Dent Blanche.

170

breaking. The next day would be perfect for the walk up to the Dent Blanche hut, but would it hold the day after that? I woke up at 03:00 to find clear sky and starlight bright enough to see by. I thought of the two previous occasions and could stand it no longer. By 04:00 I was springing up the path with a light rucksack. At the hut at 07:30 I stopped to make tea and have a second breakfast.

The easy rock rib behind the hut is followed by a snow ridge leading to a hump on the main south ridge. The snow was still excellently crisp. Several parties had started earlier from the hut and left a staircase of solid steps. The views were stunning. Though there was lumpy cloud in the valleys there seemed to be an exceptional clarity about the light. The Matterhorn and the Dent d'Hérens were particularly impressive. Several times I stopped to look, started moving, and stopped again almost immediately.

There were no difficulties until the traverse, on the west side, round the grand gendarme. For a few feet the slope is exposed and quite steep. If it had been either bare rock or snow covered I would hardly have noticed it. Instead there was smooth opaque ice. Climbing on front points was needed for about ten metres, across and then up towards the ridge. Had the slope been steeper or the icy section longer it would have been serious. I was halfway, delicately balanced but comfortable, and wondering which way the earlier parties had gone. Several lumps of icy snow smashed down announcing the first party descending. Their leader promptly launched into a lecture on the dangers and foolishness of climbing solo. Naturally enough the other members of his party crowded together to look down the slope. They gave substance to his oratory by dislodging more projectiles in my direction. He was right of course; my situation was dangerous. If they all came crashing through the cornice they were standing on, they would take me with them. I climbed urgently to the ridge and went past them tapping the side of my forehead. They probably thought that was a confession.

The remainder of the ridge was pleasant and straightforward yet wonderful. On some of the little traverses round obstacles on the ridge the verglassed rock provided interest and variety rather than difficulty. I met several more descending parties. They were cheerful and helpful. Their enchantment with the route, the weather and the views resonated with mine, dispelling any fatigue I might have felt. Surprisingly, I overtook two parties still going up. The first of these was a youth, his father and his grandfather. The second group reached the summit at 11:00, shortly after I did. They all said 'Berg Heil!' almost in unison; each shook hands with everyone else, including me, then they left. Their arrival and disappearance was so abrupt I wondered whether I had imagined it.

I was alone on the summit for half an hour until the family party arrived. They were overjoyed that I was still there to photograph all three of them together. Each in turn confided that he would have climbed more quickly without the other two. I had some Scotch left to hand round, which made them happier still. I was lucky to have had this important summit to myself and then to have been part of what was clearly a very special event.

At 12:00 I left and sailed smoothly down the ridge in two hours. I found there was a slightly easier way round the grand gendarme. Expecting to feel tired I lingered indulgently over lunch. When I left for Ferpècle my euphoria was undiminished and my rucksack light. It is a fast comfortable path to descend in any case. I enjoyed every step of it.

Sierre and the Sierre-Zinal Race

Not many people would choose Sierre as their favourite Swiss town. Most people know it only as somewhere to pass through on their way to and from more exotic places. I have more affection for Sierre than any other town in the Alps. Wherever I choose to climb I always contrive to spend a day or two there. Its attraction is subtle, mostly circumstantial, and to some extent, I admit, simply familiarity.

I think of Sierre as the centre of the Rhône valley. Although it is towards the western end it is the central one of the valley's five main towns: Martigny, Sion, Sierre, Visp and Brig. The Rhône valley in summer is like a vast allotment: neat, fertile and lushly fruitful. Running roughly east-west it separates the mountains of the Oberland from those of the Valais. The mountain valleys run north or south, each associated with a town or perhaps just a hamlet on the Rhône and each with its own character. Some are busy and developed and end at a major resort like the Mattertal, which runs south from Visp to Zermatt and Saas Fee. Others are quiet lonely places like the strange Baldschieder-tal which goes northwards from Visp.

Martigny is special because it signals your arrival in the Alps, or bids you farewell. Coming from Lausanne into Martigny there are three roads out: west, over the Forclaz to Chamonix and the French Alps; south, to the Grand Combin or over the Great Saint Bernard pass to Aosta and the Italian side of the Alps; and east, along the Rhône to the Inner Oberland and the Valais. Martigny station is a convenient meeting place and invariably has British newspapers. And every summer in Martigny there is a prestigious art exhibition.

Sion is special for me because it is the first of these towns that I got to know and the initial air of enchantment remains. It is the entrance to the Val d'Hérens and Arolla. Sion is a magical sight as you approach it, especially early on a morning when the Rhône valley is misty. There are two prominent hills, one capped with a monastery housing the oldest known working church organ, the other with a ruined castle. There are mysterious narrow streets and excellent places for a pleasant lunch. And every summer in Sion there is the Tibor Varga music festival.

Sierre appears to be ordinary, which is one of its virtues. It is a perfect place to relax between routes or retreat to in bad weather. When the weather in the mountains is poor it is often perfectly good in Sierre. The station square is the crucial place. Like the whole town this is busy but feels tranquil, and there is always somewhere to park. Here, shaded by lime trees, are the post office and the self-service station café, once the best place in Switzerland for a beer, a chat and a cheap meal. Excellent shops are nearby, although the first-rate supermarket is all you need. A short walk away is the Lac de Géronde. This is a tree-fringed lake, a good place for a swim. Discreet overnight stops are tolerated. If it gets crowded there is a very quiet, less pretty place a bit further away by the Rhône on the other side of the main valley road. By the Lac de Géronde is the cheerful and hospitable Auberge des Collines, more luxurious than the station café, but equally good value. And every August there is the Sierre-Zinal mountain race.

The start of the race is at 08:30 on the main road at the eastern end of the town. The winner finishes 31km, 2000m of ascent and a little over two and a half hours later in Zinal. The attraction of the race, like that of Sierre, is not immediately obvious. Over 1200 runners take part and another 2000 people walk the course as tourists, starting at 05:30. It is not a genuine fell race; the whole course is well marked and on good tracks. It is a high-profile, media-conscious occasion with helicopters, bands and lots of spectators. These, for me unpromising characteristics, are redeemed by the course itself and the splendid arrangements. The race is organised by Jean-Claude Pont and his genial efficiency pervades the whole event. There may be some aggravation at the front and there is doubtless some misery at the back but I find that competitors, helpers and spectators are amiable and have exactly the right level of seriousness. It is a truly international field and lots of local people take part.

Peripheral features add to the charm. A gang of apparent undertakers plays moronic, fife and drum tumbril music at the start. The Swiss army, deployed along the course, blows whistles at tourists to warn them to make way for runners. After the race you can have a swim as well as a shower. At the prize-giving ceremony in an enormous marquee, a band mangles the same few bars of music as each successful competitor goes up to receive an award.

The race itself begins with a murderous charge up the road. Then there is a long, unrelenting climb through dark woods. This is mostly in single file with a welcome bottleneck every so often. The first of the well-supplied drinks stations is a cheering sight in spite of the substantial ascent still to come. Occasional breaks in the trees and glimpses of open sky are both encouraging and disappointing. The transformation is unexpected even though you have been longing for it. Suddenly the trees thin out. You go round a bend and into an open sunny meadow. It is a glorious moment that colours your impression of the whole course. Now you have twenty-four kilometres left of varied, undulating terrain. If you are going well you settle down to steadily picking up places. If not you hang on and use the spectacular scenery to relieve the pain.

The Sierre-Zinal race 1981. Less than a kilometre to go to my best time so far, and 340th place. The vest is that of Dark Peak Fell Runners, the first and still the best fell-running club. The colours, brown with a yellow and purple stripe, symbolise the peat, broom and heather of the Peak District, or, more elementally, earth, sun and sky.

After twenty kilometres and the climb up to and past the Hotel Weisshorn the course is gradually downhill on rocky paths. British fell runners, used to much rougher terrain, prosper on this stretch. Then comes the steep zigzag path down to Zinal, on which they prosper even more. Some of the runners who left you behind on the uphill unexpectedly reappear, descending barely faster than they went up. The very last bit, three-hundred metres downhill on the road, is quite trying. Then you have a shock of awareness, of crowds, and heat, and sore feet. Quite unnecessary pop music blares out over loudspeakers. You revise your opinion of the undertakers' fifes and drums. The grind uphill through the cool woods seems a long time ago. For me it is.

I discovered the Sierre-Zinal race by chance in 1975. I happened to be in Zinal doing nothing in bad weather, and before I discovered what all the commotion was about, runners began to appear. It was a good year to be British. Jeff Norman and Ian Thompson were first and third. Then I did not know there was such a thing as fell running. I started in 1979, first did the Sierre- Zinal race in 1981 and have run it in most years since. It seems to have become part of the tradition of visiting Sierre.

Grand Combin from Mont Avril. The S side of the Grand Combin gives a different impression from the more familiar N flank. Although such contrasts are to be expected they often come as a surprise and change significantly your feelings about the character of a mountain.

Section 9
The Grand Combin

41	Grand Combin de Grafeneire	4314m	41b	Grand Combin de Tsessette 4141m
41a	Grand Combin de Valsorey	4184m	41c	Aiguille du Croissant 4243m

The essential quality of the Combin is elusiveness of character. This is not really a massif like Monte Rosa, yet it seems inappropriate to regard it as a single mountain like the Grandes Jorasses for example. Although isolated, it occupies an imposing central position. Its normal routes are very different yet all of a similar standard. This significant mountain offers unexceptional climbing. It is a familiar sight to all Alpinists yet few are really familiar with it. You could sum up the Combin as managing to be special despite being almost everything the Matterhorn is not.

The Combin is almost exactly midway between Les Droites in the French Alps and the Dent d'Hérens in the Valais South. These are its nearest 4000m neighbours and both are twenty-four kilometres away. The position of the Combin and its massive size are important in linking the Mont Blanc area with the Valais. Situation and size make it instantly recognisable. Although the Combin is one of the first mountains you look for from any other summit, its amorphous outline means you are not left with an immediately memorable image.

The topography of the Combin is complex, particularly on the southern and eastern sides. However, several ascent possibilities are impracticable due to objective dangers, inaccessibility or very uneven difficulties. The main summit, the Grafeneire, provides superb and unique views. If there is no wind it is a comfortable place to sit and give each direction the serious attention it merits. Because the location of the Combin is so distinct you get fresh perspectives on even the peaks you know well. Although they are worth visiting, the Valsorey and Tsessette summits are seldom deliberately climbed for themselves. They lie on either side of the Grafeneire, and one or other of them is naturally and easily climbed en route to the main summit on one of the two most popular ascent routes. As they are well separated from the Grafeneire, they quite often provide a consoling achievement when an ascent of the main summit fails. The Valsorey is the culmination of the west ridge, which is now the most reliable way to climb the Combin. Much of the rock on or near this ridge is loose but not stressful and probably no worse than anywhere else on the mountain. A fine ice climb, the north-west face, also leads directly to the Valsorey summit.

The Tsessette can be climbed easily by a minor detour from the traditional Corridor route. This traverses from west to east across the north flank of the Combin to attain the short north-east ridge. After being the trade route of the Combin, the Corridor fell into disuse when the threatening line of ice cliffs above it became dangerously unstable. This brought to the once busy Panossière hut a few years of relative tranquillity until the hut was effectively demolished by an avalanche.

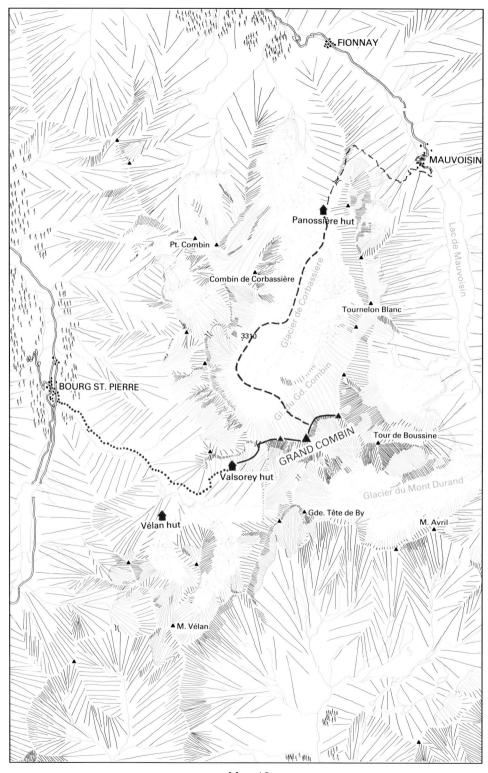

Map 13

Grand Combin from the Combin de Corbassière

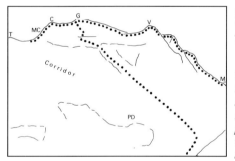

MC	Mur de la Côte	G	Combin de Grafeneire
V	Combin de Valsorey	M	Col du Meitin
T	Combin de	PD	Plateau du Déjeuner
	Tsessette	C	Aiguille du Croissant

The dangerous séracs above the traditional Corridor route are so evident it is surprising that they were ever stable enough for the Corridor to provide the normal route. The more direct line through the ice cliff will presumably vary in difficulty so using it for descent only will be a speculative venture. My impression was that the difficulties would not be substantial for independent parties, however problematic they were for guided parties. In any case they are confined to a few metres, so in descent they may provide an opportunity to indulge in a traditional technique, that of cutting an abseil bollard in ice.

The remaining 4000m peak, the Aiguille du Croissant, is an insignificant snow hump near the Grafeneire. Even as a minor top it is unworthy of attention except for a bizarre piece of historical controversy. The first English party to climb the Combin insisted that when their local guides had made the first ascent they had mistaken the Aiguille du Croissant for the main summit. Shades of Karl Blödig on Mont Brouillard!

On the south side, one ridge of very loose rock leads to the Valsorey and another to the saddle between it and the Grafeneire. The main south ridge, leading directly to the Grafeneire, is a better line but equally unsound rock. This ridge begins at the Col du Sonadon, which is a critical point on the Haute Route between Chamonix and Saas Fee. Between these ridges are sections of the dreadful

177

crumbling south face. Even worse is the steep cliff above the Glacier du Croissant. This maze of tottering earthy rock buttresses is effectively an upper-level east face. Nothing else that I have seen in the Alps has been so frightening and repulsive, although the main east face, below the Tsessette and which I have seen only in pictures, is yet more horrifying because it is much larger. These monstrous sights are the menace lurking behind the Combin's benign appearance and part of its contradictory character.

For me there is one particular mystery about the Combin. I have spent three days on the mountain and encountered nobody. On one occasion, approaching from the north side with someone else, the weather was poor and the snow laborious so we did not expect to see other people. The other two occasions were glorious days yet there were no recent footprints and I was completely alone all the time.

41 Grand Combin de Grafeneire
41a Grand Combin de Valsorey
41b Grand Combin de Tsessette
41c Aiguille du Croissant

W ridge, traverse from Valsorey to Tsessette, (PD), descent by N flank direct. Solo
Map p 176   Illustrations pp 174, 177

I remember the walk from Bourg St Pierre to the Valsorey hut as exceptionally pleasant. This must have been mostly subjective reaction because the path itself is ordinary. Being fit helped, and having started earlier than usual I was rewarded with a cool dewy sparkle everywhere. The western approach to the Grand Combin is disappointing in so far as it does not provide good views of the mountain. However Mont Vélan, 3734m, looks impressive and interesting. I met no-one else on the path and when I arrived the hut was deserted. By late afternoon I had begun to suspect that bad weather was expected but then two German climbers came in. They planned to ascend the steep north-west face, using as a guide a page of the excellent book *Im steilen Eis* by Erich Vanis. Next morning before sunrise we left the hut together and scrambled up to the Col du Meitin where we parted.

The west ridge was a strange climb. It was easy, absorbing and very enjoyable, yet frustrating. The rock was astonishingly loose. At one point it consisted of thin friable flakes almost like mica. The ridge was not well defined and much of the time I found myself wandering on to the shallowly concave face on my right. Every so often I decided that I should veer to my left until I came to the ridge crest, where there might be better rock and a definite route. I never did stick to that resolve for long enough to find out whether my guess was correct: there was always an intriguing line that meandered back to the right. This was partly because my gaze was continually drawn across the face and to the south. Although the immediate views were of nothing more than crumbling rock, far beyond the south-west ridge were the Gran Paradiso and the distant sentinel of Monte Viso.

The ridge seemed to end suddenly. There was a refreshing stretch of good rock in an open position, a short snow slope and then I was on the summit of the Grand Combin de Valsorey. On wonderful firm snow, clean and bright, I went briskly down to the col and then steadily up to the highest point, the Grand Combin de Grafeneire. The views were stunning. In whatever direction I looked my reaction was to shake my head in disbelief at the wonder of it all. For some time I kept turning to look at particular landmarks and then, distracted by everything else in sight, forgetting to locate them.

Eventually I went on, over the Aiguille du Croissant and down the short north-east ridge. This is not a ridge in the conventional sense, rather the edge of the sloping plain of smooth snow that is the upper part of the Combin's north flank. In descent these gentle snow slopes are on your left. To the right is a precipitous rocky cliff. At the end of the north-east ridge is a steeper slope called the Mur de la Côte, which descends to a similar ridge running eastwards to the Grand Combin de Tsessette. The Mur de la Côte was an unpleasant surprise. For several metres it was icy, quite exposed and steep enough to demand caution. It seemed prudent to cut a few steps, which I enjoyed doing even though my clumsiness revealed a lack of practice. Downhill is, after all, the most difficult direction for this activity.

The easy walk to the Tsessette brought two more surprises. One was the view of the repulsive tottering south-east face; the other was the absence of footprints. I had expected to find a well-trodden track to follow down through the Corridor and eventually to the Panossière hut. From the Grafeneire summit however I had noticed what appeared to be a faint line of old footprints leading directly down the north flank. That suggested there would be a way through the cliffs at the end of the upper slopes, so I abandoned my plan of descending the Corridor and instead retraced the way I had come. There were some useful steps already cut on the Mur de la Côte and instead of traversing across the north flank I climbed back up the north-east ridge. The opportunity of another visit to the main summit had proved irresistible, as I had known it would.

Descending was easy, and although it was seven kilometres to the Panossière hut along the Glacier de Corbassière, for most of the way there was just the right amount of downhill gradient for easy walking. At the hut I found a comfortable sunny corner to sit, make some tea and look at the Combin. Then I climbed slowly up to the Col des Autannes and down the stony path to Mauvoisin, wishing I had arranged to be met at Fionnay, at the end of a gentler path.

Guides

It must be wonderful to be an Alpine guide. Instead of snatching a few days each year from your other life, you spend the whole of the summer in the mountains. Your practised and detailed knowledge of approaches and descents gives you a relaxed attitude and a wide safety margin. Instead of constantly having to make choices between routes, you have opportunities to do any route and any minor variation that appeals to you. So much more of your life takes place in that enchanted world that others can only dream about. And you get paid for doing it.

It must be awful to be an Alpine guide. Instead of becoming totally involved with a route, you have to concentrate on your hapless clients. Your goal is their safe delivery from the hut to the summit and back. Instead of insight and exhilaration as you move over glaciers and ridges, through séracs and couloirs, you are haunted by the damage to your reputation and livelihood if, in spite of all your efforts to shepherd your clients, one of them contrives to kill himself.

My encounters with guides have left me with a disparaging view of them. This is partly my own fault. My original attitude based on written accounts of extraordinary events was far too idealistic. It has since been tempered by first-hand observations.

I have only climbed with guides once. That was on an Austrian Alpine Club mountaineering course, my first experience of Alpine climbing. I admired their skills and fitness. I found them charming and likeable people. What I did not like was the absence of any genuine instruction in Alpine mountaineering skills. The days were pleasant enough: up not too early, amble from one hut to another, go over a summit or two, finish by lunchtime. I was surprised that my wanting to practise things, either en route or in the afternoon, produced some aggravation. At the time their unhelpfulness towards someone keen to learn and willing to work was no more than a niggling disappointment. I did not realise then that what we were being taught was how to be taken round well-trodden paths by guides. Several years later I was resentful of the lessons I had to unlearn. Time was wasted teaching myself to be technically competent. Discovering for myself a more rewarding approach was hard and frustrating. Perhaps if I had hired a guide the year after my AAC course my experience would have been different. By the time I could afford to hire a guide I neither needed nor wanted to.

Generally I have found professional guides unhelpful towards independent climbers, sometimes positively obstructive. Their proprietorial attitude is not justified. They could without any loss of status behave with more generosity and less arrogance. This applies as much to encounters in huts and on téléphériques as to those on the mountains. There are exceptions of course. Plenty of chance meetings with guides have been friendly and pleasing. These have been mostly on harder routes, particularly when there has been time to demonstrate a degree of competence.

It might be argued that unguided parties present problems for guides because if they get into difficulties or have an accident any guide nearby must provide assistance. That is true, but it applies to all climbers, not just to guides. What distinguishes a guide is that he will present the assisted party with a substantial bill. I have been involved with a serious accident once only (See Zinalrothorn, pp 161-3). The guide on that occasion was at the bottom of a crevasse with a broken femur and I gave the assistance. Perhaps this credit balance that I can never redeem prejudices my interactions with guides.

The defensive attitudes of some guides are easy to explain. The client-guide relationship is problematic. It cannot be a simple financial transaction. For most climbers there is an emotional element that is difficult to cater for and there are dangers inherent in the undertaking, especially to guides from their clients. The service guides offer is ambiguous. Should a guide instruct or merely steer? Do clients buy expertise and insurance or just local knowledge? Is the guide's role to enable the client more skilfully and sensitively to climb the route or simply to enable the client to say he has 'done' the mountain? All this makes the guides' task genuinely difficult. These problems however are just part of the job, and not where their deepest anguish lies.

Guides are the victims of better maps and better guide-books. Their role has been usurped by freely available information. All their secret paths have been inexorably revealed. Even worse, their pioneering and exploring role has been taken over by brash outsiders, semi-professional climbers and dilettante amateurs. How hard to bear this must be for the guides. That once proud body of men, the heroes and high priests of the mountains, have become the ushers of the trade routes, shepherding the feeble along the well-trodden ways. Once, however grand and aristocratic their rich clients might have been, the guides were still the masters even if they behaved deferentially. Now, as they drag their strings of plodders along, independent spirits sail past flaunting a rhythm and harmony with the mountain that the guides seem to have lost and their parties will probably never know. Their tetchiness towards the unguided and unorthodox climbers they meet is therefore understandable.

The steady increase in accessibility and information explains why guides' behaviour is not always all it should be. Explains, but does not excuse. There is no excuse for the guide I saw on a long chimney pitch of a rock route. He had two clients – female as it happens – both of them climbing competently as I caught them up. The chimney needed a bit of thought and effort but was more intimidating than difficult. At the top of it was a fine sunny ledge. The guide arrived and began to bring up the first of his clients. After she had made a couple of pauses the guide sighed and simply hauled in the rope. The woman just sailed up, probably making a token flap at handholds as she sped past. The second woman was not allowed even a couple of pauses. It was impressive in an appalling way. I guessed that the guide had done the same thing several times before.

There is no excuse for the Saastal guides. When local councillors proposed building a rock platform on the summit of the Fletschhorn to raise its height to 4000m, did they veto such nonsense? No! I assume they happily anticipated more clients to be escorted to another easy summit.

There is no excuse for guides adding to the congestion on popular routes by taking long strings of climbers and then berating other parties trying to pass them.

There is no excuse for the Matterhorn guides who would like to prevent access by unguided parties to the Hörnli route as if they actually owned the mountain. The Matterhorn guides are well known for their antagonism towards independent parties. They have revived my interest in the Hörnli route to the extent that I feel I should choose a busy day and solo it.

As the context of Alpine mountaineering has changed, the guides' role has been downgraded and their status has inevitably diminished. They figure prominently in first ascents of many important mountains and classic routes, but their exact contribution in such events has always been unclear to me. The parties concerned were usually a mixture of guides and 'gentlemen climbers'. The written accounts, invariably by the gentlemen, always leave basic questions unanswered. The traditional version in which complementary talents are combined does not ring true. Could the gentlemen really not have succeeded without the guides? If so, their achievements are greatly overpraised because surely the guides could have made the ascents by themselves. Were the guides unable to make new ascents without a financial stimulus? Were they merely porters, or an early form of protection? Perhaps guides' attitudes have always been largely commercial. This would not distinguish them from some well-known mountaineers today, except that for the guides it would have been a case of necessity. Nevertheless all climbers are so much historically in their debt that a residue of affection remains.

Many climbers are interested only in the having done; the manner of their doing seems of no importance. Present-day guides seem to have chosen to cater for that category. Have they abandoned their responsibilities to the physical and spiritual aspects of the climbing environment? For most climbers the guides are becoming, sadly, irrelevant.

Section 10
The French Alps

For many British alpinists the Alps means the French Alps; Alpine climbing means long technical routes, mostly rock and climbed in pitches; going to the Alps means going to Chamonix. The mountains of the French Alps are an ideal place to use the skills developed and practised on British rock, except that mountains is the wrong word in this context. Aiguilles is better. It is the word used locally and it conveys the presiding spirit, which is of doing routes rather than climbing mountains, of overcoming difficulties perhaps rather than being at one with the Earth. The talk is about particular bits of particular routes, about how to do that move, about exactly which line the route follows. And the talking seems to be crucial. Do a route and then talk about it. It is not exactly competitive but there is an air of competition about Chamonix climbing that is absent elsewhere.

The focus on individual routes rather than mountains tends to devalue the approach and the descent. These become chores that have to be done in order to do the climb instead of being part of it. The climb itself can become merely an exercise in following the guide-book. Climbing in the French Alps consists of forays out of the valley whereas in other places it becomes life itself. The actual sequences of events may be much the same as in other areas, yet somehow the feeling is different.

I have not climbed much in the French Alps. I do regret that, but overall I am glad to have been led away from the crowds and the intensity to more remote places, and to have had my climbing dominated by mountains rather than routes. When you see a mountain many times from different places, as you see it in the background while concentrating on a day's climbing, it acquires a character and comes alive in your mind. As a result, when you eventually climb the mountain you remain aware of its personality however much you get absorbed in details of the climb.

The notion that Alpine climbing is like British rock-climbing, only longer and with snow and ice complications, is one I shared when I first went to Chamonix. I might share it still if the weather had been better and I had done some of the routes I had in mind. Instead I had a few days' squalid camping and did not see enough of the fantastic rock to be amazed and captivated. The sheer quantity

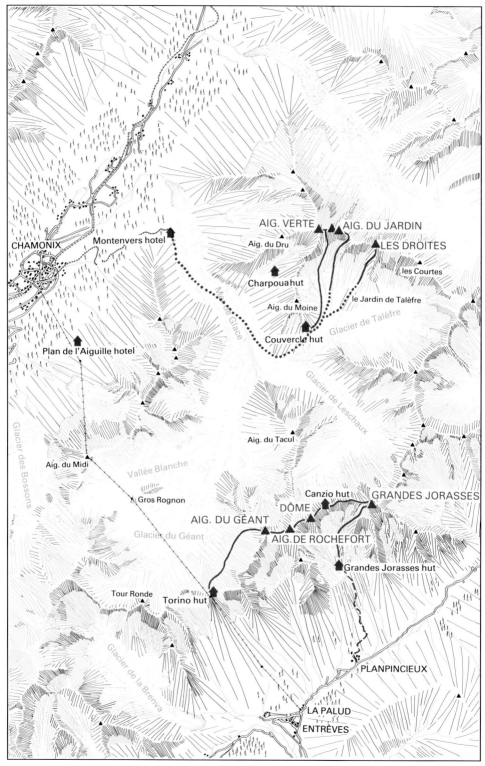

CHAMONIX

Montenvers hotel

AIG. VERTE · AIG. DU JARDIN

Aig. du Dru

LES DROITES

les Courtes

Charpoua hut

Aig. du Moine

le Jardin de Talèfre

Couvercle hut

Glacier de Talèfre

Plan de l'Aiguille hotel

Glacier de Leschaux

Mer de Glace

Aig. du Tacul

Glacier des Bossons

Vallée Blanche

Aig. du Midi

Gros Rognon

Canzio hut

GRANDES JORASSES

DÔME

AIG. DU GÉANT

AIG. DE ROCHEFORT

Glacier du Géant

Grandes Jorasses hut

Tour Ronde

Torino hut

Glacier de la Brenva

PLANPINCIEUX

LA PALUD

ENTRÈVES

Map 14

of rock is the biggest surprise on your first visit to the Alps. After Britain, where every little outcrop is studied and climbed in minute detail, the enormous towers and seemingly endless walls of steep clean rock are a stunning revelation. Although the surprise can be repeated in many other parts of the Alps, the Chamonix Aiguilles is the most concentrated and developed area for long rock routes. The second surprise is that your climbing skills are more than adequate for this vastly more exotic context. Provided, that is, that you learn to move rapidly and relentlessly.

The town of Chamonix is appalling and strangely likeable. It is crowded, noisy and aggressive but it is redeemed by a disarming insouciance. Access to the mountains begins invariably with mechanical assistance: the téléphériques from Argentière and Le Tour, the Montenvers railway and, dominating everything, the Midi-Torino téléphérique. The queues for this are enormous on fine days. The business of obtaining a ticket and an estimated departure time and then actually getting on board with equipment, a heavy rucksack and bags of food is hot, aggravating and dispiriting. You are guaranteed a stressful, and usually late, start to an expedition. The way to survive cheerfully is to find it all hysterically funny instead of frustrating. Despite the aggravation, it has to be the wonder of the Alps and given the magnitude of the problem the arrangements work quite well. The trip itself, especially across the Vallée Blanche, is truly fantastic and over all too soon.

The famous Aiguilles, from the Midi in the south-west to the Tour in the north-east, are all a bit under 4000m except for the Aiguille Verte and Les Droites, so for me they have remained of peripheral interest. I should have found time to stay in a quiet part of the valley, near Argentière perhaps, and climbed the Aiguille du Chardonnet and the Aiguille d'Argentière. This would have given me a better perspective of the French Alps because these two mountains, like the Verte, have great character and routes to match.

The Aiguille Verte is unique in the Alps for its large number of worthwhile routes, none of which is easy. Like Les Droites its north side is a tremendous face, steep and icy. The less demanding routes use the south side or the ridges. There is no straightforward way to descend the Verte unless the Whymper couloir is in good condition and you have it to yourself.

The other 4000m summits in this section I associate with Italy and I have used the Torino téléphérique station as a starting point. The Aiguille du Géant, the Aiguille and Dôme de Rochefort and the Grandes Jorasses are a totally disparate trio, yet they can be combined into a superb two-day expedition. The Géant is a fine rock tower at the western end of the Rochefort ridge. Its harder routes are seldom climbed. The least demanding route, the south-west face, is an interesting line which has been simplified and spoiled by several fixed ropes. The guides maintain them to ensure that ascent and descent can be accomplished comfortably in a day's outing from Courmayeur. The route is very popular and would be pleasant in spite of the disfigurements if it were not so crowded. Opposite, across the Glacier du Géant, is the magnificent red-brown spire of the Grand Capucin, 3839m. Its easiest route takes all day and is sustained TD+. Another 161m would make climbing the four-thousanders substantially more difficult. Except that then the Grand Capucin would be festooned with ropes and ladders so that guides could take clients up.

The west ridge of the Rochefort is usually climbed only as far as the Aiguille de Rochefort. That is the famous section, consisting of swooping knife-edged snow cornices. Combined with the

Géant it gives a day of excellent contrasting halves. The round trip from the Torino takes about ten hours in good conditions.

The Grandes Jorasses is simply one of the great mountains of the Alps and it looks the part from wherever you see it. The easy ascent, on the Italian side, has alternative top sections that provide a circuit. The summit crest is a long string of 4000m points, each quite distinctive, with nicely varied bits of ridge in between. It starts at the west end with Pointe Young, which is four metres short at 3996m. Two enormous buttresses dominate the north face. These are the Walker spur and the Croz spur. The Walker spur seems to have an obsessive fascination for the best British alpinists, perhaps rightly so. The usual approach is a long, tedious trudge across the Mer de Glace and up the Glacier de Leschaux. The first half of this is also part of the route to the Couvercle hut. The Mer de Glace is pleasant at first, as you escape from the multitudes at Montenvers, but after two or three kilometres the formless stony monotony becomes irritating and you long for the steep climb and the ladders up the Egralets cliff.

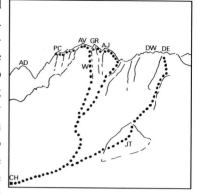

GR Grande Rocheuse
AJ Aiguille du Jardin
DW Les Droites, W summit
DE Les Droites, E summit
PC Pointe Croux
AD Aiguille du Dru
W Whymper couloir
JT Jardin de Talèfre
CH Couvercle hut
AV Aiguille Verte

When you are on your way to do the Walker spur you would hardly notice the dreary glacier in your excitement. That was probably true of the climber Brian and I met near the junction of the two glaciers. He was coming back. Slowly. The previous day he and a companion had strolled up from Montenvers and bivouacked below the spur. That morning at first light, eager to get to grips with his great ambition, he had been a bit careless crossing the bergschrund, and had fallen and fractured an ankle. Without insurance the cost of a helicopter rescue was too great to contemplate, so, with frustration hurting as much as his ankle, he had set off to retrace his steps. After eight hours of hobbling, on one leg and two ice-axes, over loose boulders and broken icy debris, he was about halfway. He hoped to reach Montenvers and get down to Chamonix the same day.

Meanwhile his partner had gone down with their gear to make the arrangements they had decided upon and would come back to meet him. He said that his anger with himself had passed. So had most of the physical pain, provided he was careful. Setting out to climb the Walker spur and falling off the bergschrund now seemed faintly amusing. It was clear that getting himself back had superseded in his mind the challenge of doing the route. He had turned his accident into a personal quest of great importance. Accomplishing it was going to be a far greater achievement than doing the route would have been. Sympathy or pity for his misfortune was inappropriate.

Aiguille Verte and Les Droites from the Grandes Jorasses Pointe Walker.

42 Aiguille Verte

42a Grande Rocheuse
42b Aiguille du Jardin, E (Jardin) ridge (AD+). Solo
42c Pointe Croux solo; via Whymper couloir (AD). With Anne Brearley
Map p 184   Illustrations pp 187, 189

The Aiguille Verte is one of the most prized fourthousanders. The choice of normal routes is much greater than usual, though most of them are climbed infrequently. All are relentlessly serious without ever being especially difficult. I still find the Couturier couloir a great attraction, but it needs a certain state of mind and good conditions, neither of which prevailed at the time I was thinking about the Verte. The Jardin ridge appealed to me more than other options on the Couvercle side because the route and its difficulties appeared to be well defined. I was not put off by its length and I thought the upper part of the ridge, traversing across the Jardin and the Rocheuse, would be exhilarating and satisfying. The reality was distinctly different.

When Brian Wood and I caught the train to Montenvers we had not decided which route we were aiming for. Our plan, what there was of it, was to go up into the Talèfre glacier so that we could see something of the possibilities. We hoped that by then the snow conditions and the next day's weather would be clearer. By the time we had walked past the Couvercle hut we had almost opted for Les Droites but then we wandered aimlessly up the glacier and bivouacked in a place more suitable for the Verte. Next morning it was clear though not cold and Brian was not feeling very bright. At the bergschrund at the bottom of the couloir up to the Col de l'Aiguille Verte it was evident that his problem was altitude so he decided to return to Montenvers and Chamonix. We exchanged various bits and pieces and I went on up the couloir. As I climbed I checked over the equipment and food I was carrying or thought I was carrying and hoped I would not suddenly remember that Brian still had some item like matches or the guide-book.

On this occasion I had too much rather than too little. Our two-man bivouac tent and a full-length, full-weight rope contributed to a heavy rucksack that soon felt oppressive. I was tense and unsettled. Soloing serious routes without careful planning is not the way to do it. If I had known how stressful the day was to become I would have have made a point of enjoying the easy climb up the couloir. If I had known what was in store I would have gone back.

The couloir is scree as much as snow, not steep, and there is almost a path. A steeper branch goes off to the left, narrows and leads to the rock chimney that is supposed to be the most difficult pitch on the route. To have it so near the beginning was very convenient for me. It looked easier than I had expected. A few metres up, about halfway, I began to change my mind. The problem was not the cold greasy rock but the rucksack. If I forced myself inside the chimney I was cramped and had no feeling for the wall at my back. Half in and half out was precarious. The solution was to loosen the waist strap, undo the inside shoulder strap and squirm up for a bit with the rucksack outside the chimney; not as bad as it sounds. After several metres I was able to bridge across comfortably and then step on to one wall. A few minutes higher I found the next awkward bit of rock. Again it was easier than I expected. The problem now was that it did not fit the guide-book description. Just continuing upwards usually leads back to a ridge but this time it did not.

The situation was irritating and persisted for some time. I had not seen the true east ridge at all, just a sequence of small vague ones. I was sure that the main ridge was on my right but the natural and easiest line took me leftwards. As I wondered whether to force a way to the right there was a sudden chill and a wisp of cloud drifted around me.

I stopped to assess what the weather would do and decided I had no idea. There was thin broken cloud everywhere, with plenty of blue sky and sunshine in transient patches. I looked back for landmarks. Retracing my route would be simple enough even if the weather got a lot worse, but would I be able to find it? I had only the vaguest notion of where I was in relation to the summit ridge and I was unable to get a clear view of what lay in between. I pressed on, looking for easy ground, still being drawn leftwards across the south side. Every so often I saw tantalising bits of

Verte chain from the Frontier Ridge at dawn

sunny rock ahead, never enough of them to know whether they would help. Then a comfortable rib I was on ended at a steeper wall split by a horrid intimidating groove. As I looked at it and shook my head the mist cleared to show it leading directly to the main ridge. The blue sky, the prospect of getting back on route and the absence of any obvious alternative drew me into the groove. I suspect it was not as bad as I remember and certainly not as long as it seemed. Perhaps there was forty metres of it. I felt least insecure bridging across but most of the groove was too shallow. It was rock, variably covered with dripping ice. Protruding bits were sometimes frozen in solidly, sometimes not.

At the ridge my relief was enhanced by a small patch of sunlight. There were no footprints and only a few metres of the ridge were clearly visible, but at least it was definitely the main east ridge. I climbed easily up a large buttress and into thin, drifting mist. Was this the Aiguille du Jardin summit? If so, some careful thought about whether to continue was needed. If not, I might as well carry on to the summit. Further progress meant descending and I was reluctant to move without seeing what was ahead. Then the mist cleared enough to show a simple bit of snowy ridge. As I descended and then began to rise, the Jardin summit appeared, then the Rocheuse and the Verte. It all looked further than I had hoped.

On top of the Aiguille du Jardin I felt tired and was fed up with the weight of the rucksack. The cloud had half cleared and half dropped away, at least locally, and I had an unobscured encouraging view of the rest of the route. My vague intention had been to descend the Whymper couloir but now I guessed it would be in poor condition. I would not want to start down it unless, when the time came, the cloud was dispersed enough to give me a clear view of it. I was not confident I could even find it, although there would surely be footprints to follow. After a few minutes in the

189

sun, sitting on my rucksack instead of carrying it, I felt sanguine again. I still could not guess what the weather would do, except that a perfect afternoon was unlikely. In my small piece of the Alps the weather was fine and seemed fairly stable. I decided on a fast trip to the Verte and to descend the way I had come, except for the groove. I took the rope and a bit of gear and some food and left the rucksack and everything else on the Jardin summit. I was at one end of a narrow island of rock and snow with a sea of cloud below and I set off for the other end.

The sunny airy traverse was delightful after the gloom and uncertainty earlier. I glanced at the pinnacle of Pointe Eveline, 4026m, as I passed it and thought I might have a closer look on the way back. The exposure on the long knife-edge of Col Armand Charlet was exhilarating in my rejuvenated mood and contrasted well with some wriggling route-finding on the Grande Rocheuse. Here I found some old footprints and there were more at the Col de l'Aiguille Verte. As I hurried up the easy snow ridge from the col the cloud closed around me. It obscured the views and revealed the fragility of my confidence. At the summit I could see nothing until a bit of wind made a gap and Mont Blanc appeared briefly. The time was exactly midday, two hours since I had left the Aiguille du Jardin. Just as I started to leave the Aiguille Verte the ridge vanished in cloud.

Getting back to the Jardin seemed to take a long time. The cold clammy mist was oppressive and several flurries of snow added to my unease. I sat on my rucksack, reluctant to put it on, well aware that when I did I would feel tired and unsteady. With a sprinkling of fresh snow the groove I had climbed to reach the ridge would now be even worse. I continued along the ridge, unsure whether to follow it or to go down on the south side to find the way I had come up. At a point where the ridge was indeterminate and several ways seemed possible I chose a rib on my right that descended steeply towards where I must have ascended. It soon became unpleasantly steep but I saw easier ground below. A quick abseil, I thought, and I would be well on my way down.

There was an obvious spike to use but the space behind it narrowed too much, to a thin crack. When I had gone down a few feet I stopped to test whether the rope would pull through and found it had jammed. I hauled myself back up and looked at the only other possible place for the rope. This would certainly not jam – there was barely enough of a spike to be secure. The one thing I realised I did not have with me was a spare sling to use as a belay. I tried unsuccessfully to wedge a suitable stone behind the first spike. Then I decided the second spike would do provided I kept the rope in tension when I abseiled. The take-off position made this very awkward. Eventually I descended into the mist. After a few metres I could see neither the rock that the rope was round nor where I was going. I stopped abseiling at the first possible place in another whirling shower of gritty snow. As I moved to a comfortable stance and fiddled with the rope it fell down around me. I took off my rucksack and calmed down by coiling the rope slowly and carefully.

With a film of new snow nothing looked familiar. I just followed the easiest line down, trying to convince myself that I recognised it. As I descended the mist thinned. I was cheered by glimpses of the glacier and occasional bits of sunshine. Then I did recognise an awkward little rib I had climbed in the morning. A convenient rock bollard encouraged me to abseil down it. The relief at ending the uncertainty about where I was and the proximity of the comfortable plod down the couloir seemed to release a flood of tiredness. Another abseil, this time clumsy and in slow motion, got me past the chimney. As I rejoined the main couloir below the Col de l'Aiguille Verte I stumbled and looked down. Beside my left boot was a large quartz crystal the size of a tangerine. It was a mysterious smoky-brown colour, shaped like a mountain, the facets smooth and shiny. I almost looked up at the sky to see whether there was a written message as well. I walked down the couloir gripping the crystal tightly in my fist and not until I reached the bergschrund did I put it into an anorak pocket.

On top of the Verte at midday I had thought about my chances of getting back to Chamonix the same day. Now it was seven hours later and I began to consider where to bivouac. About two hundred metres from the bergschrund I was still thinking about it as I unpacked the bivouac tent and my sleeping bag. I made some tea, heated some baked beans and fell asleep eating them.

Ten years later I did the Whymper couloir with Anne Brearley. This was for me to climb Pointe Croux, which I had not even seen the previous time, and partly because a simple relaxed return visit was an attractive idea. What happened was that again the weather deteriorated and again the climb was stressful. The couloir was in very poor condition, especially when we descended. The other parties were amiable but their presence during ascent and descent greatly increased the danger and general awkwardness. Anne sunbathed on the Aiguille Verte summit while I went down the west ridge. This was clean snow, far better than anything in the couloir. Pointe Croux was a disappointment. There was a short difficult bit, exposed enough to be serious, but the Pointe is insignificant. The Grande Rocheuse buttress and Pointe Eveline would have been a more worthwhile outing.

43 Les Droites
E Buttress (AD). With Brian Wood
Map p 184   Illustrations pp 187, 189

As the train load of passengers filed along the platform at Montenvers a woman standing on one side examined them closely. She was middle-aged, stern-looking, dressed mostly in black and very upright. With her, though trying to look separate, was a much younger woman, a girl really. She was more colourfully dressed and seemed amused. Brian had got off the train promptly and was out of sight. I was near the back of the procession. When it was my turn to be scrutinised the older woman stepped in front of me and launched into an earnest speech. I had no idea what she was talking about. As soon as I had an opportunity I interrupted to say I was English and did not speak French. 'English!' she exclaimed. 'You are a gentleman?' I was not sure whether this was a question or the result of a rapid assessment. In either case it was an address I had experienced so rarely that the only response I could manage was to grin and shrug my shoulders. 'You will take my daughter!' she cried. Grasping her companion's hand she held it out to me, so I took the hand to be going on with.

Between them they explained that they had missed meeting friends in Chamonix with whom the daughter was to have gone on a hut tour. The rest of the party had gone to the Couvercle hut so her mother had needed to find a strong, experienced, reliable and sympathetic climber whom she could trust to escort her daughter safely across the Mer de Glace and up to the Couvercle hut. It seemed tactful not to spoil her mother's evident satisfaction by mentioning Brian. Soon the two of us were walking through the crowds of tourists to where he was waiting at the start of the descent to the glacier. The young woman was of course perfectly competent to walk across by herself. She met her friends at the hut and charmingly declined our invitation to bivouac with us instead.

This unexpected event gave the day a special quality which lingered on. We walked across to the Jardin de Talèfre and up to the north end of it. There we found a perfect bivouac site. It was flat, sheltered and in the sun; there was running water nearby and plenty of useful flat rocks. A wonderful balmy evening was followed by a clear night.

The east buttress of Les Droites is on the south side of the mountain. The main ridge of the buttress offers a direct line to the east summit whereas the route takes a pragmatic course on the south-east flank. It makes maximum use of snowy slopes on a face that is mostly rock. The previous night had not been cold and had followed a spell of poor weather so we were expecting the route to be in bad condition. When we found that it was, we over-reacted and were more painstaking than was necessary. We climbed several bits in pitches and fiddled about arranging poor-quality protection in soft snow and crumbly ice. With another couple of years' experience we would simply have ambled up and down. Nevertheless it was a pleasantly interesting ascent.

We sat on the summit enjoying the views and the still air, telling ourselves we had done some serious climbing. This was put in perspective when a climber suddenly appeared behind us. He had soloed one of the awesome north face routes. He seemed surprised to see us but immediately showed great interest in our route up. As soon as he realised there were fresh footprints to follow he plunged down, probably less than two minutes after he first appeared.

Perhaps this apparition made us feel feeble; perhaps we just had plenty of time. For whatever reason, our descent was slow and inefficient. Going past the Couvercle hut nobody offered us a young woman to look after. This disappointment made the Mer de Glace seem dull and long.

44 Aiguille du Géant
SW face (AD). With Bob Brevitt
Map p 184   Illustrations pp 193, 196

I first climbed this route with Brian and Denise Wood. The presence of many other climbers on the route made a long, fractious day inevitable. The irritation of delays and awkward manoeuvring on small stances is aggravated by language problems. The exposure adds to the tension. It would nevertheless be possible to enjoy such situations if there were less noise. Why some parties indulge in continual shouting to each other remains a mystery to me. I suppose they are the same people who cannot cope with tranquil sunny evenings at huts without bursts of community singing. Some cold drizzly mist in the afternoon added to our discomfort.

Thirteen years later when Bob Brevitt wanted to do the Géant-Rochefort-Grandes Jorasses traverse I was equally enthusiastic even though I had done all of it before. I was keen to acquire more pleasant memories of the Géant. Two days of heavy rain were followed by superb weather and a firm forecast that it would last another two days. It was mid-afternoon when we left the Torino to walk across the Glacier du Géant. This was hard work instead of a comfortable stroll because a lot of soft snow covered the usual beaten track. In spite of brilliant sunshine a strong wind was preventing consolidation of the new snow. There were no footprints to indicate the easiest line up the broken

Aiguille du Géant from the Rochefort ridge.   The SW face route is mostly out of sight apart from a short section where it uses the edge on the right.

ridge that leads to the base of the Géant. Consequently that usually simple, little climb had its interesting moments. We reached the 'breakfast place' below the overhanging south face at 18:00, later than we had intended but perhaps not too late to do the south-west face that day. The opportunity to have the route to ourselves and then be first on the Rochefort ridge the following day decided us.

The first few minutes were idyllic. The easy movement on clean rock was delicious after the snowy scramble up the ridge carrying heavy rucksacks. The evening sun, orange-red, had already transformed the sky and the landscape. As we traversed the face and rose higher there were icy patches instead of snow. Suddenly, near the west edge of the face, we lost our sheltered aspect and were in the wind. We felt cold immediately. The first fixed rope was festooned with icicles and half frozen to the face. Bob heaved at it and a great shower of ice clattered down.

He led on, determined and vigorous, pulling and kicking off plates of ice. Cursing the presence of the fixed ropes on such fine rock he tried to avoid using them. The icy cracks, the cold wind and the rapidly setting sun made this difficult. I had no such scruples, although with numb fingers the slippery, frozen ropes were a mixed blessing. The panorama in the evening colours was magnificent. The circumstances felt distinctly curious: inspiring and a bit crazy. If Bob felt, as I did, an undercurrent of hysteria mixed in with the splendour of the situation he gave no sign of it.

The last part of the south-west face route, a steep twenty-metre wall, leads directly to Pointe Sella, the lower of the Géant's twin summits. Between them on this occasion was a thin crest of icy snow. The traverse to Pointe Graham was unexpectedly awkward. I found the move on to the snow crest distinctly difficult, without being quite sure why, and I was gratified when Bob was equally discomforted. It was no easier going back. Exactly as we left Pointe Sella to descend, the last arc of the sun disappeared.

As the sky colours faded into darkness stars began to appear, first discretely, then in a rush. The moon rose: bright, close, magical. Still whipped by the wind and bitterly cold, our sense of unreality grew. Then we were back at Mummery's ledge, below the fixed ropes and out of the wind. Feeling returned to fingers and well-being replaced unreality. A quick abseil, a scramble down and across the face and we were scuttling back to the 'breakfast place'. After dinner we settled down to sleep, cosy and pleased with ourselves. Across the Glacier du Géant were the lights of parties setting out from the Ghiglione hut for the Brenva face.

Next morning the Rochefort ridge was impossible because new snow was insecure and waist deep in places. The ridge lay before us, inviting and immaculate. We waded fifty metres through the snow before accepting what had been inevitable after ten.

Rochefort ridge from the Aiguille du Géant.   The swooping curves of the snow ridge provide a classic Alpine traverse. In good conditions the steep rock to the Aiguille de Rochefort is a delicious contrast.

Géant-Rochefort-Jorasses ridge from Mont Berio Blanc

Géant-Jorasses-Rochefort ridge from the Aiguille du Grepon

45 Dôme de Rochefort
45a Aiguille de Rochefort
W ridge (AD). With Gary Dyer

46 Grandes Jorasses Pointe Walker
46a Pointe Whymper   46c Pointe Marguerite
46b Pointe Cruz   46d Pointe Hélène
W ridge traverse, (D). With Gary Dyer

Map p 184   Illustrations pp 193, 195, 196

The complete Rochefort-Jorasses traverse is a good candidate for the best two-day expedition in the Alps. If you begin with the Géant you encounter every Alpine context except steep ice and crevassed glaciers. If you end by descending the Hirondelles ridge then the pleasant tension of anticipated difficulties persists for the whole trip. The route follows a natural and compelling line with very little deviation from the main summit ridge of the two mountains. Route-finding is straightforward unless, as we did, you invent your own problems. It is a genuine two-day affair: escape from the overnight refuge of the Canzio bivouac hut is serious in bad weather. All these qualities, together with exhilarating situations and magnificent views, make it an exceptionally satisfying route.

We caught a late téléphérique from Entrèves and bivouacked unobtrusively at the Torino station. This is not as bizarre as it may seem. The weather looked unsettled and the Torino hut had no attractions for us. The station is quiet and private after the service closes although it is not particularly comfortable. The luxury of an en suite lavatory was reduced by the smell.

After a poor night, warm and cloudy, we loitered until well after sunrise, waiting for the weather to improve. Eventually it did and we walked across the Glacier du Géant. At the little couloir that leads up to the ridge below the Aiguille du Géant we were treated to a display of incompetence by two parties from the Torino hut, which was both amusing and appalling. We hurried past them, relieved to do so unscathed.

The famous west ridge of the Aiguille de Rochefort was enjoyable yet less exciting than I had expected. Instead of following the switchback of the ridge crest, the well-trodden path took a sedate line between the troughs. The other parties in front of us on the route stopped at the Aiguille. This encouraged us to go on without a pause to the Dôme de Rochefort. The latter part of this section of the Rochefort ridge is interesting, elegant and exposed. That so few parties bother with it is inexplicable. The perfect weather, bright, clear and almost windless, added to the sense of tranquillity we felt on leaving the vicinity of the other parties. The easy traverse from the Aiguille to the Dôme was profoundly satisfying. I wish I had been aware at the time that the first ascent of the ridge was made by Karl Blödig, the first person to climb all the fourthousanders. In the circumstances I would have enjoyed the sort of sentimental reverential reflection that I rarely indulge in.

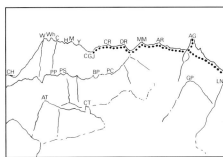

GP	Gl. des Périades	H	Pointe Hélène
PP	Pointe des Périades	M	Pointe Marguerite
PS	Pointe Simond	Y	Pointe Young
AT	Aig. du Tacul	CR	Calotte de Rochefort
PC	Pointe Cupelin	DR	Dôme de Rochefort
CH	Col des Hirondelles	AR	Aig. de Rochefort
W	Pointe Walker	MM	Mont Mallet
Wh	Pointe Whymper	LN	La Noire
C	Pointe Croz	CT	Clocher du Tacul
CGJ	Col des Grandes	BP	Brèche des Périades
	Jorasses	AG	Aig. du Géant

Grandes Jorasses summit ridge from the Dôme de Rochefort

The summit of the Dôme is a comfortable place to sit, eat a bit of lunch and take pleasure in the splendid and contrasting views. The Grandes Jorasses ridge was particularly spectacular and looked serious. It promised that the following day would provide distinctly different delights. Gary Dyer, a strong and accomplished rock-climber, was on his first visit to the Alps. His wide-eyed enthusiasm heightened my enjoyment. With plenty of time and in a properly relaxed frame of mind, we were able to make the most of our stop at the Dôme. We had an inexpert discussion on the chances of the good weather holding for another day and settled for hoping that it would. An amble across to the Calotte de Rochefort, three straightforward abseils and a bit of scrambling brought us to the Col des Grandes Jorasses and the Canzio bivouac hut at midday.

Later that afternoon we left the hut to reconnoitre the route to Pointe Young. We spent about three hours being indulgent rather than efficient, deliberately enjoying the warmth, the clean rock and the absence of rucksacks. To ensure a relaxed start next morning we left bits of protection at the awkward points and tape slings to indicate the best line. Although the steep slabby west flank of Pointe Young is not difficult enough to need this preparation it was certainly worth doing, particularly as it was such a pleasure.

The next morning was fine and we waited until after sunrise before following, at a leisurely pace, our route to the top of Pointe Young. The second summit of the main ridge, Pointe Marguerite, is gained by scrambling up a rocky scree-filled couloir on the south side. A steep spur bulges out blocking access to the couloir. Following the guide-book we abseiled down the chimney-like cleft at the south-west side of the spur to a small platform.

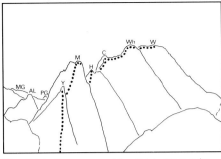

Y	Pointe Young	M	Pointe Marguerite
H	Pointe Hélène	C	Pointe Croz
Wh	Pointe Whymper	W	Pointe Walker
MG	Mont Grépillon	PG	Pointe Grépillon
AL	Aiguille de Leschaux		

The spur looked vertical and smooth and extremely difficult. There was supposed to be a finger crack to enable a horizontal traverse round the spur to the couloir, but the only crack visible petered out after four metres. After Gary had launched himself along this crack and scrambled back quivering, I went down a few metres to an easy traverse line round the spur. This ended in an icy hanging gully blocked by an overhang. Though I knew it was pointless I tried to force a way up and round the overhang and reduced myself to the state Gary had been in. For another hour and a half we alternately persuaded each other to try again at our chosen obstacles until eventually Gary fell off. This provoked a speck of intelligent behaviour. I climbed back up the cleft and soon found another horizontal finger crack across the spur. Although the crack looked as unpromising as the previous one, Gary went out of sight across the face at his first attempt and reached a scree couloir! As we scrambled easily up to Pointe Marguerite I felt weary and stupid.

The ridge to Pointe Hélène is an amazing knife-edge of rock: the thinnest and most exposed I can remember. Here we paid for our mistake of abseiling too far down the side of the spur because the weather was now overcast, cold and increasingly misty. Had we been there two hours earlier we would have felt exhilarated. Now we were apprehensive and instead of squealing with delight we mumbled about getting a move on. After Pointe Hélène the ridge is still sharp but no longer fantastic. At Pointe Croz it begins to change from rock to snow. We reached the easy ground between Pointe Croz and Pointe Whymper in a fierce storm and with zero visibility. As we struggled across the gentle snow slopes to Pointe Walker I began, only half in jest, to tell Gary about digging a survival hole in the snow. Then, as we reached the highest point of the Grandes Jorasses, the wind dropped, the hail and snow ceased and the mist partially cleared. We sat there for a few minutes enjoying the relief and hoping for a clear view of the route down the south-west flank. Making do with a hundred metres of faint, old footprints we descended into the mist and were soon lost.

By simply taking any easy option in roughly the right direction we made efficient progress, although this did not become evident until the mist began to break up. Before then we endured the nerve-racking tension inevitable when you move on a big unfamiliar mountain in mist. Sunshine and visibility came just in time. We found ourselves at the bergschrund but in the wrong place. There was an enormous drop to the bottom lip, six or seven metres. Some distance away, across easy snow slopes, was the path down to the Boccalatte hut. 'What do we do now?' Gary asked, as I stood on the edge of the bergschrund, looking along it for a place where it was possible to get across. 'Jump down' I said, and he did! My horror turned to hilarity when he plummetted into the snow without rolling forward and was stuck fast up to his armpits. Then it turned to horror as I felt obliged to jump down as well to dig him out. Laughing hysterically we sauntered down past the hut and on to the Val Ferret, occasionally looking back at the Grandes Jorasses ridge through gaps in the lifting clouds.

I	L'Isolée
Ca	Pointe Carmen
M	Pointe Médiane
Ch	Pointe Chaubert
D	Corne du Diable
CD	Col du Diable
V	Aiguille Verte
R	Grande Rocheuse
J	Aiguille du Jardin
D	Les Droites

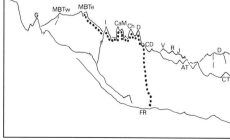

MBTw	Mont Blanc du Tacul, W summit
MBTe	Mont Blanc du Tacul, E summit
G	grand gendarme
FR	SE (Frontier) ridge of Mont Maudit
AT	Aiguille du Tacul
CT	Clocher du Tacul

Mont Blanc du Tacul from the Brenva ridge

The Shrinking Alps

I remember on my first visits to the Alps being astounded by the vastness. It was not so much the size of the mountains as the number of them and the seemingly endless vistas of villages, valleys and passes. Now the Alps seems to be a much smaller place. It is still effectively endless because I will always have new places to discover, and my most frequented haunts still produce surprises. Even so I am conscious that it seems to get ever smaller. This is partly the result of familiarity and loss of innocence. I now know what to expect of many places and my initial sense of wonder has inevitably changed. There are though specific things which contribute to the shrinking effect.

Standing on any summit looking at all the others I am still moved. Although the situation is familiar my feelings still have an element of disbelief. Yet now I know all their names and I have stood on all the summits I can see. I feel I know each of them so the sense of magnitude that comes from the mystery of the unknown has gone. Looking at any mountain you cannot but be struck by its enormousness. For some, like the Dent Blanche, the Aletschhorn, the Grand Combin, their vast bulk is a tangible quality. Yet, as I look at any of them, I know that I could start down in the valley out of sight on one side and a few hours' pleasant effort would take me up, over its summit and down out of sight on the other side. Large as they seem, they have become smaller.

In two senses, one natural and one unnatural, the Alps are literally shrinking. The retreat of glaciers is well known. Although this happens almost too slowly to be noticeable, nineteenth century prints reveal striking changes. And there is definitely less snow. The famous classic snow faces get icier and more rock shows through, as for example on the north face of the Ober Gabelhorn and the north-east face of the Lenzspitze. Many west-facing couloirs, like the one to Col Emil Rey by Mont Brouillard, or to the Dames Anglaises on the Peuterey ridge or to the Aiguilles du Diable, are now mostly bare rock. When I climbed them they might not have been too pleasant but they were genuine snow/ice couloirs. In bad weather you hardly notice that such places have changed. In periods of good weather you are only ever struck by there being less snow than you remember, or by an ice-field being smaller, never the other way round. As it is the snow and ice that 'make' the Alps, this is a literal shrinking.

The unnatural shrinking is more rapid. Everywhere there is development, an insidious euphemism for character transformation. The metalled roads go further up the valleys, the téléphériques are extended and new ones built. Quiet unspoiled places which once had their own unique charm receive their quota of crass incongruous advertisement hoardings and become distinctly unquiet. This is a familiar complaint, often selfish and merely sentimental. Even so it underlines a genuine dilemma. Progress in some eyes is despoilation in others. The observable reality is that the remote areas are made ever more accessible and less remote and hence become smaller. The Alps, at least the areas with the essential qualities that distinguish them, are diminishing.

You could argue that climbing huts are a part of the development. Well they are, and a few would be better removed, though genuine distinctions of scale and type can be made. New climbing huts are rare and usually cater for people who want to go to an area to enjoy it as it is. Climbing huts seldom disfigure the landscape and are not adorned with advertisements for cigarettes and drinks. The serious damage is being done to cater for piste skiing. This is where there is money to be made, which is the driving force that is whittling away the Alps. And rapidly. Buildings for piste skiing tend to be lurid and conspicuous, like the skiers for whom skiing is not enough and who have a need to be noticed as well. A mountain can take a climbing hut and a lot of climbers without totally losing its character. One clanking ski-tow and the accompanying hoard of shrieking, garishly clothed skiers are impossible to ignore. It only needs one and in a sense a valley is lost from the Alps and transferred to the rest of the world.

The gigantic hydro-electric schemes could be seen as developments that diminish the Alps by imposing technology. The man-made lakes do have an ugly starkness but the dams have a massive grandeur in keeping with their context. On the whole I find their influence benign and regard them as an added attraction.

Quite a different sense of diminution was provided by Paul Mackrill and John Rowlands. In the period May-September 1988 they set out to climb all the major fourthousanders entirely on foot, a concept at the same time audacious and stunningly bloody-minded. Starting with the Piz Bernina they worked roughly westwards. Although a long spell of bad weather in the Oberland effectively ended their chances of complete success they persevered for the time they had available. Paul got as far as the Grand Combin and achieved the notable feat of climbing all the 'Swiss' summits in one season. Their wives accomplished an equally impressive display of endurance. They provided valley support: encouraging, sympathising, shopping, washing, driving. And waiting.

In the later stages they must have begun to see the Alps as a single entity. The individual mountains would have seemed to get steadily smaller and climbing them a lesser undertaking. They would have realised that their concept was feasible and that given normal weather they could have done it. As the days ebbed away, indifferent to their increasing competence, their frustration must have been hard to bear.

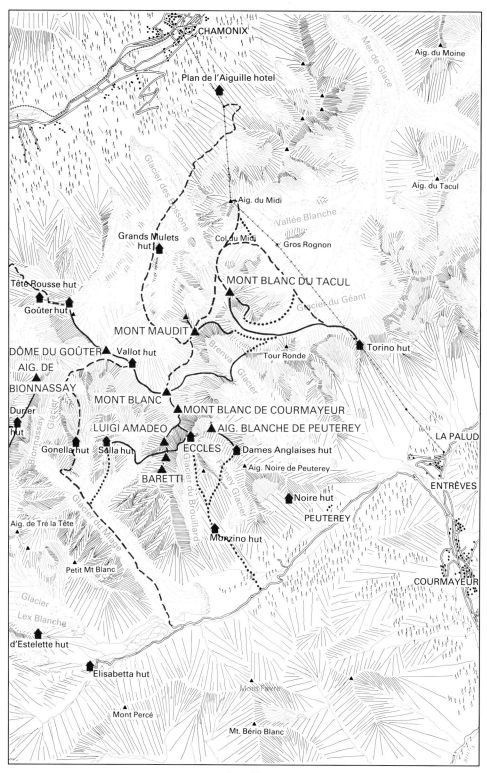

Map 15

Section 11
Mont Blanc; the French side

47	Mont Blanc du Tacul	4248m (4247m)	47e	Corne du Diable	4069m
47a	L'Isolée	4114m	48	Mont Maudit	4465m
47b	Pointe Carmen	4109m	48a	Pointe Mieulet	4287m
47c	Pointe Médiane	4097m	49	Aiguille de Bionnassay	4052m
47d	Pointe Chaubert	4074m	50	Mont Blanc	4807m

Mont Blanc is miraculous. The highest point in Europe is inevitably such a centre of attraction, both for mountaineers and for others whom climbers disdainfully call tourists, that it could easily have been spoiled. The vast potential for commercial exploitation could have ruined the mountain for the discerning alpinist. The mountain itself could have been uninteresting for serious climbers. Instead it caters for all interests and survives the enormous traffic virtually unscathed. When you consider Mont Blanc's features, what becomes clear is the amazing good fortune of the geological accident that left the highest summit in the Alps where it actually is. The mountain itself is massive so there are remote parts that are rarely climbed; the summit is spacious and safe; there are four totally separate easy routes; there is a wide variety of high-quality harder routes; there are satellite peaks which enhance the main mountain yet have their own character; the mechanical assistance is moderate and discreet and leaves some approaches unaffected. To emphasise that none of these virtues is inevitable imagine the Matterhorn or the Grand Combin, for example, enlarged by about ten-per-cent and compare the resulting mountain with the accommodating riches of Mont Blanc.

The main ridge across Mont Blanc links the major satellite peaks. It starts at the Aiguille de Bionnassay on the west side, runs roughly eastwards over the summit then turns north-east to Mont Maudit and Mont Blanc du Tacul. It is, of course, a superb high-level traverse, entirely snow. The French-Italian frontier mostly follows this ridge as far as Mont Maudit then turns down the south-east ridge of Mont Maudit towards the Grandes Jorasses. The deviation from the main ridge crest begins near the top of the Bosses ridge and consists of a loop to the south; it takes in the whole of the pleasant summit snow slopes, stopping short of the complex precipitous rock walls below them. The line of the frontier is the visual horizon from the Italian side so it is presumably the result of a smart piece of work by a French diplomat or surveyor.

The two sides of the dividing ridge are very different. The northern, or French, side is mostly snow slopes and moderate gradients. The easiest routes are on this side, with téléphériques from Chamonix and Les Houches and the railway from St Gervais to bypass the lower slopes. The southern, or Italian, side is a complicated jungle of massive ridges, which provide serious and very committing routes. There is one popular, relatively easy ascent on this side, the Grises route. This begins with a long trudge up the Miage glacier, which always seems even longer and more tiresome in descent.

On the east side of the massif the five-section téléphérique connecting Chamonix with Entrèves, above Courmayeur, has a significant influence. It makes Mont Blanc du Tacul and Mont Maudit accessible without difficulty. The south and east faces of both these mountains have a number of notable hard routes but their accessibility and the simpler topography distinguish them from the south side of Mont Blanc itself. The téléphérique to the Midi station provides the least strenuous way to climb Mont Blanc. Despite the enormous gain in height, effectively to 3532m on the Col du Midi, there is still a substantial effort to be made and interesting ground to cover on foot. Even so this option begins too far beyond the snow line to appeal to purists. The Grand Mulets route is the most authentic and includes long stretches of relatively boring snow-plodding in keeping with the character of Mont Blanc's northern slopes. It is the most efficient line if you want to do the whole climb without mechanical aid and is the route used for ascents in record time. There was a flurry of record-breaking attempts during the summer of 1988, with new fastest times being superseded before they had time to pass into legend. The shortest time to climb on foot from Chamonix to the summit of Mont Blanc was about eight and a half hours in 1970. At that time the thirteen kilometres distance and 3800m height and return was still done as a lightweight mountain walk. Since then, by treating it more as a run, the time has been reduced by over three hours. During 1988 the mountain runners attacked it seriously. Spurred on by some French-Swiss rivalry, Laurent Smagghe became the first person to complete the return trip in under five and a half hours. Two years later, Pierre Gobet, a winner of the Sierre-Zinal race, reduced the record time to five hours.

Mont Blanc du Tacul from the Tour Ronde

47 Mont Blanc du Tacul
S ridge (AD). With Brian Wood
Map p 204   Illustration p 206

This ascent really began at the Giovanni Montagna bivouac hut after an unsuccessful attempt to climb the Aiguilles de Tré-la-Tête. We had chosen the Tré-la-Tête as an ideal training route and, exactly as on a previous occasion, we were frustrated by poor weather. After a perfunctory walk up Petit Mont Blanc we waited until mid-morning before descending to the Val Veni, to be sure that the mist and drizzle were going to persist. By the time we were back at our transport a gloriously sunny afternoon had begun. Some alleviation of this turn of events was in order and a few beers seemed the appropriate remedy. We probably over estimated the correct dose and achieved euphoria instead of mere consolation. We lurched into Courmayeur, shopped for more food, drove to Entrèves and caught the last téléphérique to the Torino. We had foreseen the possibility that the dramatic improvement in the weather might be short lived so our sumptuous provisions included a large bottle of wine to soften the blow should it occur. The evening was fine and the night brilliantly clear but we drank the wine anyway.

 Next morning we went briskly across the Géant glacier past the Tour Ronde and steadily up into Cirque Maudit. At the base of the south ridge the general outline of the main rib was obvious but there were several equally plausible-looking places to begin an ascent. We waited until sunrise hoping that the 'correct line' would become clear. It did not and eventually we became fed up trying to decide. We began climbing at the spot where that happened.

The feeling of uncertainty characterised most of the route. We frequently found ourselves in steep rocky couloirs without a clear view of the ridge, so most of the time we were doing no more than gaining height and speculatively getting to the next corner. The rock was clean and warm, often very loose. The climbing was never very difficult although several pitches were unpleasantly awkward. It was impossible to avoid dislodging loose rock in places and the steepness meant that even small pieces were dangerous. At one point the rope sent two head-sized pieces crashing down close to where Brian was belayed. Our overall impression was of slow, uncomfortable progress made more dispiriting by our evident lack of fitness.

Reaching a straightforward snowy ridge that led to the west summit brought some relief, though not much of the exaltation we might have expected. Strictly we were off route by then and almost on the south-west ridge. The uncomplicated terrain meant we were able to relax more and enjoy the views, particularly of the Frontier Ridge of Mont Maudit. The impression we had previously gained from the Tour Ronde, that this was a superb route that we really must do, was confirmed. Ten days later we were able to look at our route up Mont Blanc du Tacul from the Frontier Ridge. We were quite impressed. Considering that we had climbed most of it the orthodox way, in pitches, our progress had been reasonable.

We walked across to the east summit and found a comfortable spot to eat, make some tea and recover. Descending, when we finally got ourselves moving, was at first enjoyable. By the time we had curved round below Pointe Lachenal and were heading south-east, towards the Torino, a nightmare had begun. The sun was dazzling and it was dreadfully hot. There was a path to follow

Aiguilles du Diable ridge of Mont Blanc du Tacul from near the Couvercle hut. *Beneath L'Isolée in this picture are the Gervasutti and Boccalatte pillars, with the Gervasutti couloir on their right.*

MB   Mont Blanc
MBC   Mont Blanc de Courmayeur
MBT   Mont Blanc du Tacul
BF   Brenva face
D   Corne du Diable
Ch   Pointe Chaubert
M   Pointe Médiane
Ca   Pointe Carmen
I   L'Isolée

and all we had to do was keep putting one foot in front of the other. It should have been simple. Instead we plodded on like geriatric zombies, heavy eyed and heavy legged. The snow was inconsistent ankle-deep slush, making every step an effort and a disappointment. A substantial part of our misery was not the weariness itself but our surprised dismay at the extent of it. The rocks at the foot of Pointe Adolphe Rey were the last place where we would find some shade, so we stopped for a snack and a brew of tea. The moment we sat down we were cheerful. We sipped tea elegantly and exchanged urbane remarks, anticipating merely a pleasant stroll up to the Torino. Then we realised we might miss the last téléphérique and instantly the Torino seemed far away. We trudged and slithered up with sustained determination and arrived just in time to see the last departure still descending.

We knew from a previous occasion that the first part of the descent from the Torino on foot is unpleasant. As there was no pressing need to return to the valley at once, we hardly considered it. We settled down for a second bivouac at the téléphérique station. Our provisions were adequate though scant in comparison with the previous evening's over-indulgence. On the first téléphérique down next morning, we expected to be the only passengers but were joined by several other climbers from the Torino hut. It would seem that we had not been the only party to arrive back late the previous day.

47a – 47e Mont Blanc du Tacul, Aiguilles du Diable

47a L'Isolée

47b Pointe Carmen

47c Pointe Médiane

47d Pointe Chaubert

47e Corne du Diable

SE ridge, traverse (D+). With Bob Brevitt

Map p 204   Illustrations pp 200/201, 208

There is a mystery for me about these five pinnacles. They are sharp spikes, conspicuous from many locations: from Mont Blanc and Mont Maudit, from the Aiguille Blanche de Peuterey, from the Dent du Géant and the Grandes Jorasses, from the Couvercle hut and the Aiguille du Midi. I had spent many hours at these places, and others, sometimes doing no more than deliberately gazing at the Alps. Yet before I climbed the Aiguilles du Diable I had never seen them. To be precise, I had no recollection of ever seeing them. Somehow whenever they had been in my field of vision my eye had skipped past them or my mind had ignored them. After I had completed my ascents of the fourthousanders in Blödig and Dumler's list a comprehensive and challenging article in *High*

Bob Brevitt.   At our tiny bivouac site perched above the couloir that descends from the Col du Diable, Bob characteristically took advantage of the windless evening to carry out some running repairs.

magazine appeared. This added several minor summits, of varying worth, to what I had naively accepted as the standard list. It prompted an unexpected coda of new routes and return visits and it included, bizarrely, two of the five Diable pinnacles. Since climbing them they have become impossible to overlook.

The traverse of the Aiguilles du Diable is magnificent and serious. The rock-climbing difficulties are clearly not sustained and only a couple of moves would be genuinely problematic if you and the rock were warm. Yet on the three central pinnacles the tension is kept up by several awkward situations and exceptional exposure on both sides of the ridge. Using written accounts to determine how difficult a route will actually be when you climb it is always an uncertain business, particularly when it appears to be close to your normal limits. The Aiguilles du Diable had impressed climbers as different as Miriam O'Brien (on the first complete traverse in 1928) and Gaston Rébuffat. Even Eustace Thomas was moved enough to depart from his usual matter-of-fact account. The several abseils to and from precarious places make it a committing route and not one to be undertaken lightly. When I was trying to talk Brian Wood into climbing it with me we were unfit and aware of our lack of recent rock-climbing. After two ambling preparatory routes Brian convinced himself that his participation would not help me, and I decided that I would be foolhardy to solo it.

We went to Chamonix in search of a climbing partner for me. An acquaintance of Brian's led us to an English climber who was 'plenty hard enough' and whose partner had gone home with concussion after a fall. Climbing with someone I do not know is something I do with great reluctance. This time I was very lucky. Bob Brevitt was the perfect person: strong, resourceful and an experienced alpinist. His well-worn equipment and shabby clothing reminded me of my own. Best of all he shared my predilection for bivouacs, few words and solitude. We did several routes together and I regret that I was not climbing at my best so that our collaboration was unequal. If we had met a few years earlier I could have broadened his horizons and he could have raised my standards without either of us having to compromise our attitudes.

The following afternoon we joined the crush of tourists on the Aiguille du Midi téléphérique and then were suddenly by ourselves as we crossed the Vallée Blanche and the Glacier du Géant. We soon passed the Grand Capucin then slowed as we went up into Cirque Maudit in knee-deep soft snow. We had a vague plan to bivouac below the couloir that leads directly to the Col du Diable. An intermittent stream of rocks and icy slush spewing over the top lip of the bergschrund drove us away, and we climbed up nearly vertical rocks on the right of the couloir looking for a bivouac site in the easier ground higher up. We found two possible places before discovering a tiny improbable shelf perched directly above the couloir, thirty metres or so above the bergschrund. It was just big enough for two. A few minutes hard work fitting rocks and filling cracks with gravel made a comfortable, very exposed platform. The situation was magical. We seemed to be high above the steep ice slope although the couloir was three metres away diagonally down to our right. The Diable pinnacles were in view behind us. In front, across Cirque Maudit, was the Frontier Ridge of Mont Maudit with the Aiguille Blanche de Peuterey and the Brenva face beyond. I have often thought since of going back there just to enjoy another bivouac in that enchanting spot.

Next morning we waited almost until sunrise before starting to climb the couloir. Like many others it was easier than it looked. The angle was just right for efficient interesting ascent, without being intimidating. Without its covering of well-frozen snow it could be awkward, although the rocks on its right are easy. We soon reached the ridge by traversing obliquely across the face to our left, towards the base of the Corne du Diable. The Corne is a pleasant overture for the more demanding work to follow. The climbing starts from a little saddle between the Corne and Pointe Chaubert, where we could leave our rucksacks. Although the climbing on the Corne is vertical and almost immediately feels exposed, there are plenty of good holds. The descent back to the saddle is by a comfortable abseil, which I deliberately used to get my hands warm.

The first pitch of Pointe Chaubert is a fine slabby wall. Easier, more broken rocks follow to the summit. The wall was in the sun and sheltered from the wind. Later on the wind was to be a persistent nuisance. It was never very strong, except when funnelled between the pinnacles, but it kept the temperature down and eventually brought mist and a sleety shower. The pleasure of the steep sound rock and sparse, nicely adequate, well-defined holds was repeated on the next pinnacle, Pointe Médiane. It established a feeling of confidence that survived the trying situations that followed.

The abseils down to Brèche Médiane from the top of Pointe Chaubert introduce an air of tension. They emphasise the commitment because retreat is no longer easy, and they underline the exposure. Abseiling on to a sharp ridge feels more precarious than abseiling down a steep wall, perhaps because it is a less familiar experience. The ascent of Pointe Médiane is several pitches long, steep and sustained. It begins on the south-east side in the sun, traverses right so that suddenly you are on a sharp arête, then ascends steep slabs on the north-east facet of the pinnacle. The abrupt changes of view produced by small movements is a particular pleasure on pinnacles. On this occasion there was also the unwelcome change to ice-cold rock. The summit of Pointe Médiane is an amazing collection of enormous perched blocks. They are flat-sided and rectangular, and stand on end supporting each other. They form two prominent windows, which necessitate inelegant clambering about; comical in retrospect although not quite amusing at the time.

Descent from the Médiane is a very awkward vertical abseil. We had wondered whether 'a thirty-metre abseil' meant exactly that or whether it could be split. From the window where the abseil begins it is impossible to see what you are descending to. We had brought only one forty-five-metre full-weight rope. We pretended to convince ourselves that 'we must come to something' before we ran out of rope and Bob squirmed backwards through the second window and disappeared. Sounds of anguish soon followed. Bob was almost at the ends of the rope but still several metres above the stance at Brèche Carmen. He managed to fasten himself to the face. Though there was too much wind for me to hear exactly what he shouted I could understand his message. He was not happy. I scrabbled in my rucksack for my 6mm rope and unravelled the tangles. This sounds simple, yet in the constricted jumble of blocks that formed the window, with numb fingers and the wind blowing the light rope about, it was frustrating. I pulled up one end of the abseil rope and tied the two ropes together while Bob held on to the other end. When I threw the thin rope down the wind blew it out into space, so I had to haul it in and tie on a bundle of karabiners so that it would drop to where Bob could grasp it. He endured my incompetence with the fortitude I had already come to expect of him, reinforced by the knowledge that he had no choice. Eventually we were both at Brèche Carmen, having discovered that you can abseil perfectly well with ropes of markedly unequal thickness using a Sticht plate or a figure-of-eight descendeur.

Brèche Carmen is not a col in the usual sense. It is a large block jammed in the cleft between the almost vertical walls of Pointe Médiane and Pointe Carmen. It is a fantastic platform though not an ideal place for calming down after a hair-raising abseil. Pointe Carmen has two summit spikes with a large platform between them. Steep cracks, partly ice filled, lead directly from the Brèche to the stumpy spike of the east summit. The west summit is a thin spire which gives another steep airy pitch. The rock is excellent: clean and solid, with sharp edges and good jamming cracks. The persistent exposure coupled with cold fingers and gusts of wind made it serious. This time the descent abseils were straightforward and the scramble up the main ridge to the detached Isolée was relaxing and warming.

The climbing on L'Isolée is less demanding than what has gone before, apart from the famous difficult move. Rucksacks are left behind, the tension has been broken by the easy walk from Pointe Carmen and the first pitch can be examined and discussed in comfort. Cracks on a steep wall lead to a shallow groove that is capped by an overhanging tongue of rock. This is where Armand Charlet worked wonders with a jammed ice-axe on the first ascent. Bob swung out to his left on to the main ridge with powerful assurance and a few grunts to indicate that it was not as easy as he made it look. It is a satisfying move. At Stanage, on a sunny afternoon, it would provoke squeals of delight. In the context, with cold hands and alpine boots, I only really enjoyed it afterwards.

The small airy summit of L'Isolée is surprisingly comfortable. On a balmy day, after completing the Aiguilles du Diable traverse, few places in the Alps would be more fitting for contented contemplation. Cold overcast weather and the feeling that it might get a lot worse denied us some of the pleasure we had earned. We scrambled and abseiled back to the main ridge and climbed up to the summit of Mont Blanc du Tacul, urged on by a brief flurry of thin sleet. Later on, as I laboured up the three-hundred metres of ascent from the Col du Midi to the téléphérique, I remembered my ascent of the Tacul eleven years before and realised we might miss the last departure again. I felt just a hint of nostalgic disappointment when we arrived with plenty of time in hand and were spared a symmetric misfortune.

48 Mont Maudit

SE (Frontier) ridge (D), descent via Col Maudit and Col du Midi. With Brian Wood
Map p 204   Illustrations pp 214, 216

Before walking from the Torino round towards Cirque Maudit to climb up to the Col de la Fourche bivouac hut we spent a couple of hours on the snow slopes by the Col des Flambeaux playing at 'luging' with Brian's family. This is usually done with a toboggan. Brian's idea was that a plastic bin liner is just as good. You find a nice even snow slope, sit on the bin liner, grasp the two front corners, lift your feet up and take off. You can also try it lying face down but then the absence of a toboggan does make a difference. It is surprising how tiring it is, and how hysterical and thoroughly wet you can get.

After leaving the family we reached the foot of the steep slope up to the Col de la Fourche and found a multilingual pantomime in progress. Several parties were on the slope and unexpectedly finding it very difficult because the thin snow covering was soft and they were effectively on ice. They were not enjoying themselves. The highest party was slowly hacking out enormous steps, showering those below with lumps of ice and being cursed for their pains. The lower parties were trampling on each other trying to get in front. Occasionally someone slipped, and slithered screeching down the slope for a few metres before being caught. Their frustration, aggravation and fear were almost visible. The noise was amazing. I looked at Brian and we shook our heads. We made some tea and sat on our rucksacks to watch the performance in comfort. After three quarters of an hour it was clear that the show would last some time. The hut would be uncomfortably full and even if there were room for us, two grinning Englishmen arriving late, cooking their dinner and drinking Scotch would probably be the last straw for some of the earlier arrivals.

We decided that we would walk a bit higher up the cirque and bivouac. If we started early next morning and climbed one of the couloirs further along the ridge we could still be first on the route. We spread out a large polythene emergency bivouac bag, sat on it and began to sort out sleeping gear and dinner. When our equipment was at maximum dispersal and we both had our hands full the polythene bag started to slide down the slope – a sort of team luge practice. We rolled off before we had gone far enough to distract the parties on the slope and went back, gathering up bits of gear, to dig out a level platform. When we had finished dinner it was dark. As we settled down for the night faint yelps of anguish told us that the show was still going on.

Mont Maudit and the Frontier Ridge from the Tour Ronde

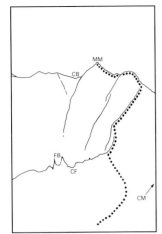

MM Mont Maudit
FB Fourche de la Brenva
CF Col de la Fourche
CM Cirque Maudit
CB Col de la Brenva

Next morning, well before sunrise, we started climbing the couloir we had chosen the previous evening. At first it was straightforward. As we went higher the snow covering became a thin sheet of brittle surface ice. There were verglassed rock and sometimes ridges of crumbly snow. I alternated progress up the slope with lateral movements looking for better ground. Fortunately when the conditions became serious we had only a few metres left to climb. I cut a few small steps to feel more secure and we were soon on the main ridge. The slope to the Col de la Fourche would have been in good condition after a cold night and it would have had large steps already cut. It would have been easier to climb that to attain the ridge. Easier but not better. Starting as we did we made the Frontier Ridge our own personal route for that day. Later events reinforced that feeling. We saw the lights of other parties on the first part of the route and after sunrise, when we were high on the ridge, we saw one party on the snow crest above the first step. They must all have turned back at some point because we did not see them again and there were several places where they would have been clearly visible.

The first step, where the ridge begins to ascend steeply, gave us the only problem we encountered. A steep wall blocks the true ridge, which continues above it as a thin snow crest looping to the left. A broader subsidiary ridge of rock begins indistinctly on the right and rises directly to merge with the true ridge. The topography is clear from the Tour Ronde. In situ, by the light of head-torches, we were unsure where the route lay. We had a few testing moments on mixed ice, snow and icy rock as we edged upwards trying to find a line we believed in. As always, the uncertainty exaggerated the technical difficulties, which were short lived. Soon we found the snowy couloir between the two ridges that led us comfortably to the snow crest of the main ridge. The sun came up, flooding the landscape and our emotions with warmth and light. If there were difficulties after that we did not notice them. We made efficient progress, elated and almost carried along by the superb situations. It was not exactly effortless yet we had no sense of strain.

The varied climbing on the Frontier Ridge is always interesting. One minute we were on an exposed crest of snow, the next weaving through jumbled icy rocks, then traversing round a gendarme on warm dry ledges, then scrambling up a little wall with ice-filled cracks and patches of snow. Short sections and many corners created suspense. In a way the route is complex but our impression was of gloriously simple mountaineering. I was aware of the mixture of apparently contradictory effects that the best days on mountains always generate. We had to be conscious of time yet our activity seemed timeless; we were moving quickly yet there was a calm stillness; I was totally absorbed in the climbing I was doing and at the same time looking across at the Brenva spur and at the south ridge of Mont Blanc du Tacul and reliving those ascents.

Before 09:00 we were enjoying the views from the summit. We basked in the sun, drinking tea for refreshment and something else for celebration. The summit of Mont Blanc du Tacul seemed

Mont Maudit from near Col Maudit. On snow slopes like this one the presence of well-trodden paths makes all the difference. Although the angle is easy, finding a trouble-free line of ascent can be difficult.

very close. We had been there only a few days before yet so different were the circumstances and our frame of mind that it seemed to have happened in another life. We descended easily on excellent snow to Col Maudit and past Mont Blanc du Tacul to the Col du Midi. I thought afterwards that we should have included an easy ascent of the Tacul. Now I feel sure we were right to keep it entirely Mont Maudit's day. This time the short stroll across the Glacier du Géant was very pleasant.

49 Aiguille de Bionnassay

      S ridge (PD+). With Denise Wood

Map p 204   Illustrations pp 217, 218

The Bionnassay is such an elegant mountain that whenever I see it I feel a pang of regret that I have never been back. The north-west face followed by the east ridge traverse to Mont Blanc is the classic option, providing great variety of snow and ice work without excessive difficulty. The drawback of this route is that the long trudge up Mont Blanc and the hordes of people there would diminish the effect of the Bionnassay's contribution to the day. Descending the south ridge to the Durier hut provides several more intimate possibilities in keeping with the Bionnassay. Continuing along the south ridge to traverse the Dômes de Miage to the Aiguille de la Bérangère would be a gentle prolonged descent. Even more esoteric, and high on my list of treasured projects, is to follow the north-west face, south ridge and Durier hut by Col Infranchissable, the Tête Carrée and a complete traverse of the Aiguilles de Tré-la-Tête. Then descend from there by Petit Mont Blanc and the Giovanni Montagna bivouac hut to the Val Veni. This expedition would make best use of the

Aiguille de Bionnassay S ridge from the Durier hut.

Aiguille de Bionnassay from the Dôme du Goûter

south-west corner of the Alps. It is nicely episodic with no dreary bits, continually interesting with nothing really demanding. For me it would meet the demands of nostalgia and sentiment and would be a satisfying way to link some familiar places.

The desire to do a grand expedition based on the Bionnassay arises partly because what I remember of climbing it is dominated by the long approach and the descent to the valley afterwards. The time spent on the Bionnassay itself was delightful but ordinary in comparison with events before and after. Brian and Denise Wood and I were staying near Les Contamines. Our first plan for the Bionnassay began with an afternoon start to the Tré-la-Tête hotel and effectively ended halfway there when it began pouring with rain. Two days later we had dried out, at least from the rain, and we made a 04:00 start from Notre Dame de la Gorge, intending to get to the Durier hut. We made good progress at first and stopped near the hotel for a second breakfast. Negotiating the Tré-la-Tête glacier outfall was awkward and tedious. We worked hard, apparently moving quite quickly and yet making slow progress. By the time we reached the Cabane des Conscrits, about halfway up the glacier, it was mid-morning and very hot.

The afternoon was strange. The scenery on the Tré-la-Tête glacier is superb. The ridges on either side, Dômes de Miage on our left, Tête Carrée, Tête Blanche and the Aiguille de la Lex Blanche on the right, are picturesque and impressive. The glacier was awful underfoot: unpredictably soft, with a lot of new snow on the surface. In spite of this we plodded on cheerfully and enjoyed the views and the context. Several badly crevassed areas gave us some unpleasant moments and gradually we became tired and fractious. The steeper climb up to the Col des Dômes, 3584m, was very hard work. When we got there Brian announced that he was going no further. Although Denise and I wanted to go on to the Durier hut we were not enthusiastic enough to argue about it. It is a fine place to camp out and we had agreed that our home-made bivouac bag would be just big enough for three.

Not quite big enough for three would have been more accurate. Denise, in the centre, slept instantly, deeply and without a break, occasionally emitting a serene grunt. On either side Brian and I were jammed against the bag with a hot inner side and a cold outer side. We squirmed about feeling claustrophobic and tense, talking and complaining and pushing Denise from side to side. When the alarm went off we were grumpy and bleary eyed and Denise leapt up bright as a button. A lovely crisp morning and magnificent sunrise colours as we walked along the easy ridge to the hut soon put things right. At least for me. Brian was still struggling with altitude acclimatisation and had needed a good night's sleep. At the hut he felt unwell and decided to rest there while Denise and I climbed the south ridge of the Bionnassay.

The ridge was in excellent condition: straightforward yet absorbing. There were longer stretches of rock than I had expected and a distinct dip before halfway. Several places that looked as if they might be difficult proved no more than pleasantly interesting. The summit ridge was a fine exposed snow crest, not sharp enough to need particular care and not corniced. The summit is too exposed to be comfortable unless you stamp out a platform. Strong winds and gathering cloud emphasised how inhospitable it was and that we needed to return promptly. By the time we were back at the Durier hut sleet was falling.

Next morning was dreary at first. The early sun gave no warmth and there was a carpet of wet slush. The rocky ribs down from the Col de Miage to the (French) Miage glacier looked repulsive. I have learned since that rotten broken rock at that angle, with or without a coating of icy slush, can be descended quickly and casually. We let the conditions intimidate us and went down in a gingerly and feeble fashion. The glacier and the moraine that followed were pleasant only because they were easier. At the first hamlet, the Chalets de Miage, we stopped for a couple of beers. When we departed it was hot and sunny. After a kilometre I realised I had left my wallet there and strode back trying to convince myself I had been lucky to remember it so soon. Denise enjoyed the delights of Les Contamines while Brian and I, hot and tired, trudged five kilometres along the road to our van. Somewhere on that tedious walk we determined that for once a grand meal in a restaurant would be in order that evening.

50 Mont Blanc
>Bosses ridge (F), descent by a variation of the Corridor route. Solo

48a Pointe Mieulet
>SE ridge (PD) from Col du Mont Maudit. Solo

Map p 204   Illustration p 221

This ascent of Mont Blanc, my fourth, was motivated in several ways. Each of the previous ascents had been by serious routes on the Italian side and had included some tense moments. I wanted to see the popular routes on the French side and to enjoy a relaxed straightforward ascent without dramatic interludes. Bivouacking on the top of Mont Blanc and watching the sunset and sunrise was a long-cherished idea that I was keen to accomplish. The Bosses ridge was the easiest way to reach the summit with a fairly heavy rucksack; descending via the Col de la Brenva would give me an opportunity to climb Pointe Mieulet and to have another look at the routes I had done on Mont Maudit and Mont Blanc du Tacul. To make the occasion even more special several friends from Dark Peak Fell Runners were planning an ascent of Mont Blanc as a way of winding down after the Sierre-Zinal race. We had met in Sierre and then in Chamonix and agreed on a day. Their enthusiasm did not extend to bivouacking on the summit, despite my promises about the crowded chaos that would await them at the Goûter hut.

I arrived at Les Houches in time for the first téléphérique to Bellevue but not early enough to get on it: too many people were there before me. It made no difference, as we all caught the same service on the Tramway du Mont Blanc from Bellevue to the Nid d'Aigle terminus. I could not believe that everyone in the long cavalcade that began plodding up the path to the Tête Rousse hut were all intending to go there or on to the Goûter hut. The volume of noise they made was depressing and I began to have misgivings. Although I was determined on a relaxed stroll all the way to the summit of Mont Blanc, some resolute walking was called for to get away. The Tête Rousse hut appeared before I expected it and soon I was crossing the big couloir before the rock rib that leads steeply up to the Goûter hut.

The only problem there, was timing the traverse movements across the couloir to avoid the parties who were descending. Sporadic rockfall down the couloir made it dangerous and people were understandably afraid. That so many reacted by standing still at an exposed point to receive or shout instructions or to proclaim their fear was disturbing. Perhaps that is what the multitudes I had left behind had been practising. I know a climber who was standing on the rickety cat-walk at the Goûter hut and dropped his helmet. It slid into the couloir and bounced down out of sight, becoming an exotic item of objective danger. To be killed by a falling helmet would be the ultimate ironic climbing accident.

I had brought less gas than I had intended so I stopped at the Goûter hut to buy a litre bottle of water. At midday, when the hut would be at its most tranquil, it was crowded and full of good-humoured noise. The well-trodden path over the Aiguille du Goûter and round beneath the Dôme du Goûter was still crisp and pleasant. I plodded on cheerfully enjoying the views, particularly of the Bionnassay, and the jumbled recollections of my previous ascents of Mont Blanc. Two descending parties went past, both looking distressed. Before the Bosses ridge I found a sunny spot

Bosses ridge leading past the Vallot hut to the summit of Mont Blanc

sheltered from the keen wind and stopped for lunch. Two climbers that I remembered seeing at Les Houches that morning, whose combined age must have been over 120, tramped past and returned my greeting with extravagant courtesy.

When I reached the broad summit crest of Mont Blanc I found its highest point embellished with a small igloo. The two veterans were sitting beside it, drinking from a thermos flask and deep in conversation. We repeated our greetings, even more theatrically than before. They left after a few minutes with the nonchalant air of two people who have just been to the corner shop. The rest of the afternoon passed quickly. Two parties came slowly along the ridge from Mont Blanc de Courmayeur with a weary gait that I remembered all too well. Pic Luigi Amadeo and the last section of the Brouillard ridge had a sprinkling of fresh snow and looked satisfyingly ferocious. Above Pic Luigi Amadeo, in the far distance was, yet again, the benign sentinel of Monte Viso. The wind made it too cold to be entirely enjoyable. As I was hacking out a level platform at the side of the igloo a Japanese popped out to see what was going on. He, or possibly she, said there were two more inside and if I got too cold in the night I would be welcome to join them.

The sunset colours were magnificent. For a few minutes the Alps appeared to be on fire. Two hours later I had decided that I was going to be warm enough although another layer would have been welcome. My contented drowsing was disturbed by the arrival of five Frenchmen. Two left almost at once. The other three dug a pit next to mine and went to sleep after a brief carousal. The volume and harshness of their snoring was appalling. If I have ever been aghast I was then. Luckily they were within reach so the farmyard impressions were soon replaced by acrimonious discussion. As usual the language difficulties made the already absurd situation almost surreal. Drawing on dim

Evening colours; the view NE from Mont Blanc

Morning colours; the view NE from Mont Blanc

222

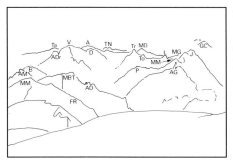

MM	Mont Maudit	FR	Frontier Ridge
AM	Aig. du Midi	AD	Aigs. du Diable
B	Aig. du Blaitière	Tr	Aig. de Triolet
To	Aig. du Tour	MD	Mont Dolent
V	Aig. Verte	Ta	Aig. de Talèfre
D	Les Droites	P	Les Périades
ADr	Aig. du Dru	L	Aig. de Leschaux
MM	Mont Mallet	A	Aig. d'Argentière
AG	Aig. du Géant	TN	Tour Noir
MG	Mont Gruetta	J	Grandes Jorasses
MBT	Mont Blanc du	GC	Grand Combin
	Tacul		

My emotional reactions to events or views in the Alps are sometimes unexpected although some are predictable. Sunrise and sunset colours, spectacular and tantalisingly brief, never leave me unmoved, however stressful or uncomfortable the circumstances. Neither provokes climbing ambitions except, of course, to return. I tend, at those times, not to conceive expeditions nor to bother identifying mountains I do not recognise. Instead I am aware of the enchantment and a sense of involvement. Perhaps the time of day and the temperature dictate my lack of detached observation.

memories of similar events in huts, eventually I was able to convey my philosophy of 'all sleep or all keep each other awake' but I do not think that my threats of kamikaze reprisals were understood. At about 02:00 they got up and left. While it was still dark parties from the Goûter hut began to arrive. Some were so cold and uncomfortable they left before they had seen the sunrise. The first of the Dark Peak Fell Runners contingent arrived and I made them some tea.

The sunrise was wonderful, as Alpine sunrises always are. Next time I will choose a quiet mountain where I will be on my own. Almost any other mountain would do. The Grand Combin seems the obvious choice. I walked away from the summit down the Petits Mulets ridge. Within two minutes the hubbub that had been so distracting at the summit faded from my mind. The mountains seemed to come alive. I had lost contact with them briefly, redeemed myself and been forgiven. I grinned at them all sheepishly.

I stopped at the Col de la Brenva to look at the Brenva spur and the Frontier Ridge of Mont Maudit. I had climbed them fourteen years earlier yet it might have been yesterday. The path contouring across the west side of Mont Maudit was neat and airy, the snow crisp. Walking round to the Col du Mont Maudit was a simple delight. At the col there were the inevitable parties finding the slope on the north side steeper and icier than they had anticipated and trying to solve their problems by shouting. I left my rucksack near the col and climbed to Pointe Mieulet, partly on the broken ridge, partly traversing on the west side. It is an undistinguished point, hardly deserving a name and not worth a visit. Nevertheless I enjoyed the little scramble across to it and sitting on top for a few minutes.

I went back along the path towards the Col de la Brenva and then plunged down to the Corridor. The snow was soft but still pleasant. I made good time down to the Grand Mulets hut and across the Glacier des Bossons. When I arrived at Chamonix on the téléphérique from the Plan de l'Aiguille I could not be bothered to find the bus to Les Houches and just walked along the road. Had I known that would happen, or had I even stopped to think, I could have avoided most of the tedious walk to the Plan de l'Aiguille and along the road, and saved the téléphérique fare, by taking a path directly down to the road.

Eustace Thomas

I knew nothing about Eustace Thomas until I had completed climbing Blödig's list of fourthousanders in 1981. When I tried to find out how many other British mountaineers had climbed them the answer was none since Eustace Thomas finished them in 1932 and he was the first. This seemed very unlikely and still does but if any British person had climbed them in the meantime nobody appeared to know about it. Blödig gets the credit for being the very first, around 1900. In fact neither of them climbed to all the summits in modern lists.

Nowadays the problem of which tops to include is an aesthetic one. When Eustace Thomas was actively involved the standard of cartography meant that heights quoted were unreliable. Most of the discrepancies involve mountains no longer deemed to be 4000m or over, like the Fletschhorn, 3993m, and the Piz Zupo, 3996m. The most serious omission from his list is the Punta Baretti, 4013m. This summit is also missing from Blödig's list. 'Serious' is overstating the case, of course, except that Eustace Thomas emphasised its absence from his list by including some much less worthy tops. Least substantial is Pointe Mieulet which he made a special trip to climb. This is one of the little rocky points on the north-west ridge of Mont Maudit. I could not be certain which one when I traversed them; they are so insignificant. The Punta Baretti is quite different. Although dominated by Mont Blanc it is a fine-looking minor peak wherever you see it from, and it is a very distinct point on the Brouillard ridge. In fact it is the peak many people settle on by mistake when looking for Mont Brouillard. Was Eustace Thomas ever aware he had accidentally omitted the Punta Baretti, and if he was, did he mind? Judging from his approach to climbing them all and what he said about it I am sure he would not have been pleased. I hope, if he did realise afterwards, he was not too disappointed.

Eustace Thomas was a remarkable man. His fell walking and mountaineering achievements are impressive enough in themselves. They become truly amazing when you realise that he began them after he was 50 years old. He also designed the Thomas stretcher for mountain rescue.

He came to Manchester from London in 1900 when he was 31 to join his brother who had started an electrical engineering firm. This became a successful family business, specialising in heavy switchgear. For ten years it absorbed all his energies. Then he began walking in the Pennines and the Lake District. This became a serious activity around 1918 when he set his sights on Wakefield's fell walking record which had stood since 1905. In 1921 he established a new record which survived until 1932 when Bob Graham did his round of 42 Lake District summits in 24 hours. Emulating this round has become a popular feat. Doing it it in 1981 led me to discover Eustace Thomas a second time. After his Alpine exploits he took to flying, first in gliders, then aeroplanes. He co-piloted his four-seater plane to Egypt when he was 70.

His interest in the Alps was not so much an emotional involvement with the mountains as with the physical achievement of climbing them. He had been to Switzerland several times and had done a number of ascents before his first major Alpine season in 1923. The idea of climbing all the 4000m peaks is said to have originated the following year, and then not from Eustace Thomas himself, but even that first season is characterised by energetic expeditions efficiently 'gathering in' several summits at a time. In the next six years until 1929 he hired the famous guide Joseph Knubel, usually with Alexander Lagger too, for five to seven weeks. They were a very competent team, especially at covering a lot of ground in a day. I suppose not carrying heavy sacks with food and bivouac gear and staying in huts and hotels made it easier, yet you have to be impressed. I would like to think that when I am 55 I will be able to start at the Gnifetti hut, traverse Liskamm and Castor, climb Pollux and the Breithorn and get down to the Schwarzee hotel. An eighteen-and-a-half-hour day from the Torino hut, traversing the Aiguilles du Diable and descending to the Requin hut when I am 62 will cheer me up even more.

Eustace Thomas's approach was very different from mine. He expressed regret for the times he was inefficient and would not have approved of my serendipitous behaviour. Notions like climbing a mountain by a route that does it justice rather than the easiest or most efficient route do not appear in his accounts in the Alpine Journal. Perhaps such ideas are rather

Eustace Thomas between the guides Alexander Taugwalder and Georges Cachat, 1932.

fanciful anyway. There is plenty of evidence of his determination and careful planning but not much of his charm and good humour. This is a pity for it makes his expeditions seem soulless, with him largely unmoved by the mountains he ascended so relentlessly. I find it strange that he should have omitted the Punta Baretti. The Grande Rocheuse is also puzzling because he initially ignored it while going to some trouble to climb the Aiguille Verte and the Aiguille du Jardin on either side. I can only assume that neither was on the first list he was given and so he simply disregarded them. It seems to me he was ill served by Joseph Knubel here. His friends are said to have mischievously sought out obscure 4000m points that he had missed. He displayed cheerful unconcern at these researches but climbed the additional tops nevertheless, and they included the Grande Rocheuse. Missing out the Punta Baretti that should have been included is unimportant and yet I wish his friends had been more thorough in their mischief.

Perhaps there is something about the remote obscurity of the Brouillard ridge that encourages oversights and disputes. Karl Blödig claimed the first ascent of Mont Brouillard and produced some lofty thoughts about the honour of being the person to climb the last unclimbed fourthousander. His claim rests on his rejection of Baretti's account of climbing it twelve years earlier because when he, Blödig, reached the summit there were no signs of an earlier ascent!

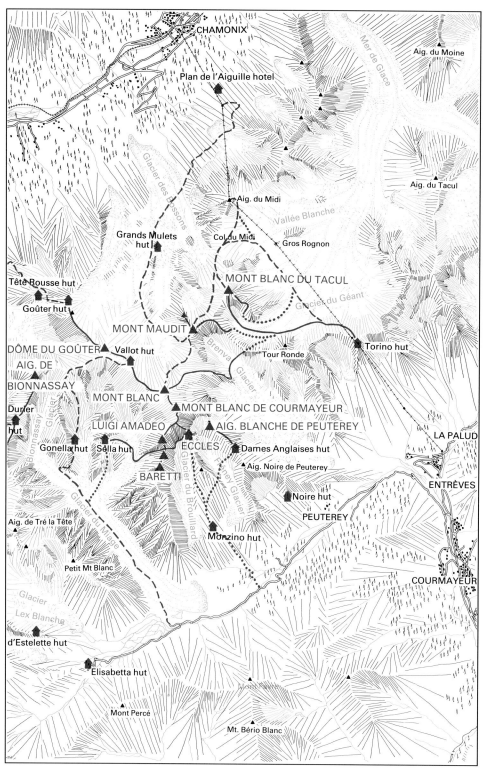

Map 15 (repeat)

226

Section 12
Mont Blanc; the Italian side

The southern side of Mont Blanc has an air of seriousness that is matched nowhere else in the Alps. The Miage glacier and Grises ridge provide the only fairly easy ascent; otherwise the routes for climbing Mont Blanc on the Italian side are long and strenuous and allow no easy escape. On the classic routes the technical difficulties are not excessive. What makes them demanding is the cumulative effect of sustained mixed climbing at high altitude, route-finding problems and arduous approaches.

There are two distinct sections: the Brenva face and the three great ridges of Brouillard, Innominata and Peuterey. On maps the three ridges seem to offer obvious and well-defined routes. This is deceptive. The Brouillard and Innominata routes begin at Col Emil Rey and Col Eccles respectively. These are small cols higher up the ridges than Mont Brouillard and Punta Innominata and close to the main mass of Mont Blanc. The Peuterey route begins at the col between the Aiguille Noire and the Aiguille Blanche de Peuterey. In each case attaining the starting col is a substantial undertaking. Routes on the long lower sections of the ridges are regarded as separate or, in the case of the Brouillard ridge, disregarded altogether. The Brenva face routes can be climbed from the French side by crossing the Glacier du Géant from the Midi téléphérique station. This has the minor advantage of easier descents and the major disadvantage as far as I am concerned of replacing Courmayeur with Chamonix.

For me, climbing Mont Blanc has come to mean being involved with the big routes on the Italian side and staying quietly and simply in the Val Veni. It means enjoying the enduring delights of Courmayeur and being strangely tolerant of its shortcomings. Above all it has come to mean a sense of adventure and a feeling of preoccupation with the mountain. The decision to set out has to be carefully weighed because it is necessary to be particularly sure of the weather. On these routes I am nearer to my limits of ability and ambition so there is more living with them in my mind beforehand. Climbing here is never casual or uneventful.

Whether Courmayeur in spite of its cosmopolitan grandeur has managed to retain a village-like charm or whether its virtues so effortlessly beguile me that I am incapable of critical judgement, I cannot tell. I look to it for the usual amenities, the most important being places to buy food.

Half-a-dozen shops close together satisfy my needs with an unselfconscious magnificence that renews a shock of pleasure on every visit. Wine and spirits, cheese, fruit and vegetables, fresh meat, preserved meats, bread: each shop is a candidate for the best of its kind I know and each has the relaxed helpfulness that comes from a confident awareness of its own excellence. Remarkably, although the proprietors have become a little less agile and their geniality more mannered, these favourite shops have hardly changed in sixteen years. The bread and confectionery shop is an exception. This expanded to a second site, so now my first minute in Courmayeur involves a choice. There are two places to buy a flat crusty triangular loaf and be tempted to tear off a corner almost before leaving the shop.

This constancy is the key to Courmayeur's attraction. Although it has grown and changed it seems to be the same as ever because its points of reference continue to flourish. Less important features have the same air of immortality. These include the Alpine museum with its balustrade of ice-axes and statue of Emil Rey, 'Prince of Guides'. There is Gobbi's climbing shop, where you can buy forty different ice-axes but usually all you go there for is to talk about the weather. There is the rambling procession on guides' day when the local mountain guides, wearing ceremonial garb and carrying coils of rope, parade through the town. They are led by a cheerfully unprofessional wind band, approximately in uniform, and are accompanied by local dignitaries, colourfully robed priests, small children and stray dogs.

The Val Veni is not a pretty valley and the views it offers of Mont Blanc are disappointing. This is presumably its salvation because it is still relatively undeveloped and is remarkably quiet considering its importance. Not so on public holidays however, when the road gets spectacularly jammed. Solitary camping, officially prohibited in the best spots, can still be practised with discretion. One unique attraction has gone. The small Italian-army barracks used to be occupied during August by a detachment of British soldiers practising the esoteric Alpine activities so vital for Britain's defence. If you were accompanied by a woman wearing a bikini you could talk your way into their amazing shower tent where jets of hot water gushed forth extravagantly in all directions.

The ridge on the south side of the valley provides good walking on poor weather days and important opportunities for examining the complicated topography of the Brouillard, Innominata and Peuterey ridges. Set further back is a mysterious mountain, Mont Berio Blanc, 3252m. This dark, regular pyramid, particularly intriguing in the hazy early-morning sun, is conspicuous from routes on the south side of Mont Blanc. I had long intended to climb it, without ever finding the right occasion. I was inhibited by the lack of paths on maps and by the possibility, in the absence of any information, that it was harder than it looked. Then one morning I got up early for a run on Mont Fortin and Mont Favre to see the sunrise. I found myself unable to resist the temptation to continue on to Mont Berio Blanc. It was amazingly loose, as if it had been tipped out of the sky: not difficult but eerily surreal. The cairn on top consisted of three stones, so for the only time in my life I added a couple more.

Another important vantage point, completely different in character from Mont Berio Blanc, is the Tour Ronde. This is a popular expedition from the Torino and very worthwhile. Its elegant north face tempts and eludes me. When I have felt in the mood to climb it there have been ice and bare patches of rock instead of steep crisp snow. On the summit of the Tour Ronde you can sit like T. Graham Brown and become obsessed with the Brenva face. You can look at the vast complex of buttresses, icy gullies and hanging snow-fields, and discover something about yourself as a mountaineer. Do you shudder in awe or do you instinctively start to think 'I could go up there, then get to that couloir, move across to those rocks, then...'? You can also look at the route that starts just below the Torino at the Helbronner téléphérique station and goes across the Glacier du Géant, over the Brenva ridge and on to Col Moore. Then follow the intimidating line of the Pear up the Brenva face to the summit of Mont Blanc and contemplate the audacious exploit of Robert Chéré, a Chamonix guide. One day in July 1977 he caught the first téléphérique from Chamonix to the Helbronner and soloed it all in five hours.

50 Mont Blanc

  Brenva ridge (AD+). Solo
50a Dôme du Goûter
  traverse SE to SW (F). Solo
Map p 226 Illustration p 230

  The situation that greeted Brian Wood and me when we arrived at the small Ghiglione hut on the Arête de la Brenva shocked us. There were so many people that none could be comfortable. The floor was awash with melted snow that had been carelessly carried in on boots. Every bit of horizontal surface above floor level was occupied by recumbent climbers and their rucksacks. The atmosphere was heavy with frustration and recrimination. Early arrivals resented being disturbed and tried to protect their territory. Late arrivals resented being confined to wet areas of floor and demanded that people vacate table-tops. Participants in bilingual disputes tried to make themselves understood by raising their voices. Rest, let alone sleep, was impossible.

  We had arrived during the afternoon and had cooked and eaten our dinner early. The noisy squalor and continual aggravation had begun to get us down when the door burst open and two climbers stepped through the entrance. Their surprising late appearance produced a sudden silence in the hut, but their own surprise was even greater. Their eyes and mouths opened together as they took in the scene. Then, with great feeling and in a broad Lancashire accent, one said 'Fookin' stroll on!' This unexpected friendly voice cheered us up. We had some breakfast, packed our rucksacks, and went across to Col Moore, arriving there at midnight. There was little to be said for sitting there in the dark, so although there was no need to start up the Brenva ridge so early we began climbing almost at once. In retrospect this was the wrong decision. We should have taken advantage of being there so early to climb the Route Major, or at least the Sentinelle Rouge.

  After a few metres, as we scrambled up a short steep wall, Brian fell off. The hinge part of one of his crampons had snapped. He was shaken rather than hurt and decided not to go on with only one crampon. We had a hasty exchange of equipment and I continued up the ridge. I progressed at a feverish rate and arrived at the famous snow arête in what felt like no time at all. I rested briefly.

Brenva face of Mont Blanc from the Ghiglione (Trident) hut

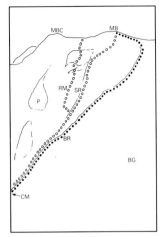

MB   Mont Blanc
MBC Mont Blanc de Courmayeur
P   Pear buttress
RM   Route Major
SR   Sentinelle Rouge
BR   Brenva ridge/spur
CM   Col Moore
BG   Brenva glacier

Sunrise was still a long time away. The conditions were good and there was plenty of moonlight so once again there seemed no reason to wait. Another wrong decision.

The snow covering was adequate at first. Then, as soon as I was well established on the arête, it steadily thinned until I was essentially climbing on ice. The angle of ascent up the broad arête was quite comfortable but the slight slope to my right rapidly steepened. I became very conscious that if I came off I would go a long way. Intermittently there were strong gusts of wind. In the dim light, intimidated by the exposure, I moved more slowly and began to feel cold. I was cutting small steps about two metres apart, front-pointing between them and finding it increasingly difficult to make myself move from one step to the next. I could make out the end of the arête above me and beyond it the beginning of the sérac band. I forced myself to keep moving towards a tiny rock outcrop just below the séracs. I reached it eventually with my nerves in shreds. There was an incipient spike to belay to and then I found a good crack for a metal chockstone. I almost fell asleep with relief. I wriggled into my sleeping bag and duvet jacket and settled down to wait for the sunrise. I discovered I had the stove and plenty of gas but no food.

It would have seemed entirely appropriate if the sunrise had been announced by fanfares of celestial trumpets. I suppose the colours and the warmth were much the same as in other sunrises but that was not my impression at the time.

Two climbers approaching did not notice me until they were quite close. They were surprised to find someone there. We managed to exchange a few words of explanation in a mixture of English and German and they thanked me for the steps. I let them get well in front to find a way through the séracs, which they did either expertly or fortuitously. In spite of suddenly feeling very tired I enjoyed the slow plod to the summit.

There were too many people and I was too conscious of my lack of food to stay as long as I would have liked. I traversed the Dôme du Goûter and sauntered cheerfully down the Grises route. When I stopped at the Gonella hut for some water I was made very welcome by the guardian and his family. They were keen to overcome the language barrier to find out what I had done. When my laborious explanation reached the 'no food' stage they immediately produced bread and salami. I suppose the food and the water, like the sunrise, were quite ordinary but again that was not my impression at the time.

The S side of Mont Blanc, with the Brouillard,
Innominata and Peuterey ridges, from Mont Favre

ABP Aig. Blanche de Peuterey
ANP Aig. Noire de Peuterey
GC   Glacier de Châtelet

FMH	Franco Monzino hut	MB	Mont Brouillard	CI	Col de l'Innominata
EBH	Eccles bivouac hut	CER	Col Emil Rey	PI	Punta Innominata
GPA	Grand Pilier d'Angle	PB	Punta Baretti	IR	Innominata ridge
AC	Aig. Croz	ARB	Aigs. Rouges du Brouillard	DA	Dames Anglaises
PLA	Pic Luigi Amadeo	MBC	Mont Blanc de Courmayeur	SW	SW ridge of Dôme du Goûter
GB	Glacier du Brouillard	GF	Glacier de Frêney	MBT	Mont Blanc du Tacul

Anne Brearley.   Afternoon tea at the Quintino Sella hut: a tranquil, almost elegant, hour spent enjoying the remoteness of the situation and balmy sunshine.

51 Mont Brouillard

Col Emil Rey and N ridge (AD). With Anne Brearley

51a Punta Baretti

N ridge from Mont Brouillard (PD). Solo

Map p 226   Illustrations pp 235, 232/233, 236, 240

An efficient collector of 4000m summits would climb Mont Brouillard and the Punta Baretti as a pleasant diversion from Col Emil Rey before ascending Mont Blanc by the Brouillard ridge. This would have the significant bonus of avoiding the descent from Col Emil Rey. I do not regret having made three visits to this remote col, because each one was a memorable adventure, but to be positively glad about it would be perverse. It is a difficult and unpleasant place to get to and Anne is unlucky to have had it inflicted on her three times. The first time was from the west side. We had an enjoyable climb to the little Quintino Sella hut, reaching it just when we were getting tired and the pleasure was wearing off. The hut is rarely visited. According to the visitors book we were only the seventh party that year and the first British one for five years. After we had laid some of the bedding on the roof to dry out we had an elegant tea at the back of the hut in a warm sheltered spot that caught the afternoon sun.

The events next morning were unpleasant although the weather was good. The traverse line from the Quintino Sella hut across and down the Glacier du Mont Blanc to the couloir up to Col Emil Rey is ill defined, and the glacier is nastily crevassed. There was a thick layer of unconsolidated new snow. Every few steps I sank suddenly into a softer patch. Each time this felt momentarily as

Mont Brouillard and Punta Baretti from the Pic Eccles.   The approach couloirs on both sides to Col Emil Rey are not friendly places. However neither is as steep as this view of the E side suggests.

PB Punta Baretti	CER Col Emil Rey
AG Aig. des Glaciers	PO Pointe des Ouillons
MB Mont Brouillard	CS Col de la Seigne
T Aig. Nord	
de Tré-la-Tête	

if I were falling into a crevasse. The couloir leads directly to the col and is narrow and dark. We were glad to reach it after our slow enervating descent of the glacier. It seemed slightly less evil than it looks from Petit Mont Blanc across the Miage glacier. We climbed as fast as we could urged on by persistent small projectiles whining past.

At Col Emil Rey any residual thoughts we had about continuing up the Brouillard ridge vanished when we saw and heard the amount of debris falling down it. We scrambled up the short interesting ridge to the summit of Mont Brouillard and restored our spirits with the views, which are superb and totally different in each direction. Like others before us we were too absorbed with the magnificent Brouillard pillars and the Peuterey ridge and with looking far to the south to give the Punta Baretti the attention it warranted. When we visited Mont Brouillard again especially to climb the Punta Baretti I saw what a fine little mountain it is and I was amazed that on the previous occasion I could virtually have overlooked it.

After the interlude on the summit of Mont Brouillard we had the morning's horrors to repeat in reverse. The couloir, with bits of stonefall rattling down it, looked steep and unpleasant to descend.

Punta Baretti from Mont Brouillard. This is definitely my favourite picture of me in the Alps.

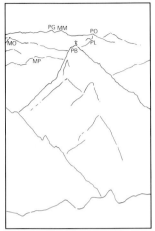

PB Punta Baretti
MO Mont Ouille
MP Mont Perce
PG Pointe des Glaciers
MM Mont de Miranda
PL Pointe Léchaud
PO Pointe des Ouillons

As we stood at the col procrastinating there was a loud whirr and a stone the size of a dinner plate smashed into the snow four metres away. This put the small particles in the couloir in perspective. We descended briskly and emerged completely unharmed. The climb back up the glacier, using our descent footprints with some judicious variations, was merely tiring. As we traversed back to the hut we climbed out of a steep gully and paused on the flank of a buttress to choose the best line. There was a rumble above us and blocks of ice the size of small caravans thundered into view and crashed past us down the gully.

Four years later we were back on the summit of Mont Brouillard. This time we had reached Col Emil Rey from the Brouillard glacier. I had stubbornly tried to force a direct route diagonally across the upper part of the glacier after an excellent bivouac at about 3400m on its left bank. Eventually we used a circuitous route that climbed almost up to the Eccles bivouac hut and then traversed adventurously across the head of the glacier through unstable-looking séracs. A steep bulging ice-wall led us to an unstable buttress of loose rock below the Brouillard pillars. The final slope leading to the col was soft snow over ice. The Punta Baretti did not have the same attraction for Anne as it had for me so she did not experience its recuperative influence. She decided to enjoy the panorama from the summit of Mont Brouillard while I ambled across the ridge to the Punta Baretti.

After a few metres my attention wandered from the immediate details of the ridge itself. The ridge was airy and well defined, the climbing uncomplicated, the rock warm and clean. My feet, with an occasional helping hand, could manage by themselves. I began to think of the Punta Baretti's special significance for me and its curious situation, close to the activity and importance of Mont Blanc yet remote and esoteric. Looking south, along and beyond the ridge, nothing of the Alps was in view. I felt as if I were in a strange, unknown place and on untrodden ground.

My serenity was interrupted by a short, nearly vertical wall, just interesting enough for the ridge to reassert itself. Then a small slab, glittering in the sunlight, caught my eye. It was about a metre square and evenly covered with a crust of quartz crystals. I instinctively reached out to touch it and a piece came away into the palm of my hand. I looked at it and made the crystals flash in the sun. I had a sudden feeling of uneasiness, as if this had all been prearranged, and I looked around and above me. Then I scrambled to the summit of the Punta Baretti and held the piece of rock up to the sun to show I had found it. I sat there for a few minutes smiling at myself, without completely losing the sense of the mountain's presence. Then I became conscious of the length and possible complications of the descent and walked back, reluctantly, to Mont Brouillard.

We slithered insecurely down the snow slope to the rock buttress. To avoid the frequent stonefall from the Brouillard pillars we left the easiest line to descend by a slightly more awkward route on the west side. Then we had to wait for a quiet break in the stonefall and dash across the exposed ledgy slopes to the comparative sanctuary of the glacier. The jumbled tottering séracs looked unstable and it was almost a comfort when they were swallowed up in mist. Gradually we worked across eastwards and began to relax. The mist probably helped by shading the snow and slowing its further deterioriation, although the poor visibility would have caused us serious problems without our ascent footprints to retrace.

50 Mont Blanc

50b Mont Blanc de Courmayeur
50c Pic Luigi Amadeo
      Brouillard ridge (AD+). With Anne Brearley
Map p 226   Illustrations pp 239, 232/233, 240

If there is one expedition I have done in the Alps that I would like to do again, to correct the mistakes, to discover the exhilaration I missed, to ease the embarrassing memories or simply to do the route justice, then this is it. I doubt whether I would dare suggest a return visit to Anne. She refers to the route as 'Pig Luigi'.

We knew that conditions would be poor following recent indifferent weather so we set out expecting a high-level bivouac. We decided that a gentle late-afternoon walk to the Franco Monzino hut and an overnight stop there was the most efficient approach. This would give us good conditions to Col Emil Rey and on the lower part of the ridge. If the weather changed the next day we should be past the difficult sections or still be able to retreat. If the weather changed overnight we had only to descend from the hut. As a fitting preamble to what followed on the route the hut was noisy and very crowded, with some sort of celebration and a film show. The night was warm and overcast and we slept, or rather did not sleep, outside.

Getting to Col Emil Rey in poor snow took eight hours' hard work and had several tricky moments. We kept to the true left bank of the Brouillard glacier until close to the Eccles bivouac hut and then traversed across the head of the glacier. This is probably the best line because we never saw a plausible route directly across towards the col. Quite small changes in the configuration of the fallen séracs however could make this approach very difficult. Our uncertainty about getting through to the col made the approach seem even longer and more tiring than it actually was. The ascent of Pic Luigi Amadeo begins in a groove at the end of a downward traverse from Col Emil Rey across the east flank. Two thirds of the way across the traverse is a large flat block, where we stopped for a long lunch. The groove was festooned with wet snow and uninviting but as the good weather seemed set we decided to press on.

The first awkward section was a smooth bulging slab covered in several centimetres of slush. Above the slab the groove became broader and straightforward. The snow seemed secure even though it was soft. Eventually I found an awkward constricted stance and arranged a belay with three uncertain chockstone runners. I had pushed my ice-axe obliquely between my rucksack and my shoulder blades. As I tried to wriggle into a comfortable position facing outwards I slid down a bit and the spike of the axe caught on the rock behind me. The axe was pushed upwards and at the moment I realised what was happening I felt it topple forward over my shoulder. My grab at it, with

Brouillard ridge and Pic Luigi Amadeo from Mont Blanc

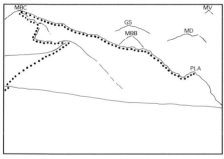

MBC	Mont Blanc de	MD	Mont Ouille
	Courmayeur	GS	Grande Sassière
MBB	Mont Berio Blanc	MV	Monte Viso
PLA	Pic Luigi Amadeo		

a hand full of rope, served only to increase the severity of the parting clip the pick gave my knee. The axe cartwheeled down directly towards Anne. It thudded into the bulging slab and bounced over her head. Anne has a way of saying 'Bloody Hell!' that conveys both outrage and reprimand with great efficiency.

Ironically my spare, short axe was a better implement for parts of the slope above. I wanted to get to the ridge proper to find somewhere in sunshine to settle down for a bivouac but the sun went down faster than we went up. When we reached the ridge crest it was cold and in shadow. We continued to ascend feebly, looking unsuccessfully for a satisfactory bivouac site. We stopped at some rough rocks that provided a seat and some shelter. Frazzled, embarrassed about my ice-axe and aware that if the weather turned overnight we would be in a very serious position, I was not good company. The night was clear and cold. Before dawn we decided to make some progress up the ridge then stop for breakfast when the sun came up. When it did there was a strong wind as well, so our stop was cold and uncomfortable. After holding the stove in a precarious position while we heated some water for tea I dropped it, losing all the hot water, nearly losing the pan and prompting another 'Bloody Hell!'.

Brouillard ridge from Petit Mont Blanc.   In contrast with the illustration on page 235 this view makes the approach couloir on the W side of Col Emil Rey appear more benign than it really is – or at least than it seemed when I climbed it. What the picture does not convey is the feeling of confinement in a narrow channel and what it cannot show is the stonefall. However, when there is plenty of well-compacted snow and progress is comfortable both these drawbacks may be absent.

Most of the remainder of the ridge was a tediously pleasant jumble of rock boulders. It was made awkward by a coating of ice and frozen snow, so for much of the way we found it easier, albeit more delicate, to climb the smooth slopes of icy snow on the east flank. The harsh summit of Pic Luigi Amadeo had an air of wild remoteness. The ridge to Mont Blanc de Courmayeur, descending from the summit towards a small col, narrows and becomes a fantastic undercut fin of rock. A previous party had obviously found this difficult because a new-looking full-weight rope had been tied to the top of the fin and to a bollard lower down the ridge and abandoned. This was very useful although there was no need for such extravagance. We were tempted to take it with us.

After a step in the ridge, which I found difficult without being able to understand why, we plodded on slowly, past the point where the Innominata ridge emerges and on to Mont Blanc de Courmayeur. My enjoyment of this splendid high-level traverse was reduced by a cold biting wind. Having to walk with my face turned down away from the wind made me more conscious of my tiredness. My problem was merely irritation: Anne's was serious. She felt ill and very weak. Our guess at the time was blood-poisoning from an infected grazed foot, which had certainly looked nasty before we started. Two days later when it was examined at the hospital in Aosta the staff, to our amusement, made her sit in a wheelchair while she waited for treatment. Much later, after a recurrence, her condition was diagnosed as a pulmonary oedema.

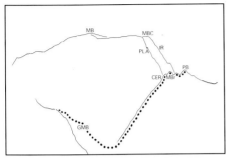

MB Mont Blanc	MBr Mont Brouillard
MBC Mont Blanc de	PB Punta Baretti
Courmayeur	CER Col Emil Rey
PLA Pic Luigi Amadeo	GMB Glacier du Mont
IR Innominata ridge	Blanc

Our stay on the summit of Mont Blanc was shorter and less satisfying than I had anticipated. I could not tell whether Anne needed just a rest or descent and medical treatment. We thought she might feel less exhausted going downhill and that we had a chance of reaching the Midi téléphérique station in time to get down to Entrèves that day. By the time we were passing Mont Maudit it was clear that we were moving much too slowly so we stopped to bivouac opposite Pointe Mieulet. Whether sitting on her rucksack or lying down, Anne was asleep instantly. Again the night was clear and very cold but this time we waited until after sunrise before stirring. As we walked slowly past Mont Blanc du Tacul we were in the perfect position to see crash down below us an enormous sérac perhaps forty metres high. The debris rolled down the slope and crossed the path neatly between two parties ascending.

The climb up to the Midi took us a long time but as soon as it was over things improved. Anne felt better and we both felt relieved. The cable car journey across the Vallée Blanche to the Torino was superb. In contrast to what had gone before we seemed to move at extraordinary speed and the journey ended all too soon. When we finally arrived at Entrèves we luckily met an acquaintance who gave us a lift to where we had left my van in the Val Veni.

50 Mont Blanc
52 Pic Eccles
Innominata ridge (D+). With Bob Brevitt
Map p 226 Illustrations pp 232/233, 244

I reacted to the long ascent from the Val Veni to the Eccles bivouac hut with furtive enjoyment. I was not as fit as I would have wished so I was pleased to find myself coping with Bob's relentless yet charitable pace. Both the old hut and the new one nearby were full when we arrived, with some climbers standing ostensibly in the entrances and others constructing sheltered corners outside to bivouac. With our instinctive preference for solitude we were unperturbed to find there was no room for us and almost without a pause continued climbing the south-west ridge of Pic Eccles. We expected to come across suitable bivouac sites on the ridge but none materialised. Towards the end of the ridge we mistakenly traversed to the right because it looked easier. The result was several problematic moments and some entertaining rock-climbing before we reached the summit.

Pic Eccles is rarely climbed for itself and is usually ignored by climbers intent on the Innominata ridge. A direct ascent from the valley makes it a worthy fourthousander. At the time I thought it was the only one I had not previously climbed so our brief visit seemed full of significance. Since then I have climbed some additional minor 4000m points and there are yet more. I like to think I will never climb the final one so that the mountains will have the last word.

Robert Denis Brevitt, 18.10.1951 – 24.12.1989
Bob Brevitt died following a climbing accident in the Dauphiné Alps.

While descending from Tête de Colombe, Bob and Andy Poole were
struck by an avalanche. They were taken to hospital by a French
mountain rescue team but died shortly after arrival.

The descent to the col had its moments and the col itself was knife-edged and inhospitable so, with the sun already set, we began climbing the Innominata ridge. We were tired and hungry and it was cold and getting dark. I wondered why I felt almost reckless optimism instead of concern. At the foot of the first steep rock step there was a vague platform. Some imaginative heaving of rocks produced a place where two people could half sit and half lie back to back, and worry about themselves or bits of gear falling into the darkness below. The manoeuvring to cook and eat dinner was awkward enough to be funny.

There was no point in starting before sunrise next morning because we would immediately encounter the section of difficult rock-climbing. Before we had finished breakfast, parties from the Eccles hut arrived. They had climbed directly up the snow slope to Col Eccles using a wire-hawser fixed rope. There was not much room where we had bivouacked and to get to grips with the curving chimney crack of the first steep rock pitch they more or less trampled over us. Bob's response was to climb directly up the much harder wall beside the crack. The overall line of the Innominata ridge is more direct than the Brouillard or Peuterey ridges on either side. Although it appears well defined from distant viewpoints it is indefinite in several places. This led to several moments of aggravation because the party that knew the route best was moving most slowly. The fastest-moving party seemed to have the least idea of where to go, so no sooner had they fought their way to the front than they went wrong and were overtaken. Curiously the five parties on the Innominata that day were of different nationalities: Italian, German, French, English and Dutch.

The last section of the Innominata is a plain steep snow slope that leads to the final, almost level, part of the Brouillard ridge. Our exertions of the previous day began to take effect when we reached it and we suddenly felt tired. Even so we kept strictly to the ridge and traversed all the minor outcrops to Mont Blanc de Courmayeur and on to Mont Blanc. When we left the summit I absent-mindedly wandered round to the right of the Dôme du Goûter and found myself looking at the Goûter hut instead of along the east ridge of the Aiguille de Bionnassay. Bob did not share my amusement at this piece of whimsy. The Grises route provided an easy and efficient descent to the Gonella hut. We stopped nearby for a welcome rest and a meal of tea, soup, bread, salami, raw carrots and raisins. When we reached the Miage glacier it seemed every bit as long and tedious as I remembered it.

53 Aiguille Blanche de Peuterey
53a Aiguille Blanche de Peuterey South-East
53b Aiguille Blanche de Peuterey North-West
SE ridge (D). Solo
Map p 226   Illustrations pp 232/233, 244

Of the recognised major 4000m peaks the Aiguille Blanche is the most serious to climb. There are two long sections exposed to stonefall, there is an abseil to reach the Frêney glacier and the glacier itself is complicated and badly crevassed. Although I did not deliberately climb the Aiguille Blanche last of the mountains in Blödig and Dumler's list, it was an appropriate finale.

Aiguille Blanche de Peuterey from the Punta Baretti.   The arduous business of getting to Col Emil Rey is amply rewarded by one of the most magical views in the Alps. When you finally reach the col the difficulties and uncertainties are soon forgotten. As they disappear the nature of life seems to change and to take on a sense of enchantment, which is sustained by the airy ridge to the Punta Baretti.

Twice before, I had walked past the Franco Monzino hut and up to the Col de l'Innominata. I had sat there looking down at the Frêney glacier's maze of séracs and crevasses. The complicated col opposite, between the Aiguille Noire de Peuterey and the Aiguille Blanche, is divided into the Brèche Nord and Brèche Sud by some rock pinnacles called the Dames Anglaises. I had looked across at the couloir that leads directly to the Brèche Nord des Dames Anglaises and wondered whether it would be easier than the diagonal Schneider couloir and which would have the most stonefall. I had looked at the sky and wondered about the weather. I had been uncertain about how to tackle the route and where to bivouac. At the Col de l'Innominata there is a memorial plaque to Andreas Oggioni. He was Walter Bonatti's partner on many routes and died nearby when they were caught in a storm that lasted several days. You need to feel very confident to solo routes in the face of a warning like that. I had felt feeble and uncertain on the two previous occasions and had retraced my steps to the Val Veni. To disguise my lack of self-confidence I had magnified my doubts about the weather, although each time they were justified the following night by a fierce storm.

My third attempt was very different. I just knew the weather would stay fine and I greeted Andreas Oggioni's plaque like an old friend. I had decided to climb the Aiguille Blanche and then reverse the route instead of continuing on to Mont Blanc. For the abseil down to the glacier I tied a single rope to a spike in an inconspicuous place and left it there. This would enable me to climb up to the col on my way back. I meandered blithely across the glacier, scrambling past fallen séracs and leaping over crevasses, and reached the far side without difficulty. I sorted out a straightforward way

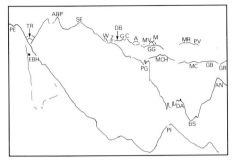

PE   Pic Eccles
EBH Eccles bivouac hut
TR   Tour Ronde
ABP Aig. Blanche de Peuterey, main summit
SE   Aig. Blanche de Peuterey, SE summit
W   Weisshorn
Z   Zinalrothorn
DB   Dent Blanche
GC   Grand Combin
A   Alphubel
MV   Mont Vélan
M   Matterhorn
GG   Grand Golliat
PG   Pointe Gugliermina
MCH Mont Chéarfière
MR   Monte Rosa
PV   Piramide Vincent
MC   Mont Chichet
GB   Ga. di Bonale
GR   Grande Rochère
AN   Aig. Noire de Peuterey
DA   Dames Anglaises
BS   Brèche Sud des Dames Anglaises
PI   Punta Innominata

to reach the bottom of the Schneider couloir and was tempted to continue up it. Instead, I kept to my plan of bivouacking by the glacier. A detached hump of rock nearby, the size of a house, had a flat gravel-filled groove on top. It provided a perfect bivouac site, safe from falling debris.

The night was still and clear with a wonderful bright moon. I was too excited and not tired enough to sleep. At the same time I felt relaxed and was quite content looking at the sky and the dark outlines of the mountains. For a long time there were shouts, flashes of torchlight and the sound of falling rocks on the north face of the Aiguille Noire de Peuterey. A party was negotiating the tricky sequence of abseils that lead from the summit of the Noire to the Brèche Sud. This is a serious descent that needs great care even in daylight.

Next morning I enjoyed a deliberate and leisurely breakfast waiting for the sunrise. When it was imminent and the light was good I scrambled up the chimney-like crevice to the Schneider couloir. I began climbing the bed of the couloir, trying to move steadily and calmly. It is narrow, almost claustrophobic at times. There are two places where it is blocked by small overhangs. I squirmed past the first one fairly easily. At the second I moved out to the exposed rocks on my right. I found them easier than I expected but because they were smooth and rounded I felt more secure in the couloir, even though the crisp snow was shallow and icy in places. The couloir was acting as a channel for some irritating small-scale stonefall. The irritation reminded me of rock-climbing at Stanage when there are midges about, except that here there was the possibility of a much larger item descending.

The couloir brought me above the Brèche Nord to broken rocks below a steep rock wall which is the south-east face of Pointe Gugliermina. This is the direct line from the Brèche but the south-east ridge of the Aiguille Blanche is reached by a much easier subsidiary ridge further round to the east. I wandered about for a few minutes looking for signs to indicate the 'correct' route and then decided it did not matter because any easy rising traverse would do. The subsidiary ridge is reached by crossing a steep concave amphitheatre of broken ledges. There are several small intermediate ridges and gullies. All were loose and all were raked by stonefall generated by a party higher up that I heard yet never saw. It was an absorbing activity: listening for a quiet lull then picking my way to the next ridge, hoping it would turn out to be the subsidiary ridge I was aiming for on the far side. This ridge was vague and broken and gave easy entertaining scrambling back to the main south-east ridge beyond Pointe Gugliermina. More easy rocks then snow took me to the first of the Aiguille Blanche's three summits.

I wriggled down an icy chimney of broken rocks and crossed a dazzling airy arête of hard snow to the central and highest summit. It was four hours since I had left my bivouac. The time had flashed past and yet it felt longer, almost as if it had been a different day when I started. During the ascent I had been so preoccupied anticipating possible difficulties that I had almost forgotten that this was the last Alpine fourthousander. There had been no substantial technical problems so the ascent had not absorbed any emotional energy. As I stood on the central summit the significance of the occasion returned and I began to feel light headed. To calm down I went over to the north-west summit. The Eckpfeiler buttress and the Peuterey ridge looked straightforward. I was very tempted to continue on to Mont Blanc but I had deliberately left all my bivouac gear by the Frêney glacier and I convinced myself of the virtues of a relaxed unhurried descent.

I went back to the central summit, arranged a comfortable seat and had a drink and something to eat. I had it in mind to think back deliberately to past ascents and all the other fourthousanders, but the Aiguille Blanche wanted no part in such pretentiousness. This was just another summit, no more wonderful and no less inconsequential than all the others. My thoughts were dreamily incoherent. I felt very emotional yet it was mostly the usual emotion that comes with a good route climbed well. I had no need to evoke the presence of other mountains to share the occasion: they were already there because they always are. Every route has echoes of previous routes and anticipates future ones. I looked across to Mont Brouillard and Col Emil Rey. My recollection of being there and gazing entranced at the Aiguille Blanche was so clear that I felt I was back there again. That ascent seemed not separate but part of this day's events. I stood up to look round at the French Alps and the Grand Combin and the mountains of the Valais and saw something of what was actually there mixed inextricably with other, earlier, images of them. It is like meeting a friend: you see the person and part of the history of your relationship.

I was reluctant to leave yet mindful that it was a long way and no mere stroll back to the Val Veni. I knew that the summit and the views would be left behind in only the simple literal sense. In more important ways they would stay with me. At the south-east summit I heard another party approaching and that gave me an excuse to sit and look for another few minutes. I had seen their head-torches crossing the Frêney glacier as I breakfasted. They were two climbers with a guide. All three seemed tense and were grim faced. In descent the route was a sequence of little problems, particularly of small-scale route-finding. It demanded concentration and my thoughts were all over the place. I kept repeating to myself 'No heroics; do the simple thing; take the easy option'. In the Schneider couloir I used my 6mm rope to abseil past the two awkward places. I experienced very little stonefall although I heard plenty. I scrambled up to my bivouac platform and brewed a lot of tea.

Crossing the Frêney glacier was easy with two nearly coincident sets of footprints to follow. I was glad to see my abseil rope where I had left it. I tied my rucksack to its end and climbed up to the Col de l'Innominata using the rope for aid. Although the rocks are steep and loose, the rope was a luxury rather than a necessity. With the extra weight of the rope to carry and the last problematic section done I suddenly felt tired so I was grateful for the comfortable snow slope on the little Châtelet glacier and the smooth moraine path.

Loping down to the Franco Monzino hut on automatic pilot I could dwell on my achievement. I began to feel elated and pleased with myself. There were a few people at the hut enjoying the afternoon sunshine and none of them took the slightest notice of my approach. This was the proper antidote to any feelings of self-importance I might have had. Nevertheless something about the world had changed even if I was the only person who knew. It felt strange buying fresh food in Courmayeur on such a momentous day when everybody was carrying on as if nothing had happened. So I bought a bottle of champagne to go with my evening meal. In spite of this and my tiredness I was too euphoric to sleep well.

At 02:00, restless and still excited, I got up and sat outside. I looked at the moon and the stars and thought about bivouacs and the anticipation of days climbing. I watched thin cloud, like gauze, drift across the sky. As the stars disappeared and the brightness of the moon dimmed I grew calm.

Conclusion

I have not said much about dead days: days spent huddled in a bivouac bag or marooned in a bivouac hut waiting for the weather to improve. Long hours of peering into mist, hoping that tantalising glimpses of clear sky will stabilise and lengthen, and wondering what to do for the best are an inevitable part of mountaineering. Whether to press on, so as to capitalise on the height gained with such effort, or to accept that a prudent retreat is called for, is a recurring dilemma. It mirrors everyday decisions and both illuminates and diminishes them. Some dead days are as memorable as successful ones, and equally instructive. Misfortune, when it stops short of disaster, is a better teacher than success.

Sitting alone through bad weather and enduring the more monotonous sections of routes, like afternoon plodding across a snow-field, are starkly existential situations. This makes them particularly good times for thinking, in the context of an activity that is generally well suited to contemplation. At such times friends come to mind and imaginary conversations take place. In that sense some people who do not think of themselves as mountaineers have been with me to many Alpine summits.

I could have climbed all the fourthousanders much more efficiently but I do not regret the long span of years or the erratic serendipity of the time I spend in the Alps. While it was pleasing to have an overall objective I am glad that my progress feels now as though it has been dictated by the mountains. Now that I have accepted that frequent changes of mind are almost inevitable, allowing the mountains and circumstances to dictate them seems to me to be the right approach. Although Alpine mountaineering is a vacation activity for me, the time I spend climbing feels, in common I suspect with most alpinists, like real time, the part of my life when I am most meaningfully alive. In the Alps everything I do elsewhere seems unreal, as if it were little more than filling in gaps. This feeling lingers on in the time between visits to the Alps. No matter where I am or how involved I am with everyday matters, be they humdrum or tense, my reaction to a clear cold night is always to think it would be a good night in the Alps. Good days and nights in the Alps are much more than pleasant intervals punctuating real life; they colour everything else I do. They affect my approach to the conventions of so-called civilised life and are with me always. Days in the mountains are days to live by.

List of 4000m ascents in chronological order

This list covers the climbs described in the text. To be consistent, all the identified 4000m tops are included even the relatively insignificant ridge points. In most cases these ascents were my first of that mountain. Exceptions appear in brackets. Subsequent ascents are not listed, including those mentioned in connection with minor 4000m points. Ascents of other summits in the Alps are not listed.

1966	(Allalinhorn, Strahlhorn, Nadelhorn)
1969	(Rimpfischhorn),Strahlhorn, Weissmies, Barre des Ecrins, Pic Lory
1970	Mönch, Lenzspitze, Nadelhorn, Stecknadelhorn,Hohberghorn, Dürrenhorn, Lagginhorn, Alphubel, Täschhorn, Bishorn, Weisshorn
1971	Piz Bernina, La Spalla, Il Roc, Gran Paradiso, Matterhorn, Dom
1972	(Aiguille du Géant), Aiguille de Bionnassay, Aiguille du Jardin, Grand Rocheuse, Aiguille Verte, Les Droites, Aiguille de Rochefort, Dôme de Rochefort, Pointe Hélène, Pointe Marguerite, Pointe Croz, Pointe Whymper, Grandes Jorasses Pointe Walker
1974	Mont Blanc du Tacul, Mont Maudit, Mont Blanc Brenva Ridge, Dôme du Goûter, (Grand Combin de Grafeneire, Grand Combin de Valsorey)
1975	Zinalrothorn
1976	Piramide Vincent, Punta Giordani, Schwarzhorn, Ludwigshöhe, Parrotspitze, Signalkuppe, Zumsteinspitze, Dufourspitze, Grenzgipfel, Nordend, Liskamm, Liskamm West, Felikhorn, Castor, Pollux, Roccia Nera, Breithorn East, Breithorn Central, Breithorn
1978	Lauteraarhorn, Aletschhorn, Gross Grünhorn, Finsteraarhorn, Dent Blanche, Ober Gabelhorn
1980	(Monte Viso), Dent d'Hérens, Mont Brouillard
1981	Gross Fiescherhorn, Hinter Fiescherhorn, Gross Schreckhorn, Pic Luigi Amadeo, Mont Blanc de Courmayeur, Jungfrau, Aiguille Blanche de Peuterey, Aiguille Blanche de Peuterey South-East, Aiguille Blanche de Peuterey North-West
1983	Allalinhorn
1984	Grand Combin de Valsorey, Grand Combin de Grafeneire, Aiguille du Croissant, Grand Combin de Tsessette, Dôme de Neige des Ecrins, Pointe Croux, Punta Baretti
1985	Corne du Diable, Pointe Chaubert, Pointe Médiane, Pointe Carmen, L'Isolée, Aiguille du Géant
1987	Pic Eccles, Mont Blanc Innominata Ridge
1988	Rimpfischhorn, Mont Blanc Goûter Ridge, Pointe Mieulet, Il Naso

Guide-Books

Most of the national Alpine clubs in Europe produce their own series of guide-books on climbing routes on the mountains of the Alps. The most comprehensive, if you can read German, French or Italian, are those produced by the Swiss, French and Italian Alpine clubs (SAC/CAS, CAF, CAI). A corresponding series of revised guides in English, edited by Les Swindin, is currently being published by the Alpine Club:

Ecrins Massif; John Brailsford, 1987.
Mont Blanc Massif, Volume I; Lindsay Griffin, 1990.
Mont Blanc Massif, Volume II; Lindsay Griffin, 1991.
Valais Alps, two volumes; Roger Payne, due to be published in 1991/1992.
Further volumes covering the Bernese Alps and the Bernina and Bregaglia are in preparation.

The Alpine Club series includes guide-books on other areas, the Dolomites for example. Although the series supersedes previous texts the pioneering contributions of earlier authors, particularly Robin Collomb, should not be forgotten. They have been crucially important for many climbers.

The English-language guide-books contain selections of routes chosen to suit the needs of British Alpinists. They cover larger areas and are more efficient than their continental counterparts, whose comprehensiveness is rarely useful. That said, it is important to remember that they are selective. Occasionally it is helpful to have seen the complete range of routes for which information and grade are available. Bear in mind that almost any feasible line on a popular mountain will have been climbed, and also that evidence of previous climbers, like slings, scratches and footprints, is just that. These signs are often encouraging but they may denote uncomfortable retreats, or that other parties have been equally off route.

INDEX

The **bold** face entries for 4000m summits indicate the first page of the relevant section and also, for major peaks, the first page of the sub-section devoted to the peak. Subsequent references in these sections are omitted.

Italic entries refer to illustrations; roman entries refer to text.

Many index entries point to no more than a brief mention in passing or to a minute but identified appearance in an illustration.